SPY AGAINST SPY

"We'll rest here a bit," grunted the Englishman, keeping the small pistol pointed firmly at young Matt Bell's heart. The English spy had lost considerable blood, but showed no sign of weakening. And Matt *must* get away and carry word to Washington immediately, or all would be lost.

"We're going to watch all the action up here, lad," gazing down from the knoll toward the British campfires. Shortly, the Battle of Long Island would begin, and all Matt Bell could do was watch in frustration.

"You miserable cur," he growled at the Britisher.

"Aye, cur indeed! But mind this, lad, the old cur knows some tricks the young cur doesn't."

He paused to catch his wind. "If I die, you die with me—if it's my last breath."

The FREEDOM FIGHTERS *Series*

TOMAHAWKS AND LONG RIFLES
MUSKETS OF '76

MUSKETS OF '76

Jonathan Scofield

A DELL/BRYANS BOOK

MUSKETS
OF '76

1

DEBORAH BELL cast a sidelong glance at her younger brother. It wasn't the weather that made her tuck her chin deeply into the velvet collar of her jacket. By mid-morning the sun's warmth was noticeable and welcome. It had been a late spring, the last patches of snow disappearing only after the first two weeks of April.

Her brother's serious expression brought an affectionate smile to her face, although she did her best to conceal it. Matthew Bell's handsome profile was stern and hard-set as he sat next to her on the cushioned seat of the shay. She had won her argument with her father, and Matthew had offered to drive her. He would have been much happier on horseback, she thought, noticing how stiff and ill-at-ease he seemed. But she hadn't sewn this velvet suit to have it shed upon by a horse or jostled about on the long horseback ride to Hartford. Besides, it wasn't dignified for a young woman to travel to the city on the rump of a horse. Matthew knew as well as she, of course, that at any other time she wouldn't have minded riding horseback; but not this time, not for this occasion.

She glanced back at Mark, the youngest of the Bells, who rode behind them. Even he had made a to-do about the trip, insisting on accompanying them on horseback, as if he were a gallant knight protecting "two royal la-de-dahs," as he had called them.

Royalty . . . It was a sore subject in their household, as indeed it was in more and more households in the colonies. Not that she was sympathetic to the Tories, but she couldn't help being glad that her family lived in such a peaceful community as Wethersfield, where they were insulated from all the uproar over King George's taxes. There was only secondhand talk, and it seemed most of the rioting was over. The tales Mark had brought back with him five years ago were a thing of the past—and would remain so, or so she had often prayed.

"Innocent people were murdered," Mark had told them, his voice hushed, his eyes wide with the terror of it. He had gone to Boston to visit with Cousins Merideth and Joshua five years ago in 1770. It would be shocking to witness the slaughter of innocent people at any age, Deborah knew, but Mark had been only twelve, hardly out of childhood. His outrage had given way to depression for a time, and he had only gradually regained his spirits. But the carefree boy was gone. The rift between the colonies and England had grown ever larger in the years following the massacre, and Deborah had seen Mark's grim satisfaction in each tale of harrassment against the crown. It seemed all he could think about was talk against the Tories and Royalists. She suspected that he knew about the Whig organization and all the fuss they were stirring against England.

She even suspected Matthew was in on it, too. She could pretty well name all the men of Wethersfield who were Whigs. The British detachment in Wethersfield could barely move without being watched, and she knew from John Langley Hunter that the British had met much the same reception wherever they stationed their men. Dangerous times, John Langley had said. And perhaps he was right, she thought, if there were undercurrents of tension and wariness even in a village like Wethersfield.

"Matthew," she asked suddenly, "you don't think there'll be another confrontation with the British, do you? Not another Boston Slaughter?"

"Why do you ask?" he said, glancing at her in surprise.

"I'm sorry," she answered softly, giving him a quick smile. "It's just foolishness. I've been listening to too many of Mark's tales."

She lapsed into silence again and scolded herself for having asked the question. There were times when she forgot that Matthew had no more answers than she. Deborah, near ten years his senior, had helped raise him and Mark, but she had always felt a special closeness with Matthew. They shared not only the raven hair and azure eyes of the Bells but were fiercely independent. At thirty-one, Deborah might have been considered an old maid schoolteacher, but the spirit and intelligence under her quiet beauty resisted any such labelling and she was universally respected, if not always understood, by the people of Wethersfield. Matthew too was respected, in spite of his youth. People sensed the strength behind his thoughtful countenance, and there were few who saw that he still retained the uncertainty and, occasionally, the headstrong nature of a young man.

They rode in silence until Matthew let out a long, slow breath and leaned back against the cushioned backrest, his eyes set straight on the road ahead of the flickering black ears of the horse. "It's not really foolishness," he said quietly. "It's a question we all ask. I don't think there's a man among us who really wants to go to war." He hesitated a moment before adding, "They want to fight for their rights, that's all. And if keeping their rights means war, then I guess it's very likely to happen."

"But the King can't really want it to come to that."

Matthew shrugged his shoulders. "No one knows what England wants. That's one of the troubles— England doesn't seem to know what we want, we don't know what England wants. As a result, we might have to take things into our own hands to get them resolved."

Deborah studied Matthew's profile. "Are you part of 'they'?"

He shrugged again. He really didn't know. He hoped it would never come to a major decision. There was no doubt in his mind that England cared little for the welfare and rights of the colonies. "I'm putting my faith in our representatives being able to talk some sense into the King. I don't see how he can dare do anything against us, knowing we're prepared to fight."

"Then there could be a war?"

"A war?" Matthew turned a smiling face to Deborah. "I doubt that. Neither side wants a war."

"But it will only take another incident like the one

in Boston to set off the fireworks." She turned to look behind them at the lone rider. Young Mark Bell saw but only waved his hand, content to be alone to himself.

"Y'mean fireworks from the likes of Mark?"

Deborah grimaced and nodded. "I'm afraid he'd like nothing better than to take up arms against the British."

"He's always been like that. Loves reading history books about wars, loves tales about wars." He paused and eyed Deborah. "He can hardly keep himself away from your Mr. Hunter friend. He's giving you pretty strong competition."

Deborah smiled at her brother's arch look but did not pursue the subject she knew was on his mind. "I must admit Mr. Hunter has some interesting tales."

"The wars with the Indians must have been hell," Matthew commented. "Different kind of fighting than what we'd meet with the British."

If she had heard him, she gave little indication. Not that he was surprised she had headed him off from any discussion of John Langley. His sister had always been polite but firm in warding off the inevitable question about her baffling friendship. Deborah's girlhood had had its share of romances with the boys of Wethersfield, but never anything serious, and the death of Mrs. Bell had left her with little time for anything other than housework and teaching. But then there had been John Langley Hunter, a Virginian who had passed through their village toward the end of the French and Indian War and who had figured in their lives ever since.

In the years following the war, John Langley had stopped in Wethersfield as often as his travels permitted and it was plain to the family that he and

Deborah had an understanding. What was not plain was the nature of the understanding. If it was a court- ship, it was one of the longest in history and had yet to result in the declaration of any intention to marry. Had John Langley lived in Wethersfield, Matthew sus- pected that he and Deborah might long ago have become a subject of gossip, but the Virginian's com- ings and goings and his closeness with Deborah's father and brothers created the impression that he was a relation of the family. That and the fact of Deborah's status as a well-respected teacher and member of the small community seemed to blind people to the nature of the relationship Matthew was almost sure existed. But if Robert Bell and his sons were often mystified that the couple seemed content to continue as they were, they shared a tacit recognition that both Deb- orah and John Langley were unconventional and somehow special, commanding enough of the Bells' love and respect so that the subject was never pressed. Besides, none of them were eager to lose her to mar- riage, although Matthew guessed that even Deborah and John Langley would eventually succumb.

The knowledge that she might soon marry and be off to Virginia left him feeling lonely and somehow very old—much older than he would like to admit. He had taken charge of the Bell family two years ago when their father had first fallen ill. Now, at age twenty-one, he felt as old as he guessed his father did. And Mark . . . Matthew could not help but smile. At seventeen, he was the baby of the clan, and occasion- ally he still gave way to boyish high spirits and mis- chief. But already he drew the stares of many young lasses of the town and it would not be too long before some wench would chain his heart. His mind had al- ready been claimed, Matthew often thought, given a precocious gravity and purpose by the shocking event he had witnessed in Boston.

Matthew settled back, let his mind rest a moment, as he gazed over the greening hills, the dark brown trees still wet from the morning dew, ready to burst with new seed. The road followed a stone wall of Connecticut shale, white and tan, rolling with the terrain until it broke off in a southerly direction. It was a good time of the year—a new awakening, Matthew always thought, a new time for new ventures, new ideas, new work. What lay ahead of them in this year of seventy-five? What adventures lay ahead for *him*, he wondered.

His thoughts came back again to his brother and sister. Maybe it was time for him to begin thinking of marriage and a family. Most of his friends had already started families and businesses of their own. He wondered whether Chaning Wilson was the girl for him. Or maybe, maybe someone like Louisa Scott.

"My husband is so absorbed in his work," she had confided last summer. "He has neglected me." She had turned her dark eyes up at him and held his gaze briefly before looking away.

He had been working extra hours at the pond, chopping wood for the new British commandant of Wethersfield. A brash young lieutenant fresh from some military academy in England, stiffly starched, a trifle of a bore, but a man with high principles and even higher ambition. Fitchley Scott was eagerly accepted by the Tory faction of the town. He was not only a symbol of England's almighty power, but served as a reminder that Wethersfield was capable of holding down rioting, should anyone get any ideas from the stories filtering back from Massachusetts.

To the Whigs, Scott was someone to tolerate, to

watch and spy upon, his every move noted, along with those of the Tory sympathizers. The rebels were only waiting patiently for the right moment, the right command.

The Bells had needed the extra money, and so Matthew had accepted the chore of chopping the winter wood for the lieutenant and his new bride. Scott had introduced his wife only because he would in all likelihood be detained in town with his military affairs, and his wife would therefore be directing Matthew. But all of this was explained to Louisa Scott rather than to Matthew, who stood to one side and heard himself referred to as "the colonist" in a tone that accorded him no higher status than that of a slave. But he could put aside the insinuations of the English just as he could ignore the slurs and gibes of those colonists loyal to the king. He had long ago learned to set aside his pride to survive. He was a hard worker and did well at whatever task he set his mind to. Chopping fallen limbs and clearing the wooded area around the pond at the south end of the Britisher's property was man's work. Wood was essential for warmth and survival during the long winter months. No man should suffer, no matter his political beliefs. Winter took no sides.

During the late summer months he had spotted her several times out of the corner of his eye as he bent to his work, but it was not until the middle of October, with only a few more weeks' worth of work left, that she stepped from her usual hiding place and openly sat to watch him. He had come to sense her secretive appearances and had become puzzled and self-conscious whenever he felt her eyes upon him, but her brazen scrutiny angered him.

He had chopped a few more logs, pondering whether he should go over to her and inquire what her purpose was in studying him all this time. Surely, since he was not being paid by the hour, she was not spying on him to make sure he was working. Perhaps she distrusted him and feared he might steal something from the house. Or maybe, having been raised in England, she had to see for herself what kind of a creature lived in this alien country.

"Is the water safe to swim in?" Her voice startled him so that his aim almost cut off his foot.

He hunched over the axe, silently cursing her for making him appear so clumsy. Angrily he wedged the sharp blade out of the log and turned to her. "It is safe enough," he answered curtly.

"I am surprised you have not taken advantage of it, especially on some of the hot days." Her voice was low and husky.

"I have my work to do," he answered, feeling awkward in her presence. She wore a light yellow dress, with a bodice that fit snugly against her full breasts, and his eyes wandered to the soft cleavage revealed at the low neckline.

He heard her chuckle and was suddenly aware that she had caught his inspection of her body. Red-faced, he sought her eyes, which stared back at him in amused boldness after flickering over his half-naked body.

They had stared at each other, mesmerized. Matthew could feel his heart pounding, the blood flowing in his veins. There was a tightness in his legs, an even more pronounced tightness in his crotch. The more he tried to fight the expanding hardness, the worse it became. His eyes undressed her and he could feel hers undressing him.

She got to her feet and came to him slowly, their eyes locked hungrily. She approached him until they were almost touching and he could feel the heat of her presence. Slowly, her hands came up, touching him gently, tentatively, and then pressing against his glistening chest.

She was there for the taking, he knew that. In the back of his mind he knew it was wrong but he could not back away from the devouring need that washed over him with her nearness. She was beautiful and voluptuous and he ached to cup the soft breasts that began to press into him.

With a small cry of anguish, he encircled her waist and pulled her to him, his lips crushing down on hers, sucking those wet and pliable lips into his.

Her body was soft and yielding and she shivered as she pressed herself to him. His hands pushed into the small of her back, grinding pelvis into pelvis. Their mouths absorbed one another, tongues hungrily searching. Quickly, his fingers found the small pearl buttons to her gown. As he unbuttoned her clothes, she undid his, both of them fumbling in their haste, tossing aside their garments until they were both naked in the warm autumn light filtering through the trees.

They stood apart, gazing at each other in rapt silence. Louisa suddenly seemed so vulnerable, so small and fragile, yet so passionate. He slowly reached out for her. She took his hand with tremulous fingers and followed him to a small patch of soft green grass where they lay down, side by side.

Wordlessly, he turned to her and traced her body with the tips of his fingers. Her breasts were small and compact, the dark nipples erect so tempting, so sweet to his lips as he kissed them. Her stomach was flat and small, so young and innocent in his eyes, rounding out to soft hips and long legs. The patch of coarse brown hair glistened in the light and he gently pressed his palm over it. He felt her give a slight lift of her hips as her arms went about his shoulders.

"Please . . ." she whispered, spreading her thighs.

His fingers felt the moistness between her legs and he responded by lifting himself gently upon her, looking down into her eyes as he slowly entered her.

They had met several times after that, each time as eagerly and wordlessly as the first, but the sweetness of that first encounter could never be recaptured for Matthew. He began to brood about his behavior and had a difficult time meeting Fitchley Scott's eyes at the next roll call on the commons.

When he came to the house to collect his wages at the end of that fall, Louisa stood demurely behind her husband. Matthew was flustered and could not look up at either husband or wife. In a way, he was thankful that his labors were finished. He would miss Louisa and the release he found in her arms, but he had been plagued by their adulterous affair. He wanted desperately to convince himself that it was Louisa who had initiated the affair, who was responsible for it. Yet no matter how one looked at it, he was as guilty as she.

Maybe it was time he sought out a wife. He could not afford the pain and guilt of another such affair. The scar would heal and life would go on, he told himself. One learned from one's experiences. The problem with this one was, he wasn't quite sure what he had learned.

2

THE STONE BRIDGE into Hartford came into sight just ahead, with large elms, weeping willows and white birches lining the lazy river that made its way through the town. As carriage and horse approached the narrowing of the road, a group of white-shirted, leather-vested men stood up from where they had been lounging and deliberately blocked the way.

Deborah clutched at Matthew's arm in alarm.

"It's all right," he murmured, but he tightened his grip on the reins.

"What do you suppose they want?" Mark asked, nudging his mount in closer to the side of the buggy.

"We'll see in a moment."

As they approached the group, one of the bigger men raised his hand and caught the bridle of the carriage horse. The others surrounded the buggy and looked up at the three newcomers.

"What kind of welcome is this?" Matthew asked guardedly, trying to find some kind of answer in the sour faces.

They stared up into the carriage, inspecting Matthew and Deborah suspiciously, only a brief glance at the younger horseman.

"Where are you coming from?" the man nearest inquired.

"Wethersfield," Matthew answered impatiently. "What is this all about?"

The only reply was another question from the same grim-faced man. "Where you headed for?"

"We're not going to answer any more questions," Matthew answered gruffly, "until you start answering some of ours."

"We want to know your sympathies," a red-bearded man asked, stepping forward.

"Sympathies?" Matthew straightened in the seat and studied them once again. "We're the Bells from Wethersfield. What's the reason for your question?"

The red-bearded one squinted up at Matthew, studied them once again. "We're the Bells from look at Mark before turning his attention back to Matthew. "We want to know what your heart be. Whig or Tory?"

"By God, we're Whig," Mark exclaimed, drawing himself up as if in challenge.

There seemed to be a shift of relaxation among the group and one or two appeared to smile. But the red-bearded man still looked up at Matthew for an answer. "And you, lad?"

"That's a dangerous question to be asking nowadays," Matthew answered evenly.

"Depends on the answer." There was a sly smile on the man's face and he still waited for Matthew's reply.

"What's the reason for this? I've been to Hartford before and never found such a reception."

"Then you must have come here some time ago. And as for an answer—which is a mite more than what you're giving, I might add—let's just say Tories aren't too welcome here in Hartford."

"Good for you!" Mark spoke up and grinned. There was a laugh from the men and a few backed off to lean against the walls of the bridge.

"You think you can keep Tories out of Hartford?" Matthew asked curiously.

The man cocked his head and looked up at him with one eye closed. "Let's just say we're trying to suggest they go elsewhere to do their business."

"Yeah," someone else cried out. "It's about time we do something to let England know we're not going to take their taxes!" The others murmured their approval.

Matthew relaxed and even smiled. "I'm putting my faith in our representatives. Once they're heard from, England will change the law."

"Well, just in case they don't, we want to make it plain to them that we're ready to do our worst!"

"We're with you," Mark answered eagerly. "We'll fight if we have to!"

"That's the way, boy!"

Matthew turned and scowled at Mark. "Let's hope it doesn't get to that," he answered as he turned back to the group of men.

"Amen to that, brother. But if you're from Wethersfield, you'll probably be seeing things here in Hartford you ain't seen before."

Deborah grasped Matthew's arm. "What do you mean?"

"Nothing you need be frightened of," came the answer, "but we're putting the scare to royal sympathizers. We're sort of a tame bunch, you might say, though there's groups in town who are a mite rougher than us. You see any fracas, my advice is to stay clear. We don't want innocent people getting hurt—just Tories."

"Maybe it's best we not visit your fair city," Matthew suggested, not wanting to expose his brother and sister to any danger.

"You'll be safe enough if you're quick with answers, young man," the redhead replied. "Unless, that is, you're ashamed of being a patriot."

Matthew's eyes narrowed and he took a slow deep breath. "I am a free man, as are my brother and my sister. Is it now you're forcing us to something other than what we are?"

"We're asking your allegiance, that's all, lad. We think it wrong to be ruled by a tyrant thousands of miles away from us who doesn't care a whit how we brew our tea as long as it's British tea. No man's to be telling us what we can buy or who we can buy from, governor, parliament nor king."

"And so anyone who disagrees with you is handled so?"

The red-bearded one smiled and nodded his head. "That's the way it's being done in the South, that's the way it's being done in Massachusetts and all over. And that's the way it's going to be done here in Hartford."

"It's about time we stand up for our rights!" Mark declared. His remark was greeted with several hurrahs from the men and the boy beamed down from his mount at his scowling brother. "Let's go on, Matt," he urged.

Matthew turned to Deborah. "You still want to go on?" he asked. When she nodded her head, he sighed and gave in. "So be it, then."

The group parted for the shay and soon they found themselves on a better road, winding among the wide-branched trees, expansive lawns and large white clapboard homes of Hartford.

Deborah drew a folded piece of paper from her pocket and spread it upon her lap. "Mr. Hale says we are to keep a lookout for a twin-spired church on our left." No sooner had she read the information than she looked up and excitedly pointed. "There, over there."

Slightly ahead of them on their left, two church spires rose from the trees, shining brightly with their white paint and golden crosses.

"We are to make a left on the first road after we pass the church," Deborah read on.

They followed the directions of the map Deborah held in her hand until they arrived in front of a small, white clapboard home, its blue-slated roof capped by a red brick chimney.

"This is where he lives," Deborah announced, satisfied that they had followed directions correctly. "Oh, Matthew," she exclaimed, "I am so excited."

"I hope you know what you're getting yourself into," Matthew remarked, jumping down from the carriage. "You've already learned more than most women all by yourself. What good is knowing more? You're already a good teacher."

"Oh squarebottoms!" Deborah exclaimed, gathering in her skirt and stepping down on the other side. "You men think all a woman's good for is setting up house and raising children."

"That's responsibility enough," Matthew answered, but he was only half in earnest. If ambition in a woman puzzled him, he was nonetheless proud that his sister had been singled out by Mr. Hale. The Yale graduate had arranged special classes for women who wanted to become teachers, and when he had heard of Deborah's fine reputation as a teacher he had offered her the use of his own college texts to further her education.

Deborah sighed, for Matthew had brought up an old argument, one she had first heard from her father years back, when she had announced her intention to become a schoolteacher. "How am I going to teach others if I don't know myself?" She grabbed his arm and waited until Mark dismounted and took his place beside them. "C'mon, you two," she announced, "this will do all of us some good!"

"It'll take more than you and your friend to convince me differently," Matthew said good-naturedly.

The man who answered the door was perhaps only a couple of years older than Matthew. He was of a slight build but carried himself with the grace of someone who knew his own strengths and convictions. His face was marked badly by smallpox scars, yet he had a handsomeness and gentleness that outweighed such mars.

"Miss Bell?" His voice was a soft baritone that betrayed a serious nature. "You are most punctual."

"I have my brothers to thank for that," Deborah answered with a slight curtsey. "My brothers Matthew and Mark."

Nathan Hale shook their hands vigorously, a slight sparkle coming to his eyes. "Good Christian names," he responded. Without waiting for a reply, he turned and led the way into a small, immaculate living room. After waiting patiently for them to be seated, he studied them meticulously, but his manner was somehow neither discomforting nor embarrassing.

He gave a sudden smile, as if pleased with what he saw, and then drew them into conversation by asking about Wethersfield. His questions revealed a lively intelligence and a sensitivity to his guests' interests, and Matthew, no less than the others, soon found himself relaxed and very much liking the man.

"But you've come to discuss adding to your education," Hale said at last, turning to Deborah. "I've heard much about you, and have no doubt you put your talents to good use. When all is said and done, there is nothing in this world more important than teaching."

"Except having one's rights," Mark spoke up, his young voice slightly quivering with boldness.

Hale started at the unexpected remark and then smiled. "Ah, so we have a patriot, do we?"

"A *fervent* patriot," Matthew corrected.

Hale studied the younger brother with serious eyes. "That is good," he finally answered. "We need as many patriots as we can get."

"I shall be one of the first to enlist," Mark stated proudly, encouraged by Hale's response.

"It is early," their host answered. "There are some of us who have started a nucleus of an organization in case there is need, but as yet—".

"You're part of the new army?" Mark interrupted excitedly.

"I wouldn't call it an army yet," Hale answered. "But if it comes to a fight, we have a Connecticut regiment ready."

Mark looked at Nathan Hale with new admiration. "I wish I could join."

"You have no reason to join yet," Matthew answered quickly, trying to think of a way to stop this conversation.

"Your brother is right," Hale said to Mark. "But if the time does come, you be sure to look me up."

"I think we are getting away from why we are here," Matthew remarked, giving Mark a reproving look. "Our trip is on Deborah's behalf."

"You are most correct," Hale answered and turned his attention to Deborah with a small bow from the waist. "Please pardon my ardor for the politics of the day, but it has become a recent passion of mine." He turned to Matthew also to see if his apology had been accepted. "I have found myself concentrating on recent events with more vigor than I sometimes thought I possessed."

"We have already met some of the vigor here in Hartford," Matthew commented. When Hale's eyebrows raised in question he explained about their encounter with the group of men at the bridge.

"And they are the tamer ones," Hale replied lightly. "I should take you around so that you might witnesss some of the bolder groups."

"Can we?" Mark asked, sitting forward in his chair in anticipation.

Matthew frowned. Lately, all conversation seemed to wander back to the rioting of the times. "I doubt Mr. Hale has the time to show us around Hartford. Besides, we came here for Deborah's benefit."

"But what could be more important than the future of our country?" Mark asked innocently.

Hale shook his head, then winked at Matthew

"Fervent, indeed. I see what you mean," he murmured before turning to Mark.

"Perhaps we should discuss things with your sister. Then, time permitting, I can take you around our city —but only for sightseeing."

Mark started to say something, but a warning glance from Matthew quickly silenced him. They sat quietly, each pursuing his own thoughts while Hale outlined the course of study he was proposing to Deborah. Her excitement was evident, and Hale was gratified with her response.

"I firmly believe that one can never have enough education," he said as they closed their discussion. "There are no laws in Connecticut spelling out how much education is required for a teacher. But there will be. Education is needed not only for the upper classes, but for all classes of people. I wouldn't be a bit surprised if one of these days even slaves were given an education."

"But how will a man learn his trade if he has to go to school?" Matthew said, leaning forward to join in the conversation. "I was taking up my father's trade almost as soon as I could walk. I learned all I had to learn in coopering. But if I had had to go to school I surely wouldn't be able to do what I can today."

"Can you read and write?" Hale asked.

"Enough to do my job," Matthew replied defensively.

Their host studied the wooden floor planks thoughtfully before answering. "I know, especially for the tradesmen, the task will be difficult. But I think in time, if certain hours of the day were put aside for learning, everyone would benefit."

"And who will do the chores?"

Their host shrugged. "This is a new nation. It's also a nation of new ideas and new ways. People will find a way. Look about you. In Massachusetts, they are already requiring towns to have schools. Can you imagine that? I know Connecticut is thinking of doing the same thing."

"But college education—like you're giving Deborah —that's even more special," Mark said, looking at Hale respectfully.

"Yes, I have been very lucky."

"Could I see your college certificate?" Mark asked sheepishly.

Hale smiled and got up, returning with a small, red, lacquered gentleman's chest, which he rested on his knees. As though opening Pandora's box, he slowly lifted the lid and lifted out a rolled parchment. "Here it is," he said, unrolling the scroll. The three crowded around him and studied the fancy inking.

"It *is* beautiful!" Deborah breathed.

"So, that is a college diploma," Mark whispered in awe. "I reckon that piece of paper can just about let you do anything."

Hale carefully rolled the document back and slipped a thing blue ribbon around it again. "It should open the doors for me, I'll grant you that."

"Does that mean you know everything there is to know?" Mark asked curiously, edging back to his chair.

"Lord, no!" Hale said, laughing. "But I hope it will eventually allow me to teach at some college. For right now, my duties in the militia are taking most of my time," he added, turning to Deborah, "and I am only too happy to know that my books are being of some use."

"Then I shall keep good care of them, and when all this fussing is over, I shall return them good as new," Deborah answered, giving him a grateful smile.

Matthew stood up, feeling awkward about voicing the question that had been in the back of his mind ever since his sister had heard from Hale. "I feel there should be something in repayment," he stammered.

Nathan Hale clasped a firm hand to Matthew's shoulder. "Your sister brought that up in her reply to my letter, and I shall tell you what I told her. Teaching is my true love, Mr. Bell, and the fact that I personally cannot teach at the moment is somewhat offset by being able to pass my own education on to a teacher as capable and deserving as your sister." He looked at all three of them with serious eyes. "And three new friends is thrice good fortune."

"Then you have our gratitude for as long as we live, Nathan Hale. Friendship with the likes of you is something we could never repay," Matthew replied warmly. He hesitated, fearing that his words must sound woefully inadequate to this learned person. "I doubt whether you will ever have need of a solid barrel, but if you do, you will have one of the finest made by these hands. I can do most anything with wood and a sharp blade, and if ever a time comes when you are in need of a good craftsman I would be grateful if you would keep me in mind."

"Be assured, Matthew Bell, that I shall keep you in mind," Hale answered respectfully. "For when all this —fuss— is over," he said, bowing to Deborah in deference to her choice of words, "I plan to return to Hartford and build a schoolhouse. It is then I shall be sure to look you up, my friend."

Matthew was pleased and he stuck out his hand and grasped Nathan Hale's. There was an embarrassed silence until their host smiled and turned to Mark. "And now—if there are no further questions, perhaps you would like to see my small city."

Mark grinned. "Will you show us those mobs we were talking about?"

"We may not have much choice," Hale replied. "Lately, they've become most bold and have taken to doing their mischief in daylight."

"Will my sister be safe?" Matthew inquired.

"All of you will be safe, especially since you'll be with me. But if we do meet any mobs, I would advise that we stay close together."

"Can we take part?" Mark asked suddenly.

"Take part?" Deborah exclaimed, annoyed. "You *are* eager for a fight, aren't you?"

"Why shouldn't we show how strongly we feel?" Mark protested.

"We're talking about more than just voicing opinions, I'm afraid," Hale remarked. "These mobs have caused quite a bit of damage to Tory homes lately, and even to a few Tories."

"Have you ever seen a tar and feathering?"

Hale nodded. "It goes a little too far, to my mind. I'm all for making our viewpoint known and drawing attention to our aims. But I must admit that some of the personal violence I cannot condone."

"But the more Tories we can get to leave the country, the better the chance we will have of getting our rights."

"Maybe so. But it will eventually lead to a confrontation—not against civilians, but against the British army. And I might remind you that they are what many historians consider the finest army the world has ever seen."

"What? Those lobsterbacks?" Mark sneered. "All

they know is how to kill innocent, defenseless people."

"Ah, yes," Hale said quietly. "I do believe your sister mentioned your witnessing the massacre in Boston. That was a most unfortunate affair, I admit." There was a silence that sobered them all.

Matthew cleared his throat. "Maybe this is not the time," he said, starting to lead Deborah to the door.

"No," Hale objected. "I am sorry our conversation got carried away. But even if we were to encounter a mob, I believe it might be important for you three to see what is actually happening, how strongly the patriots feel about their freedom. Our freedom. Wethersfield is perhaps not as up to date on current events as Hartford. You might be witnessing an historical event, in a sense."

"I don't understand," Matthew answered.

"Throughout history," Hale explained, "people have suffered through tyranny before rising to fight for their rights. For the last several hundred years, people have been content to listen to the law of tyranny—or to the aristocratic few. Here in the colonies, we have tasted certain freedoms and have found the taste to our liking. We are ready to fight for those rights. And, if history proves right, our destiny just might be to break that mold that has prevailed for so many centuries. For the first time, the common man, people such as you and me, have just as much right to say how we should live as Lord North, or The East India Company, or even George III." He looked at them seriously. "That's what is so important about knowing what's going on out there. It could be our future. You, Deborah, will have a chance to give a first-hand account of political turmoil to your students. And you, my fiery young madcap, you should want to look and witness how ugly some things can be, what even civilized, well-intentioned men can be driven to do, and to be able to draw your own conclusions as to how to act for your beliefs." Hale turned to Matthew and studied him a long moment. "And you, Matthew Bell, I feel a hesitation on your part—a division of purpose. You too should come and see for yourself, not to be persuaded to either point of view, necessarily, but certainly to add to your knowledge of both sides. When the time comes, you will be better able to choose wisely which stand to take."

3

HALE JOINED Matthew and Deborah in the shay for the tour of Hartford. Their host had thought it best he ride in the buggy rather than horseback, not only so he could point out the sights but to be closer to them. He had already warned Mark to keep as close as possible to them.

Deborah could not hide her appreciation of the houses, most fresh white with dark shutters, white picket fences and clean as the spring air, with carefully tended bushes and flower beds showing the first color of the season.

Her glance was noticeably full every time they passed women strolling along the walkways, and she took special note of the fashions, colors and fanciful embroideries.

Matthew detected the direction of his older sister's

thoughts and wished he had the money to go into a millinery shop and buy her all the material, lacework and sewing needs she wanted. Maybe someday, if she married John Langley, she would be able to afford such things. Not that they did without too much. Coopering was a good profession, and their barrels were in demand, a result of hard and skillful work. Granted, the recent embargo on trade had hurt them some, but there were enough privateers still shipping so that business wasn't too bad. However, now that their father was no longer able to use the hammer and chisel, the burden had fallen upon Matthew's broad shoulders. Mark was coming of age and had the strength to help out, but his heart was not in barrel-making. It was a lean time for the Bell family, and as Matthew watched the affluent walking about Hartford he could not help but wonder what it would be like to have frittered away his time. Today's trip was an all-too-rare luxury and he intended to take full advantage, dismissing all worries from his mind.

He was impressed by Nathan Hale, who sat on the skirt of the floor, feet dangling out along the road as they approached the busier part of Hartford. From the casual handwaves passed between Hale and people in the street, the man was obviously well known and well liked.

"It's an advantage of being a teacher," Hale explained. "Everyone knows who the teacher is and everyone knows it's a job that helps others. Hardly anyone can find argument against what I do." He broke off as he noticed commotion ahead of them. A small crowd of people was gathering at the next cross street, their voices raised in excitement.

"You had better slow down," Hale suggested and stood up for a better view. "It appears we might have a glimpse of a mob," he muttered, as they approached the fringe of the crowd. Halfway down the cross street there was a large group of men, white-shirted, dark-vested, most with tri-cornered hats, making much noise in front of a two-story brick building. Several older men leaned far out of the second story windows to address those below.

"They found Hanson Parker," one of the onlookers close to the buggy explained to Hale.

Hale smiled and turned to his guests, "Parker is one of Hartford's more illustrious loyalists. We've been looking for him for some time now."

"Good Lord," Deborah exclaimed. "What has the man done to warrant all this ruckus?"

"We suspect Mr. Parker is an associate of the Indian Bay Company. Besides, he has been an outspoken critic of the rebellion. It was only a matter of time before he was found."

"Let us hope they string him up by the neck," Mark announced vehemently.

"Mark!" Matthew turned to the boy angrily. "This country has not come to that kind of barbarism. It is one thing to tar someone, quite another to hang him."

"Your brother is right," Hale added. "We don't want to kill these people. They have as much right to live as we do. But this *is* our country, and we think we have the right to determine how it should be run. That is the difference between the way the patriots and the loyalists think."

"They should all go back to England then," Mark muttered.

"Aye, that they should, and many are. But remember that their ancestors came over here with ours. This is their country too. It is a difficult situation, to say the least."

Their talk was interrupted by the swelling of noise from the crowd. Several men appeared at the doorway of the house, dragging out a rotund, middle-aged man who was red-faced in obvious fear and frustration.

"There's Parker now," Hale announced, and stood up on the buggy step to get a better view.

Both Deborah and Matthew also stood to observe. The crowd had drawn back to allow men carrying a long piece of wood to come closer. They hefted the beam onto their shoulders and braced themselves as others boosted the Loyalist onto the narrow beam, his white-stockinged legs dangling helplessly on either side. A loud cheer was heard from the crowd as the man clung for balance, his face screwed tightly in obvious discomfort and embarrassment. The men lifted the beam high over their heads, then dropped it to their shoulders. Parker uttered a small cry and leaned forward to hang on tightly.

Men came forward and tied his ankles together. The audience now began to jeer and point at the pathetic figure. Slowly the crowd began to move forward through the streets. Little boys began to run alongside, poking their fingers into the soft thighs of the loyalist. The older boys followed, waving their fists, shouting derisive remarks and encouraging others to join in the ridicule.

The mob passed in front of the buggy, and as the din slowly ebbed away the three in the wagon sighed and sat down. "The poor man," Deborah finally said softly.

"It is a degrading scene," Hale admitted. "I doubt Mr. Parker will want to stay in Hartford after this event."

"If he had anything to do with our taxation," Mark grumbled, "I say nothing was too degrading for him.

And it will be a good enough warning for any of his friends too."

"I see no satisfaction one gets at the expense of another helpless victim," Matthew answered. "I would not want such humiliation cast on any enemy."

Hale shook his head. "And it gets worse at night time. The mob roams the street, hunting for Tories. They have burned and looted too many homes."

The rest of their tour passed without event and without any further discussion of politics. It was late afternoon when Matthew turned to their new friend and reluctantly said, "I am afraid it is time we start heading back to Wethersfield. I appreciate your showing us your fair city."

Hale frowned. "I am afraid fair Hartford has shown its tarnished side today."

"Nonsense," Matthew protested, "I am glad you showed us what is happening. I was not aware that such things really existed—and so near to Wethersfield. Things are more serious than I had thought."

"More serious than *anyone* thinks," Nathan Hale answered. "I doubt whether Ambassador Franklin can convince England to give in to our demands. After defeating a mighty nation like France, England is not likely to take us very seriously."

"Then you think the worst is in store for the colonies?"

Hale studied Matthew for a long moment. "I don't know whether I really should tell you this or not. But friends of mine have said there is talk at the Colonial Congress of renouncing all ties with England if the king does not meet our grievances."

"Why, that's treason!" Deborah gasped.

"Yes, and that's why you should not repeat what I have said."

"But surely our delegates won't let it come to that," Matthew exclaimed.

Hale shrugged. "All I have heard is that while many are reluctant to think that far ahead, there are those who are speaking out for independence. And if that happens, the result will undoubtedly be war."

"Do you really think it will go that far?" Deborah asked.

"Did you see the faces in that crowd? Are you not aware of the anger and determination the issue of freedom has raised? I tell you this. England has finally overstepped her authority with her foolish Acts. She has unknowingly nurtured the idea that the colonies might do better without any control from England. We might very well be ready for self-government."

"But there are too many differences," Matthew answered. "I can see the colonies becoming separate nations, but certainly not uniting as one nation."

"At this moment you are right, my friend. There is only one thing that could unite us all."

"War," Deborah said with a grimace.

"It the one thing that could unite everyone under a common cause," Hale agreed. "Not only the various colonies, but very possibly all the varied classes of people, different religious sects, everyone to one cause."

Matthew shook his head slowly. "It's too great a thing to comprehend. It's going to take some careful thinking before I can set my mind to even visualizing such a thing."

Hale laughed. "You will not be the only one, Matthew. I imagine that a great many important men are pondering that very thing, right at this moment. And it should not be just them, but all of us. We all have a stake in what might happen—and we should all be thinking about which is the right road to take."

They had arrived back at Hale's home and he stepped down from the shay. "I appreciate your coming to me, Miss Bell." He grasped her hand warmly in his. "You're more than equal to the texts I have given you, and I consider that in giving them to you I am contributing to all of the students who will pass through your schoolhouse. To the future of the country, if you will," he added with a smile.

Without hesitation she leaned down and kissed his cheek. "I am so glad we came to see you," she answered. "I owe you a great deal and I shall always remember your generosity. Thank you."

Coloring with embarrassment, Hale turned and held out a hand to Matthew. "If you or your fiery young brother have need of me, please do not hesitate to look me up. If war breaks out I shall be with the Connecticut regiment. We shall be only too glad to have two more for our ranks."

"And I can think of no one I would rather have leading us," Matthew responded. "But for all our sakes, let us hope we meet under more pleasant circumstances."

"We shall drink to that, sir," Hale responded, stepping back. "I shall go get Miss Bell's books, and then you had better be off before nightfall besets you."

4

ROBERT BELL, his white hair thinning, yet long enough to cascade a lock or two into his eyes every once in a while, listened intently as his three children related their adventures in Hartford. He waited patiently for each one's account of what had happened, never once betraying his own thoughts until they had finished.

To Deborah he turned first, his face soft and warm. Robert Bell held a special place in his heart for this handsome daughter of <u>his</u>. Her face was that of his beloved wife, lately so much on his mind. There were times, when looking at Deborah, that years slipped away and his world became that of fifty years past.

"You may store Mr. Hale's books in the chest for safe-keeping if you wish," he said in his low voice.

"You might also keep in mind that your younger brother might make use of them once in a while."

"But I already know enough to read and write," Mark objected, wincing at the prospect of more learning.

"If we Bells are going to have a teacher as one of us, the least we can do is try to know something about what she teaches," his father answered curtly. "Time was when just knowing how to read and write was enough. But, things being the way they are, it's going to take more than just reading and writing and one's profession to keep alive." He pursed his lips and turned his attention to Matthew.

"And you, lad, so silent through all of this. The crease on your forehead tells me there is something bothering you."

Matthew studied his father. It was not that he wanted to keep anything from the old man; the truth was that he really didn't know what he was feeling about the things he had witnessed and discussed with Nathan Hale.

"I don't know for sure," he answered with a sigh. "I guess maybe I'm worried about the future."

Robert Bell nodded. "I am glad to see one of us is worried," he said, casting a meaningful glance at Mark. "I fear that some of today's youth does not realize the gravity of a decision to bear arms. They have no idea what a war is like. They have no idea the hardships involved."

"But the colonies cannot let England have their will with us," Mark answered stubbornly. "It is time we put our foot down."

"And the colonies will place their feet in a pile of cow dung, is what they'll do," Robert Bell answered, his voice rising. "They're marching blindly into a field they know nothing about."

Mark was about to speak but Matthew gave him a stern glance. "Blind or not," he spoke up, "I don't see where we can stop them. And I don't see how we can stay out of it."

"We can stay out of it by minding our own business, that's how," their father answered.

"But England's not letting us mind our own business," Mark spoke up, this time rising to his feet.

"And I'll not have you to speak to me in that tone," his father answered, squaring his shoulders and glaring at his youngest.

"Father, I'm sorry," Mark answered in a strained voice. "But if England does not stop placing those intolerable laws upon us, then I and a great many others are perfectly willing to stand up and fight for our rights. I know you and Matt would never allow anyone to dictate to us what we can or cannot do. Neither will I, and I am not afraid to admit it!" With those words, Mark spun around and left the house.

It was quiet for several moments as the others sat motionless, absorbed by the impassioned words they had just heard. Finally, it was the elder Bell who stirred in his chair and started to shake his head. "I would not want either one of you to tell him," he said, "but I am proud of that young patriot. I only wish there was some way we could harness all that energy."

Matthew smiled and leaned back in the rocker. "If he put as much energy into making barrels, we could both sit back and enjoy life." They all chuckled.

"You know he will try to run off and join the army if there is a war," Deborah reminded them quietly.

"Aye," Matthew answered. "And we cannot keep

him in chains, either. Frankly, I don't know what we can do about it."

"Speaking of warring," their father answered, clearing his throat, "our new lobstertail has called roll call for tomorrow morning."

"What, again?" Matthew objected. It was usually only on Tuesdays that the men of Wethersfield were called together for instruction on the manual of arms and close order drill. "He's so bloody hungry for a command that he has to call out the militia again?"

"I think he is impressed with himself," Deborah answered.

"He's impressed with that damn red uniform of his, that's what," Matthew answered. "He and his two sergeants think they carry the might of England on their shoulders.

"There's more than the three of 'em," his father reminded him.

"How well we all know," Matthew answered, his anger rising. "That's what the purpose of these formations has been lately, y'know—to see who kisses his hand."

"At least it's good training for the others," Deborah observed.

"That's the only reason the patriots attend. That, and to keep an eye on Scott and the other Tories. Lately there have been two different ranks. Sympathies are that clearly drawn now."

"And which rank do you stand in?" his father asked curiously.

"I'm no Tory," came the quick answer. "You, of all people, should know that." There was a moment of hesitation before he added, "But I'm not as enthusiastic about the cause as the others."

His father cocked his head. "It is good to have a

cool head in such a group. Besides, you will come about in your own good time."

"Come about?" Matthew shook his head and smiled. There were times he did not understand the way his father thought. "Are you trying to tell us that Mark's way is right?"

Robert Bell snorted in amusement. "Youth tends to run headfirst into trouble without thinking. But it will be the likes of Mark who will come rallying to battle if it is war."

"Well then, let's hope older heads will lead them," Matthew commented. "Or the likes of Nathan Hale."

"He's not too much older than you, Matthew," Deborah reminded him. "It is largely his education that makes the difference."

Matthew grinned openly. "Y'mean if I'd had a bit more teaching, I'd be more like Mr. Hale?"

"It's not that you're uneducated," she answered, her tone serious. "You are every bit as smart as any man I know. It's just that people with education are more likely to get good positions."

"The teacher again!" Matthew smirked and winked at his father.

"Well, it's true," she responded.

"Aye," her father interjected on her behalf. "We cannot argue with that, lass. It has been that way for centuries. It is the ones that have the money, the land or the learning who get the leadership."

"And they can have all those things along with all their worries too," Matthew added. "We do all right with our coopering."

"Indeed you do," Deborah replied firmly. "I'm just trying to point out that there's not so very much difference between you and Nathan Hale, if you but knew it."

Matthew glanced at her in sprprise, then looked away, embarrassed. "Well, be that as it may," he said at length, "the leadership here is that pompous Scott. The man will do anything for advancement. He's trying to make us into some kind of a grenadier regiment so he can get a higher rank."

"He wants to make all of you Tommy Lobsters," Deborah laughed. One morning she had found some of her tardy students watching the menfolk parade on the commons, giggling at their deliberate awkwardness while Scott and his two sergeants bellowed their disapproval and anger.

"He's having his hands full, that's for sure," Matthew acknowledged. Wethersfield boasted a handful of loyalist families, but most of the militia was made up of patriots, waiting for a signal from their Whig leaders to bear arms.

"Well, some of you are certainly not making it easy on the lieutenant," Deborah added.

They all smiled. "There are some who are outright rude, I admit. A lot of it is done in good fun, for if it came to a confrontation, we outnumber the Tories five to one. I think Scott knows that and that's why he hasn't really borne down on us."

"I hope someone's keeping a steady hand on that group," the elder Bell stated. "We don't want this town to become another Boston."

"Most of it depends upon Scott," Matthew said. "As long as he doesn't push too hard, there will be no trouble."

But Scott was not in a good mood the next morning. It was obvious, as the men assembled on the grass in the center of town, that the lieutenant was agitated about something. He came out of the small one-room cabin he had confiscated as his headquarters, bent forward in a brisk pace which had earned him the nickname "the Red Bantam."

He came within about ten feet of the group and stopped, all six foot six of his lanky frame still bent forward as he scrutinized those in front of him. Even from that distance, all could see the anger in his dark eyes.

"Sergeant!" His crisp staccato voice bit through the morning air and the group quieted. The command brought one of his aides forward, snapping the heels of his boots together in an exaggerated precision that always brought a snicker or two from the crowd.

"Form a line in two ranks!"

A front line was quickly formed by seven older men and five youngsters, stiffly attending to the order, muskets held rigidly to their sides. The others watched sourly as the town's loyalists lined in rank, making no move to follow suit.

The sergeant hesitated, then puffed up his chest and bellowed more loudly, "Form a line in two ranks!"

Matthew stood quietly with Mark and the others, watching the reaction of the soldier. It was a testing to see how far they could push the English, a small but definite demonstration of defiance against their rule.

Scott had not budged a muscle. Only his eyes moved, darting from man to man, taking note of those who disobeyed.

In desperation, the sergeant came around the front file of men and confronted the other group. "You there," he bellowed. "Start rank here," and he pulled on the arm of the nearest patriot.

There was a hesitant shuffling as the men reluctantly nudged each other to form a ragged long rank behind the Tories. There were a few snickers as the sergeant tried to straighten out the line. Finally, realizing the futility of his efforts, the soldier backed away and eyed the formation.

"Some of you form in with the front row," he ordered, pointing to the Tory line, but no one responded. "You, you—form next to that one." He tugged at arms but was shrugged away.

A voice from behind called out. "We'll not form with the likes of them Tories!" There was a hum of approval.

The sergeant cast a furtive look at his superior and must have received some kind of silent communication, for he gave up his efforts and returned to the front of the two uneven files. He looked at them resignedly, and his voice was a low monotone when he continued. "When in file, musket and rod will be in the right hand, stock alongside the right foot, with powder horn slung over shoulder snug on the left hip."

A few of the muskets in the second file were shifted slowly in some semblance of cooperation. Finally, satisfied that he had done as much with the men as he could, the sergeant swiveled about and faced his officer.

"Sir! The militia is formed!" Without waiting for any further command, the soldier marched to a position behind Scott, turned about and stood at a parade rest, obviously relieved that his duties were finished for the time being.

Lieutenant Fitchley Scott clasped both hands behind his back and stepped forward, his head lowered as he affected a stern expression. "Commencing now, the militia is to meet two times per week, every Tuesday and every Thursday at this time." He waited until the murmuring died down. "I have received instructions from Boston that, at any moment, militias from every New England state shall be inducted into His Majesty's service." He waited again for the din to diminish. "Of course, as always, volunteers will have not only first preference in treatment and rank, but their pay will be substantially higher." He looked especially meaningfully at the first rank of men in front of him.

"And what if we don't want to join up?" one of the back row men called out.

Scott stepped closer. "Every one of you has been training in this militia for the very purpose of possible draft into the service."

"And who are we supposed to be fighting?" another voice asked.

"It is hoped that His Majesty will not have to go that far."

"Why not? He's done just about everything else!"

Scott's head snapped up at the words and he looked angrily at the second row to find who had spoken.

"You men had better remember you are in the service of the King!"

Someone from the first rank turned to face the others. "Long live the King!" he proclaimed and shook his fist at them.

The gesture was met with catcalls and oaths by the patriot file. "Long live our freedom!" Mark cried out.

Matthew yanked at his brother's arm to quiet him, but not before the others yelled out their approval.

"Your brother has an impetuous tongue, Mr. Bell," Scott called out. "It smacks of treason and disloyalty!"

Matthew's fingers dug deeply into Mark's arm, warning him to be still. "My brother is young and only voices his dislike for military discipline," Matthew answered.

"Perhaps that is exactly what the boy needs, Mr. Bell—discipline!"

Matthew took a deep breath to ease the tension from his voice. "We are farmers and tradesmen," he answered evenly. "Guns, formations and military orders are not our natural way."

"I would then advise that some of you had better keep that in mind," Scott stated. "These small rebellions we are hearing about are no match for the strength of England's armies." He took a step backward and placed hands on hips, his expression becoming contemptuous. "Look at you. Do you think this militia or any other colonial militia is capable of even cleaning the dishes of our armies?"

"We might not be capable of cleaning dishes, your honour," a voice rang out, "but we sure in hell know where to throw the garbage!"

"Or how to give rides!"

"How 'bout fluffing feathers?"

"Or what to do with your tea!"

Scott stepped forward, head once more down. "Hold your tongues!" he warned tightly. He waited until it was quiet. "I remind you again that this is a military formation under military instruction, and thus, you are all under the military disciplinary rules." He waited for his warning to sink in. "I have not used my prerogative to enforce military discipline. I have tried to get along with this town as best I could. I realize that neither you nor I want to be here. But orders have been given, and by the might of His Majesty I shall see that those orders are carried out to the fullest, even if it means imprisonment for every one of you!"

He turned and slowly paced the entire length of the line, wordlessly staring at each man. Matthew watched in fascination. Certainly the man was braver than most. Scott and the Tories were far outnumbered, and yet the officer had had the presence to silence the jeering group and achieve a standoff. For the time being, Matthew reminded himself.

"Now, the next man who voices his opinions without my permission shall be carted away!"

Matthew tightened his grip on Mark's sleeve as a warning to the youth to remain quiet. There would be plenty of opportunities to let one's feelings be known. But here, in Scott's little army, was not the place.

5

I SAY that lobsterback Scott is due for a ride on a rail," Jacob Miller announced in a solemn voice. Miller was one of the oldest and most respected men in the group that gathered in the livery barn at dusk.

It was a meeting as regular as the roll call on the commons, an agreed upon arrangement among the patriots.

"We rail a British soldier, and we'll really have our hands full," warned Samuel Marsues, white goatee twitching in the dull light.

"There will be plenty of time to deal with the lieutenant," Matthew agreed. "What we should talk about is what we should do if Scott does try to imprison one of us."

"I say we should take over," a voice from somewhere

in the crowd stated. There was a murmur of agreement.

"Our instructions were to wait and be patient," old Samuel replied. "We don't want to foul any plans the Whig party might be setting up by some rash act on our part."

"Maybe it's about time Connecticut starts things instead of Massachusetts. Why should them people be the ones telling us what to do?"

"For one thing," Samuel Marsues answered, "they're closer to the British army. For another thing, we got our representatives up there right alongside their leaders."

"We heard they's gone into hiding."

"Warren and Adams, I think, are hiding out at Lexington," Jacob Miller answered. "Things are stirring up and the only word we're getting is for us to be ready."

"That's all we been hearing for the last couple of years," someone complained.

"And we're all the better prepared for it, too," Jacob answered belligerently. "We're all anxious to strike a blow for freedom—and we all suffer listening to the likes of Scott and his Tory friends. But our time will come. And come soon, if I have my guess at it."

"And in the meantime, we have to suffer Scott?" an irate voice called out.

Samuel rose to his feet and glanced about at the ring of solemn-faced men. They wore the simple clothes of farmers and tradesmen, modest and hardworking men. But in their faces he saw the pride and determination that had rallied them to stand up for their rights, and their spirit made him proud of the community they had all built together.

"Aye, we suffer Scott. As we have suffered the in-justices of English law for half a decade, so we can suffer him. For when all is accounted for, he too will be taken care of. That is the knowledge that will enable us to suffer such roll calls every other day. That's why we can take the effrontery and the insinuations of them loyalists. 'Cause we know what is really happening. The ground beneath them is being worked on and it won't be too long before it will open up and swallow them with all the other dung."

"What about Matthew's question?" someone asked. "He has a good point and one we should prepare for."

Jacob Miller raised a hand for silence. "The question is, how can we save a comrade from going to prison. Assuming we get orders not to start a war ourselves, overpowering Scott will be out of the question."

"Maybe Matthew has thought of an answer to his own question," Samuel suggested.

They turned to Matthew and he rose to his feet. "Frankly, I haven't given it much thought until to-day. I agree with Jacob that if we all try something against Scott we'll have the entire British army in Wethersfield before we know it."

"Then what's your idea?"

Matthew shrugged his shoulders. "I can think of only two alternatives," he answered. "We would either have to attempt a rescue while the prisoner was locked up in Scott's office, or else while they were taking him to Boston."

"It would have to be done in the middle of the night, with disguises," Jacob stated.

"Another Indian raid?" someone chuckled.

"All right," Samuel said, again rising to his feet for attention. "I suggest that Matthew form a committee for safety, whose responsibility it will be to handle any such emergency. The less known by the rest of us, the better it will be. Matthew, you select secretly four or five others to help you in forming this committee."

Matthew was flustered. He hadn't expected this responsibility and was figuring out a way to back down from the duty when Mark came up to him and slapped his back.

"Matthew," he said, smiling proudly, "I want to be part of your vigilante group. It is good to know we are all in such good hands."

"I don't think I should be the one for the job," Matthew said uncomfortably.

"Why not?" Mark asked, alarmed. "I would feel safe if I were put in irons, knowing you were the one setting me free."

"I just don't think I should be the one," Matthew added and glanced over to Samuel sheepishly.

"And why not, Matthew?" the older man asked. "It was your suggestion and a good one at that. You have a good imagination and know Wethersfield as well as any of us. What makes you think you're not qualified?"

Silence fell over the group, and Matthew turned to face them, feeling uneasy and uncertain. "To be honest with all of you, I don't know how I am going to react if anything should happen."

There was an embarrassing moment of silence. Samuel Marsues came closer to Matthew and studied him carefully. "None of us know exactly how we'll react to the future," he said reassuringly.

"It's more than that," Matthew said. He stared at the old man with troubled eyes, conscious of the others looking at him. "You all are so hell-bent on taking up arms against England. If there is going to be a fight, you all know what you're going to do." He hesitated, wrestling with his emotions. "I'm not quite sure what I will do," he said softly.

Samuel smiled and touched his shoulder. "Matthew," he said slowly. "You're no Tory. We all know that, just as I know you know it, too. And I guess if we all dig deeply, there's a touch of loyalty to England and the King in all of us. Loyalty to the King has been imbedded in all of us from birth." He then turned to the rest of them and raised his voice for all to hear. "But we aren't raising our arms in disloyalty to the King or to England, but because we feel we have rights worth fighting to protect. And it's not just me nor you, nor you, nor you—but all of us, from Maine all the way down to the southern colonies. They all came to Philly with the same voice. And by God, we are ready to fight for what we believe in!"

The others gave a loud hurrah but were quickly quieted when Samuel raised his arm for silence and turned to Matthew. "I put by faith in you, boy," he said with a firm hand on Matthew's shoulder. "You, of all of us, probably have a more firm head on your shoulders 'cause you're thinking deep and long about what's happening. This thing is a serious matter and does take a heap of wondering to make sense. That's why you're good to have with us. You balance the hotheads among us."

There was a nervous outbreak of laughter in the group.

"I just want to be honest with you, Samuel," Matthew responded.

"Maybe he's got a reason for not siding with us," a voice called out.

Marsues spun around and tried to pinpoint the

source of the accusation. "What is meant by that remark?" he asked, his voice rising quickly in anger.

John Wilson, muscular from plowing in the fields of his farm just at the outskirts of Wethersfield, did not stand, but he met Samuel's eyes evenly. "Maybe Bell has reasons why he couldn't do nothing against Scott!"

All eyes turned back to Matthew. There had been a time when Matthew and John Wilson had been on friendly terms. Rumors had swept through Wethersfield that the eldest of the Bells and the eldest daughter of John Wilson, Chaning, were to be engaged. There was no doubt in Matthew's mind that John Wilson would have been only too happy for the marriage, and the man had several times flavored the pudding by hinting of a more than generous dowry for the young couple.

Chaning Wilson had been the talk of most of the young men of Wethersfield for as long as Matthew could remember. She had matured earlier than most girls and it was obvious that she enjoyed every moment of the attention she received. It wasn't until she was eighteen that she seemed to notice Matthew Bell was the one boy in town who was not paying her homage, and she had accordingly set her sights on him.

At first he had wanted little to do with her since, in his eyes, she was such a flirt. But Chaning Wilson was too sweet a morsel to be ignored, and once she had captured his attention she had enticed him in so brazen a manner that he had become all but obsessed with her.

He had courted her all through the winter before last, trudging through the snow in the dark evenings to spend a few minutes in front of the Wilson fireplace with her at his side. By the time the snows had melted, they had both been anxious to find a place where they could be alone. The first warm spring day had found them sitting quietly after a picnic lunch and looking out over the newly green landscape. Matthew had turned his head slowly to look into her eyes and he had seen the moistness, the surrender she could no longer hide.

He could not hold back. His eyes darted to the full curve of her bodice and Chaning leaned close so that the roundness came to his lips. He crushed her to him, his mouth encircling the material, staining the fabric. His fingers found their way up her slim waist until they cupped her bodice, kneading into the softness. She had put up little resistance as he began to unfasten the buttons of her dress.

Their lovemaking had been a disappointment to Matthew. He was aware of his awkwardness compared to her obvious experience, although that realization did not come to him until later that night when he was alone in bed, recalling the sensations and details. And after their lovemaking, Chaning had quickly dressed and begun a casual conversation, as though nothing special had occurred. But the greatest disappointment had come later. They had met several times after that, but Matthew came to feel that she was granting him a favor in which she took little pleasure. He began to realize that he had been merely a challenge to the flirtatious Chaning Wilson.

Then it had stopped, almost as abruptly as it had started. He had taken Scott's offer of cutting winter wood next to the river, and there he had met Louisa Scott. At least Louisa had the desire which Chaning had lacked.

Now, as he stood before Chaning's father and his

insinuations, Matthew suddenly wondered if his illicit affair with Scott's wife was known to others.

"It has nothing to do with Scott," Matthew answered tightly.

"And I never said it had anything to do with the man," John Wilson answered. If the man knew, he was never going to make it public, for his daughter's reputation was also at stake. But his eyes bore into Matthew's.

"I don't see what your point is, sir," Samuel Marsues answered, confused.

"It's not for you to see," Wilson answered. "It's strictly for him!" He pointed an accusing finger at Matthew.

"My brother is as much a patriot as any of us," Mark cried out, standing to challenge Wilson.

"And I say he's too close to Scott to suit my purpose," Wilson shouted back.

"Just what are you trying to say?" Mark asked. He stepped forward, but Matthew put a restraining hand on his shoulder. "Are you calling him a spy?"

"I'm saying if he can't make up his mind on how he stands, he has no business knowing what we do," Wilson answered. He looked about him and found encouragement from a few others who nodded their heads. "If by his own admission he doesn't know where he stands, to me that means he could go to their side. And if he does, he knows all about us."

"You're a low-minded man, John Wilson," Mark exploded. "Just because my brother broke off with your—" Matthew jerked Mark around and pushed him roughly into his seat, glaring at him until he was satisfied the youth would be quiet. Then, slowly, Matthew straightened and turned to the others.

"I do not want to be the cause of any division in this group," he said, his voice low, constrained. "If there is one thing you all need more than anything, it is unity." He surveyed the men of Wethersfield calmly. "I am no spy for England, nor will I ever be. If there is a hesitation on my part, it is only whether I can take up arms, not on where my heart lies." He paused, taking a deep breath before going on. "But perhaps John Wilson is right. As long as I cannot make a firm commitment, I should not be part of the minutemen."

He turned to Samuel Marsues. "It is better this way, Samuel. I shall continue to support you as best I can. My brother here shall represent the Bell family, for his commitment is true and sure. God speed to all of you!"

He jammed the tricorn on his head, swiveled about and walked out into the night air. He hesitated, looking up at the dark sky and taking a deep breath. Had he taken the right step? He knew he had to follow his own instincts, that everyone had their own path to follow. But must his always be so alone?

6

LEAVE YOUR BROTHER BE," Robert Bell chided the youngest of his offspring.

Mark Bell looked up from his place at the dinner table and pointed his pewter fork towards Matthew. "Well, I'd still like to know why he didn't face down John Wilson's slandering words."

"I'm sure Matthew has his reasons," the elder Bell answered and glanced at Matthew in hopes that there would be clarification of the episode related by Mark. "John Wilson is a good Christian and would not slur our name. Perhaps there was a misunderstanding."

"He all but called Matthew a Loyalist," Mark exclaimed. They all looked at Matthew for a reply.

He had heard their words as though off in the distance, his thoughts roiling in confusion. Although he stared at the rigid designs his fork made in the fluffy white potatoes Deborah had prepared, all he could envision was the disappointment in Samuel Marsue's eyes. Perhaps he had been as foolish and unthinking in becoming involved with the minutemen as with either Chaning Wilson or Louisa Scott.

"It is better that I stay out of the group for awhile," Matthew admitted. He looked up to meet the inquiring eyes of his family. "Somehow I cannot bring myself to a full commitment. I fear that there are too many who are too eager to take up their muskets and fight."

"But our Continental Congress has made it clear that we will fight for our rights," Mark stated.

"But war?" Matthew asked. "Egads, Mark, do you realize what that means? Does anyone?" He looked around at them. "I'm sorry, but I can't go around whooping and hollering about killing British soldiers."

"I bet you could if they came marching up that road out there," Mark exclaimed.

Matthew shrugged. "Maybe. I really don't know. In some instances I envy you, Mark, for knowing what you want. I don't—at least not yet, I don't."

Robert Bell reached over and gripped Matthew's wrist tightly. "You will," he said firmly. "I have all the faith that you will find your way solidly. Things that grow taller and stronger and are more solid take more time to sink into their roots. That may be you, Matthew, so I wouldn't worry 'bout it none. Have the strength to stand by your convictions—just as strongly as Mark here stands by his. I am proud of both of you, of all three of you," he said, looking at each of his children in turn. "I am a very lucky man indeed."

"Whatever we are, we got it from you, Papa," Deborah said with a warm smile.

"And from your mother," he reminded her.

Her smile widened and she clutched at his hand. "Of course from our dear mama."

They were silent for several long moments. Five years ago the smallpox had been severe, especially among the older people. The wife of Robert Bell, mother of three children, was buried among those in the small cemetery at the west end of Wethersfield.

"She would have been proud of you all," their father said soberly, head bowed.

"She's with us, Papa," Deborah said softly, squeezing his hand comfortingly. "She's right here with us, now."

Robert Bell looked up with moistened eyes and nodded, braving a small smile. "Of course she is. We talk to each other regular."

"Which side would she have taken?" Mark asked.

His father sniffed mightily and leaned back in his chair, thankful for the turn in the conversation. "No doubt about it," he answered proudly. "If the throne wasn't over such an expanse of water, you would have bet your last boot she would'a walked right up to His Majesty and curtsied the cute way she used to. She'd use all them manners she'd been taught to sidle up to the king, and then she'd tell him just how he should do away with the taxes and all those other laws." He smiled and nodded his head. "And you know what? She would'a had her way, too, just like she always used to. Wasn't a man alive who could turn down anything she asked for . . ."

An hour later, the Bell family sat around the fireplace, each in his favorite position. The dishes had been washed and dried and put away carefully in the cupboards. Robert Bell sat in the high-backed rocker with the red cushion his wife had crocheted for one of his birthdays, gently rocking, puffing on a long-stemmed pipe that gave off a sharp thick aroma into the room. Matthew had turned one of the straight-backed dining chairs around and had propped his stockinged feet on another, facing the fire, becoming mesmerized by the dancing flames.

Mark lay on his stomach, hands folded under his chin, also staring into the red embers. His sister sat closest to the fire, its light flickering on the delicate pages of the family Bible from which she read in her soft contralto voice. It was a gentle moment, revered by each one of them as a time to rest, to contemplate, to dream, to enjoy.

The hoofbeats were unmistakable, jarring them from their mood of quiet contentment. It was seldom that anyone would gallop past their house at this end of the town. It was dangerous to be traveling so fast in the darkness; only a serious call would beckon anyone on such a hazardous journey.

Matthew waited for the hoofbeats to fade away, but when they slowed and halted just outside their home he stood up and stared at the door. Deborah stopped her reading and glanced about, waiting.

The knock had been expected, yet its urgency and loudness startled them. Matthew quickly went to the door.

"It's a call to arms!" Charles Littleton, an onion grower from the east side of town, spoke breathlessly as he came into the room. "The Sons of Liberty have called for us, and we're headed for Boston!"

"Now wait, hold on!" Matthew exclaimed, seeing the man's wild-eyed excitement. "Who's calling us and why?"

Littleton shook his head, still trying to catch his

breath. "I gotta spread the word," he stammered. "All the patriots are being called to Boston, that's all I know."

"But why?" Matthew insisted.

The man shrugged. "I dunno exactly. All we heard is that British troops attacked a place outside Boston, a place called Lexington. And they're marching on to another place called Concord. We're supposed to help drive back them redcoats."

Matthew was stunned. This was not supposed to happen. What did the British think they were doing?

"Man, are you sure? Are you sure it was British soldiers?"

Charles Littleton nodded. "The Sons of Liberty been sending riders in every direction. They're asking every patriot to come to their aid. It's war!"

"God save us!" Robert Bell declared and sat down.

"We have to go!" Mark ran to his room with a loud whoop.

"Mark!" Matthew yelled out. "You're going nowhere!"

The youth returned, struggling into his jacket, his boots tucked under one arm. "What do you mean, we're not going?"

"Just as I said," Matthew answered. He turned abruptly to the messenger. "We appreciate your call. Is there anything you need?"

Littleton glanced around the room, not quite sure of what he was hearing. He shook his head and slowly backed out of the room, beginning to worry that he might have mistakenly come upon a Loyalist home. "No," he stammered, "nothing." Quickly he turned and disappeared into the night. Hoofbeats staccatoed and quickly died into the night.

"What do you mean, not going?" Mark insisted, now seated on a chair and pulling on his boots. "We've got to go. It's a call to arms!"

"It's way over near Boston," Matthew answered. "By now it's over and done with."

"But it's a call to arms!" Mark insisted. "It's the call we've been waiting for."

"Call to arms, call to arms!" Matthew answered, exasperated. "If everyone leaves for Boston, who's going to watch Connecticut?"

"The British are at Boston," Mark answered. It was obvious that his mind was made up. As he moved about grabbing his powder horn, pouch, stuffing his pockets with half a loaf of bread and other things that came to his mind, his voice was sure and solid with conviction. "This is the moment we all have been waiting for. It's force against force now. And the Sons of Liberty will need every man they can get."

Matthew watched his brother helplessly. He turned to his father but the old man was bent over in his chair, head in his hands, silently weeping for the future. "I'm not going to let you go, Mark!"

The boy stopped and turned to face his brother. "You can't stop me, Matthew, not this time." He met Matthew's eyes evenly and unwaveringly. "We could do wonders side by side, y'know, you and me." He waited and when Matthew refused to answer, he slowly nodded his head. "It comes as no surprise that you won't be coming, but I'm not holding it against you, Matthew. I know you'll do what you've got to do. And it's the same with me. I am a Son of Liberty and I'm proud of it. I think this is one of the best things I've ever done in my life."

Matthew's shoulders sunk in dejection. "My God, you're too young to be fighting in a war!"

"Someone's got to fight."

"Would you stay if I took your place?" Matthew asked, without fully realizing why he had asked the question.

Mark smiled and moved to take the long-barreled musket from the wall pegs. "But you won't, we both know that—so there's no use in answering."

"Mark—" Deborah grasped his arm. "Please, please don't go. You're needed here."

"I'm needed there more," Mark answered and stooped to kiss her on the cheek. "Don't you worry none. We're fighting for our rights. And knowing that, we're hell-bent on giving them lobsterbacks a fight for the money. I imagine this scuffle will be over sooner than you'll know."

Deborah released her hold and stepped back. She no longer tried to stop the tears that started to stream down the sides of her face as she watched Mark make his final preparations. Suddenly she rushed up to him, took his head in her hands and kissed him tenderly. "God be with you, Mark Bell. We shall pray every day for your safe return."

"A safe return it will be," he answered, trying to brave a smile through his own tears. "I too shall think of all of you every day and my own prayers will be with you." He turned to Matthew and hesitantly stuck out his hand. "God-speed, Matthew. I fear you will have the harder time."

Matthew clenched his teeth and tried to scowl. "I never could stop you from doing anything you wanted to do."

Mark grinned and wiped the tears from his eyes with his sleeve. "I hope this isn't one time I wish you had. But I know I'm doing the right thing. I know that, Matthew!"

Matthew nodded. "Yes, I know you do. It's just that I wish I knew in my own heart what is right. I don't agree with your going, and yet I feel I should be at your side. Or that I should be going and not you."

Mark tried to laugh. "And you think you're so much better than me? Who was it who hit the bull's-eye first? And who was it who beat you in loading the musket?"

Matthew smiled. "It's true enough that you are better when it comes to guns, Mark, but don't let that swell-headedness get in the way of a sane and clear mind."

"Don't worry about me, Matthew. There's thousands of us to protect each other. I want to live to see the result of all our efforts."

"Then I guess there is nothing more to be said. I want to hold you back, I want to tie you to that chair, I want to lock the door and throw away the key. But I know your determination and I know that eventually you would find a way to escape. So I cannot hold you back, Mark. All I can do is wish you Godspeed and remind you of our love for you." Matthew tightened his hold on Mark's hand and clasped his shoulder. He was hurting inside, so much that it was difficult to speak, difficult to see in the dimness of the cabin. It was going to be a sleepless night.

Mark turned to his father and knelt on the floor beside his chair. "It is not easy to leave a place where there is so much love. You probably know that as well as I do. Just as you know that this is something I have to do, I want you to know, too, that I will be coming back."

Robert Bell slowly raised his head. There were no tears on the old man's face, though it was solemn and full of sadness. Slowly he lifted his hand and gently touched Mark's cheek, his eyes taking in the boy's face as though trying to memorize every detail.

"We shall set your place at the eating table and leave it, knowing that you will return one of these days, safe and sound. Whatever strengths we have, we all give to protect you. And our joy will never return until you are back with us." He sighed heavily and nodded his head. "Go with God, my son—my patriot."

Mark rose to his feet, head hung low in sadness. "Don't you worry—any of you. I shall return, you wait and see." Before they knew what had happened, Mark ran to the door and stepped out into the night, gone.

The room was quiet, its occupants unmoving as they stared at the oblong hole of darkness which had swallowed Mark. It was many minutes before Matthew stepped to the door and gently closed it.

Matthew slowly turned and surveyed the others. His father had begun to rock slowly, his head to the side as he stared forlornly into the dying embers of the fire. Deborah slowly sank into the comfort of her chair, her face streaked with tears, her eyes red-rimmed and vacantly staring.

Matthew was already beginning to feel guilty, and he had to fight the urge to run after Mark and drag him back home. It was he, Matthew, who should have gone. Mark was young and untried. Matthew and his father had handled all the worries and problems the family faced. Even Deborah had once taken on an older boy who had beaten up on Mark at a young age. Yet it was Mark who now met the challenge, a challenge far more serious than any the Bells had ever encountered, and he was too determined to be held back.

Matthew slumped in a corner chair, chin on his chest, his arms folded on his chest for warmth. It was he who should have gone, who should have cried out for freedom and liberty. Was he such a worthless specimen, such a coward that he could allow a young and innocent lad to take his place? What kind of torture was he to live each day, knowing these things? What was it that Mark had said? The boy feared that Matthew would have the more difficult time of it?

Probably so. There was a hollowness, an emptiness that had opened up in his soul. He was following his beliefs, as Mark had said. But at what cost, he could only wonder.

7

IT WAS JUST the next day when Matthew began to realize how difficult his life was going to be. Deborah returned from the village store with news that Lieutenant Scott was calling together the militia the very next morning.

"But you certainly can't go," Deborah insisted, "not with everyone else gone."

"Scott and his Tory friends will be there," his father added severely.

"I'm not afraid of them," Matthew answered soberly. "Besides, we don't want to give the British any cause against us by my not showing up."

"But you'll get in trouble going there without any patriots being around."

Matthew shook his head stubbornly. "They can't hold me responsible for everyone leaving. And I suspect that I'm probably the only patriot still in Wethersfield, so the least I can do is stand up against them."

The next morning dawned with a mist that cast an eerie white haze low on the meadows. The group of Tory sympathizers huddled close together, mumbling among themselves about the absence of the other men of the town, casting curious glances at Matthew who stood to one side, by himself.

Matthew knew Scott must be aware of the absence of the patriots. He was sure the officer had been warned last evening, not only by the unmistakable clamor of hoofbeats, but undoubtedly by the swift talk of Tory neighbors left behind.

It was a good five minutes later when the door of Scott's office burst open and the officer and his two sergeants strode briskly towards them. As though nothing out of the ordinary had happened, the same military procedures were followed. At a nod from Scott, one of the sergeants came forward and barked out the orders. Immediately, the Tory townsmen formed their front row file. Matthew hesitated, not sure what he should do, but decided to form a file of one behind the front row. The sergeant looked nervously to the edge of the commons as if hoping to see reinforcements for their depleted ranks. Then he did a brisk turnabout to face Scott, who dismissed him with a nod.

Scott took his time, surveying those in the front row, making sure all were accounted for. Then he stepped forward and eyed Matthew.

"Well, Mr. Bell," he said, his tone brittle and patronizing. "I must say you do surprise me every once in awhile."

Matthew decided he would not answer the remark,

but stood his ground, one arm hooked around his mustket in a casual stance.

"I hear rumors that the renegades of this town have disappeared to do some mischief. I am only curious as to whether your friends cast you out of their lot for being undesirable, or whether the choice was yours."

"I am here of my own choosing," Matthew responded, willing himself not to allow the Britisher to goad him.

"Oh, really," came the disdainful answer. Scott backed away and slowly made his way down the line, winking at a few of the older Tory sympathizers until he rounded the end and came back to Matthew's side. "Pray tell me, sir," came the soft insinuating voice. "Was their deviltry more than you could stomach, or are we to believe that you are a loyal subject of the king?"

"We have never considered ourselves disloyal to the king," Matthew answered guardedly.

Scott's eyebrows arched quizzically. "We? We? Not disloyal to the king?" He came around to face Matthew. "My dear young lad," he intoned haughtily, "ever since I have set foot in this small hamlet, I have seen nothing but disloyalty to His Majesty. If this were England, sir, there would not be trees enough to handle the load of hangings." He paused and brought his face closer to Matthew's, giving him a cold, challenging stare. "Do you not call it treason when your confederates have taken up arms against His Majesty's army? Do you?" He backed away from Matthew and went on in a voice that was low and intense. "I do not know what game you are playing, young sir," he said, walking slowly around Matthew and looking him up and down with a scornful expression. "But I take it far more seriously than you. I know of your affiliation with the so-called Sons of Liberty and their rogue army. Let me tell you, these traitors will be caught and dealt with most severely. I know every disloyal person in this town, believe me. I have been keeping a careful watch on each of you—and your time will come too, Mr. Bell. Don't you think that I am fooled for one minute, just because you have stayed here alone. Whatever game you play, I shall be right next to you to find out. You see, Mr. Bell, I have no use for your type. I am a soldier, one who fights out in the open with musket and bayonet. You and your traitorous Sons of Liberty, on the other hand, are full of devious methods, underhanded affairs. Or perhaps you are simply a coward, Mr. Bell, a man who cannot stand tall for the things he believes in."

"I am no coward—" Matthew regretted the words instantly, knowing that Scott was baiting him and angry that he had allowed himself to react.

"No coward, he says!" Pleased with the response he had provoked, Scott turned to see if the others were listening. "Then you would have me believe that your reason for staying behind is that you are a spy?" He smirked. "Somehow I doubt it. Let me tell you, lad, I have dealt with all kinds. Don't you believe for one second that I can't handle you or that you can outdo me. There's been many who have tried and failed miserably."

"I'm not trying to get the better of you, Scott," Matthew answered, trying not to show his exasperation.

"*Lieutenant* Scott, if you please," the officer corrected. "You're right, you'll never get the better of me,

Mr. Bell. Because you are a coward. And because you would not endanger your rather outspoken young brother, or even your sister."

Scott saw the anger that had been building in his victim and he ducked away just in time to avoid Matthew's furious blow. Matthew drew his fist back to strike again, but the two sergeants jumped forward and pinned his arms behind his back.

Scott stepped around and faced Matthew, a slight smile on his face. "So the cub does have small claws. Consider yourself a lucky man, Mr. Bell," he said coolly. "Hitting an officer is punishable by imprisonment, cutting off the hand, or both." He smiled at the dark look Matthew cast him. "Let this be only a warning. I might not be so generous next time. I could say you tried to hit me. I have a great number of loyal witnesses." He flicked an imaginary speck of dust from his white sleeve. "What kind of a livelihood do you suppose you would have with the use of only one hand, eh, Mr. Bell?"

Matthew glared at the man, then cursed himself for a fool. The confusion and doubt that had dogged him ever since Mark's departure had made him easy prey, blinding him to Scott's obvious tactics. He stopped struggling and held back the anger that boiled within him, knowing that Scott was all too capable of carrying out his threat.

"That's better." Scott sighed and nodded to his men to release Matthew. "I think I should make use of you somewhere other than here, Mr. Bell, where you will be less of a hindrance. With things the way they are, I predict that I shall be spending more time this winter at my office than planned, and I shall therefore need a larger supply of firewood. Since you seem capable of *that* task, at least, your duties from now on will be chopping our winter wood rather than meeting here. But bear in mind, Mr. Bell, I shall always have one eye on you. One false step, one small shred of evidence that you were left behind to spy on us, and I shall deal with you in the strictest manner allowed. Do I make myself clear?"

Every Tuesday and Thursday morning Matthew laid axe to the trees in the grove. He took as much pleasure in the freedom and solitude of his new assignment as in the feel of the May sun filtering through the leaves overhead and warming him as he bent to his work.

Stripped to the waist, Matthew was too absorbed to notice the figure tentatively approaching from behind.

"We haven't seen each other for some time," Louisa Scott said quietly.

He started and turned at the sound of her voice, and she gave a low laugh at his look of surprise.

"I like to watch you work," she murmured, walking slowly toward him, undoing her flared yellow hat and shaking out her auburn hair. "I've missed you, Matthew."

He said nothing, his surprise giving way to discomfort with the memory of their affair, but she didn't sense his feelings until he flinched from the hand she raised to caress his face. She backed away a step, her eyebrows raised at the wariness she read in his stance.

"Matthew, Matthew," he whispered, shaking her head. "I came here only to warn you about Fitchley." She hesitated until she saw the change in his expression.

"He talks about you, Matthew. I am afraid for your

life. He somehow blames you for all the others having left Wethersfield."

"I am the only one he *can* accuse," Matthew explained. "I remind him of the others."

"He doesn't like you. I would have come sooner," she answered, "but I wanted to make sure I wouldn't be followed. If he ever caught us it would surely be the end for you. Probably for both of us."

"Surely he would not harm his own wife," Matthew replied.

"I am not too sure. Fitchley is a proud man. To know his wife has been having an affair with a commoner—especially a patriot—might be too much for him." She laughed. "If we were in England and you were an English gentleman or a fellow officer, I dare say Fitchley would only raise an eyebrow. But I don't think he would take it too kindly here." She paused and eyed him affectionately. "It was enjoyable, was it not?"

Matthew nodded and gave her a sad smile. "But it is no good now." He hesitated and took a deep breath. "We cannot meet again, Louisa," he said softly, not wanting to hurt her.

"And why not?" she asked, glaring at him petulantly.

"It is too dangerous—for both of us," he answered, hoping his answer would satisfy her.

"But we have been most careful, haven't we? And we haven't been caught yet."

"Your husband could very well have someone watching me," Matthew answered. "I, for one, cannot afford to go to prison. I have others who are depending on me."

She studied him silently for a moment. Finally, a mischievous smile curved on her lips. "You are afraid of my husband!"

"I am afraid of what he can do to me, yes," Matthew agreed.

She looked up at him, her smile becoming more self-assured. "Well then, my pet," she answered with fresh vigor, "I shall have to figure out some way for us to meet unnoticed."

"It's no good, Louisa," Matthew answered gently. "I don't think we should be seeing each other again."

She eyed him carefully. "Just you watch, Mr. Bell," she answered. "One way or another, I will make sure we get together again."

Matthew watched as she whirled and walked defiantly back to the house. Knowing Louisa, he was afraid she would keep her word. Somehow, some way, he would have to stay away from her. There was trouble enough brewing in the air, without her adding to the pot.

8

IT HARDLY SEEMED possible that over two months had passed since they had traveled to Hartford, and yet it was already well into June, with the first hints of a hot summer to come.

Matthew and his father worked long, hard hours in the barn, cutting oak slats, curing them with fire and finally binding them into barrels. Even though trading with England and the East India Company had been boycotted by the colonists, there was still plenty of business, thanks to the privateers and smugglers slipping past the few British men-o-war with their cargoes. Although the British had bottled up Boston Harbor, there were more than enough safe ports nearby to lay anchor in.

The three Bells missed Mark. Hardly a day passed that there wasn't talk of the youngest. News from

Massachusetts had filtered back in bits and pieces. The British army had suffered seriously at Concord, where the quickly gathered Minutemen had fought using tactics learned from the French and Indian Wars. Humbled, the redcoats had retreated to Boston.

"Drive 'em out to the sea!" Robert Bell muttered as he and Matthew sat down for a rest from their work.

Matthew frowned. "We have no navy to do that. Besides, I doubt Gage will withdraw much further."

His father spat into the dust. "That Britisher is as bad as the rest of 'em! And now England's sending the two Howe brothers to test how far we'll go."

Matthew nodded glumly. "The Lord Howes have quite a record and I fear things will not go well with us. They've also brought two other generals."

"Don't you worry," Robert Bell answered. "This is our soil we're fighting on. We'll send those lords back to where they belong!"

That night, it was Deborah who brought the latest news.

"A messenger stopped at the Deane house last night," she reported excitedly. "Apparently the Continental Congress has voted to form an army."

"That's what we already have," the elder Bell snorted.

"Only a militia," Matthew corrected. "I don't like the sound of this. We're getting closer and closer to all-out war."

"Mercy!" his sister answered. "They provoked it, passing all those unjust laws and then marching on us that way. We're only fighting to defend ourselves and our beliefs."

"Fighting for what we believe in is all well and good," Matthew answered. "But when we start forming an army it means we're prepared to declared war on England. My God, there's been stronger and older nations in Europe defeated by England. Look at France! Do those people in Philadelphia think we're better equipped than France was?"

"There have been times in history," Deborah spoke up, "when people have risen up against their governments and overthrown them."

Matthew sighed. "I know, and I'm not saying that this is wrong or that it shouldn't be done. It's just . . . it's just that I hope those people have thought things out, that they know what they're doing."

Robert Bell shook his head. "You always were the cautious one, Matthew. But I am sure those good men the colonies sent to Philadelphia know what they're doing and what must be done."

"Let's hope so. In one way or another, the rest of us will have to pay for the actions of those few men."

"Don't you think what they're doing is worth fighting for?" Deborah asked curiously.

Matthew thought about it for a moment. "Yes, when all else fails. But it seems to me that fighting one another should be the last resort. Have we used all of our alternatives? That's all I'm asking. It's too easy to strike out." He thought about it some more. "Maybe we should move out." He let it trail away.

His father shook his head. "Why should we move? Why should any man have to move away because of his beliefs? We settled this piece of land, we bought it with our hard-earned money. My wife is buried in this land, as are our parents and their parents before them. Why should we leave when all we ask is fair treatment and fair representation?"

"But it is an alternative, isn't it?" Matthew asked.

"I mean, rather than fighting, we could move westward and do what we want, make our own laws and rules to live by."

"Until someone different moves in to rule us," Robert Bell answered. "When does a person stop moving? There comes a time when a man just stops, puts his foot down and says—no more. I've been pushed far enough."

"Is that the way here?" Matthew asked. "Have we been pushed far enough?"

"Probably," came the answer. "Five, six years ago England started taxing us on little things. Then they started taxing us on bigger things, began to tell us what to do and what not to do. Five years they been slowly pushing us to our limit. I guess the time's come when we just got pushed too far and now we're ready to make our stand."

Matthew sighed heavily. "I wish I could feel that, Father. I really do."

"Father! Matthew!" Deborah rushed into the barn, her eyes bright with excitement. "Come, it's Mark!"

Father and son had only to exchange glances before they dashed out of the barn and ran to the house. They were barely conscious of the horse tied to the front rail, even less conscious of Deborah trying to keep up with them, half crying and half shouting their names.

"Mark!" Matthew rushed into the living room and stopped short, one quick glance traveling over the smiling form that lay on the couch.

Robert Bell came into the room, breathing heavily, and pushed past Matthew to make his way to Mark. "Son!" he mumbled and got down on his knees to grasp the boy into his arms.

The two hugged each other, eyes squeezed shut, silently weeping. Deborah came in and slid her arm about Matthew's waist as the two watched silently. Glancing from her father to Matthew's stricken face, she knew they had seen what she'd tried to warn them about.

"I'm okay, Father," Mark finally said, teary eyes opening and trying bravely to smile. "Really I am!" He sat back to try and look at the old man, but his father kept his head tight to the boy's chest. Helplessly, Mark looked up at Matthew.

"Give him time," Matthew said softly, his eyes searching the boy's ashen face. "We're thankful you are back!"

"I told you I'd be back," Mark answered. "A little the worse for wear, but I'm back."

"Oh, Mark . . ." Deborah left Matthew's side and slipped down next to her father to grasp Mark around the neck. "Thank God you're back with us."

"I've got to admit, it does feel good," the boy answered, kissing the top of her head. "I know I've been gone only a short time, but it feels like ages."

"It's been ages to us too. You look so worn," she murmured, pushing the dark hair away from his eyes.

"Aye," he answered, striking a lighter tone as he added, "I should be worn out. I've been in a real battle, I have. And it was a beastly one at that!"

"Where?" Robert Bell asked, composed now and rising to seat himself across from his young son.

"A couple of hills in Boston," Mark answered. "It was a terrible fight for both sides. There were many —so many killed." His voice wavered as he recalled the incident. "Dr. Warren was killed there, we heard."

"Joseph Warren?" Robert Bell shook his head sadly. "He was one of our best people."

"A great many good people died, Father," Mark answered heavily. "I was one of the lucky ones." His eyes met Matthew's. "I *was* lucky, y'know."

Matthew had been stunned. He had noticed the hollow where Mark's leg should have been under the blanket first thing, and had recognized the pain that was still on Mark's pale face, hidden underneath his smile.

"We're all glad that you're home," he finally said softly. "And I know that in a way you are a lucky young man." He hesitated, feeling the tears welling up inside him, the anger beginning to press against his heart and chest, the metallic taste in his mouth from his own panic. "But I've got to know, Mark, was it worth it?"

They all turned to Matthew in surprise. "Was it worth it?" Mark repeated hoarsely. "I tell you, Matthew, I would do it all over again, given the chance, just as I know all those who died in Boston and all the other places would gladly do it again." His eyes brightened and his face set in determination. "Matthew, you have never seen such brave men. Half the time, none of us knew what we were doing, but we all knew *why* we were doing it. And that was the important thing. And that's why we're going to win, too— because every last man out there was willing to die if necessary, for liberty." Mark looked down at Deborah, grasping her hand tightly in his before he looked over at his father. "Have you heard what we're doing, Father? Did you hear about Fort Ticonderoga and Crown Point? And General Arnold in Canada? We're doing it! We're beating the English army! And now we've become a real army ourselves. I hear tell we're getting a commander-in-chief and generals and we'll be better than the Redcoats. We're going to win, Father, we're going to win!"

"I'm proud of you boy," Robert Bell answered quietly, moved by his son's spirit. "We're all proud of you!" His eyes began to tear and he quickly wiped an elbow at them. "And we know your army is going to win!"

Mark beamed and pressed his head to Deborah's. "We'll show 'em!" His eyes found Matthew again, and he slowly sobered. "What is it, Matthew?"

His brother stared solemnly and shook his head. "Oh Mark," he groaned, and shook his head again. "How can you talk that way?"

"What way?" Mark asked, his voice rising quickly. "What's wrong with you?"

"How can you talk that way, after what's happened to you?"

Mark's brows furrowed together. "I've only lost a leg. You would rather I'd lost my life, as the others?"

"You shouldn't have lost anything, damn it!" He spun and rushed out onto the front porch. He felt weak and grabbed the post for support. He wanted to cry out, to scream out the agony and rage that boiled inside of him. Oh, God, why did it have to be Mark? He buried his head in his elbow and closed his eyes.

He felt gentle fingers touch his back, and then Deborah's arm circled his shoulders and she pressed herself close to him in comfort. "I know you care for him greatly, Matthew," she murmured. "And I know the hurt that you must have inside you." There was silence as neither moved.

"I am so sorry for you," she said softly, bowing her head on his shoulder, her tears staining the back of his shirt.

"God, I didn't want that to happen to him," he moaned. Why couldn't he cry and be relieved of the pressure? It was so easy for a woman to weep, so much more difficult for a man. "It should have been me. . . ."

Deborah forced him to turn around and face her. "No," she answered severely. "It was not your fault, Matthew!"

"But it was I who should have gone!"

"No! You mustn't think that," she chided. "You each did what you thought had to be done. There was no telling what was going to happen to Mark. You mustn't blame yourself!"

"But he would be well and whole now."

"And you mght have been one of those dead. Would that have made it better?" Deborah took his head in her hands and looked squarely into his eyes. "You are not to blame, Matthew. Mark isn't even to blame!"

He stared at her unseeingly. All he could think of was that hollow under the blanket where Mark's leg should have been.

"It was I who should have gone. Mark should have stayed home," Matthew responded tightly.

Deborah looked into Matthew's eyes and saw the determined look. She released her hold on him and stepped back with a sigh. "You will get over this, Matthew, just as I am sure Mark will be able to handle the loss of his leg. All I know is that I'm thankful that Mark is here. I don't care about his leg, I only care about Mark."

Matthew looked at his sister. He knew she was trying to ease the burden and he was thankful for her efforts, but again he felt the guilt and pain swell within him and he spun around to stare out into the distance.

He felt her slight pressure on his shoulder as she reached forward to touch him briefly. "I'll be inside."

When she realized he wasn't going to respond, she turned and went back into the house.

Matthew took a long quivering breath of air. The pain inside him was a nightmare of torture. It was a tightness that tore away at his insides. He could never make this up to Mark; there could never be repayment of a lost limb.

This was something he would have to live with for the rest of his life. It would gnaw at him every time he saw Mark hobbling around. It would fester inside him, never to heal. No balm, salve or brew could ease this burden.

Oh, God, he thought, looking up to the sky with tear-filled eyes. Will I ever learn to live with this burden?

9

MATTHEW HAD chopped and stacked a winter's supply of wood for Scott's headquarters in record time, for he was concerned about Mark. It was only a matter of time before news of the boy's return reached the British officer, and Matthew was apprehensive about his reaction. Just to be on the safe side, he had turned his work area in the barn around so that he could have a good view of the road and their home. He was, therefore, greatly surprised when he spied Deborah bounding down the back porch and running toward the barn.

"What's the matter?" he asked anxiously, meeting her half way.

"It's Lieutenant Scott!" Deborah responded breathlessly. "He just left!"

"Left?" Matthew asked and started toward the house.

"He wouldn't let me go to get you," she answered, trying to keep up with his pace. "He wanted me there while he talked to Mark."

Matthew's face was grim as he entered the living room and looked anxiously at Mark, who was resting on the couch with a faint smile on his face.

"How in hell did he get in without me seeing him?" Matthew said aloud.

"That weasel probably knew you were looking out for him, so he came up from the blind side. He as much as admitted it, said he wanted to talk to me alone." Mark seemed pleased with himself, which made Matthew curious.

"What did he want?"

Mark leaned back and gestured for Matthew to take a seat. "He tried to make all sorts of accusations, said I was in great trouble. Then he wanted to know all about the Sons of Liberty."

"And what did you say?"

Mark smirked. "I said he'd find out soon enough about us. As soon as they finish up with Boston, they'll be coming right through here on the way to New York. That lit a spark under him all right!"

"Damn, Mark," Matthew muttered. "You get Scott riled up and he could make plenty of trouble."

"I'm not afraid of him!"

Matthew scowled, wondering what move the officer might be making. "What did he say exactly?" he asked, turning to Deborah for the answer.

"He wanted to know where Mark had been," she answered.

"And I told him, too," Mark said defiantly. "I told

him how we slaughtered his army, how we appreciated all the fine military training he gave us."

Matthew got up, exasperated. "Did you really tell him that?" He turned to Deborah for confirmation and muttered an oath when she bit her lip and nodded. "He can put you in prison, you know that?"

"He and whose army?" Mark retorted, his face turning sulky.

"He and those friends of his," Matthew answered. "We're outnumbered here you know, now that the patriots have left to fight."

The information sobered Mark quickly. "It's all right, Matthew," he said after a silence. "We have friends hereabouts. He wouldn't dare."

"Scott has no love for us Bells," his brother responded angrily. "He's been itching to blame us for something, and now he's getting his chance." But even as he spoke he was chilled by the realization that it was not the Bells but he himself who had earned the officer's enmity.

"Do you really think he might try something?" Deborah asked, afraid of the answer.

Matthew only shrugged. He was too suspicious of Scott not to believe the worst, and he was bothered by the fact that the officer had deliberately hidden his approach. He closed his eyes tightly for a moment, swearing that this time he would protect his brother from harm, no matter the price to himself.

"What should we do?" Deborah touched his arm tentatively.

"I don't know what *we* should do, but I know what *I* have to do," he responded. "I've got to find out what he intends to do with Mark."

"How?"

Matthew turned to her. "By talking to him, that's

how. It's better to get this out in the open. I don't want him to surprise us again."

"Give me a musket and put me on my horse," Mark said, "and I'll show him a thing or two!"

Matthew smiled at the boy. "You've done your fighting for the time being. Besides, someone has to stay here to protect your sister and father, just in case."

"In case? In case of what?"

Matthew shrugged. "I'm going to find Scott and see what his plans are. Then we'll go from there."

Deborah came up to him and took his arm, her eyes searching his with concern. "Do you think this is the wise thing to do?"

He smiled down at her and patted her cold hand. "I wish I knew what was the wise thing to do. But I don't like leaving Scott sneaking around. I'd rather force him out in the open and know what his plans are."

"If it comes to a fight," Mark said eagerly, "you come home here. We'll put up a stand like that bobbycock has never seen."

Matthew tousled the top of the boy's head and smiled down at him. It was good to see Mark in such high spirits, far higher than his own had been lately. "Always in search of a good fight, aren't you lad?" he said with a grin. He turned to Deborah. "You'd better keep a close eye on him. He'll be setting himself up against the Tory militia, given half a chance!"

Matthew found himself more tormented than ever as he rode to the commons. His brother's return seemed to have brought the war closer to home. Mark's incessant talk of the patriot army and their deeds, the constant reminder of the horrors that war brought, the missing limb—all of these crowded Matthew's daily thoughts. He was also concerned about the

extra burden to the Bell family now that Mark was a
cripple, although no one had mentioned this trouble-
some thought. And now his family was threatened
with even more misfortune. But this was one time,
he resolved, that he would act to safeguard their lives.

Scott's small headquarters was locked. Matthew
pursed his lips as he glanced about the green park in
front, hoping to see the red-coated officer or his two
uniformed sergeants, but they were nowhere to be
seen. Little as he liked going to the man's home and
perhaps seeing Louisa, it might be better to confront
him there, Matthew reasoned, where he would catch
the officer off guard.

Matthew was more than relieved to spot the lieutenant's horse tied to the front rail of the white house
which the town had been forced to give to the officer
of the British army. A two story structure, it was
nestled at the edge of the woods of maples and elms
that swept down a slight slope to the broad Connecticut River in the distance. The thought of his trysts
with Louisa flashed through his mind as he glanced at
the woods, but he pushed the memory aside as he
dismounted and strode to the front door.

"Mr. Bell!" Scott opened the door upon Matthew's
knock and stood there with one arched eyebrow and
a stance that hinted of impatience. He had taken off
his red jacket and stood in white knee breeches, white
shirt and white wig, looking more the fine English
landlord than soldier.

Matthew nodded curtly, refusing to be cowed by
the man's superior manner or to show him the deference he expected as his due. "I've come to find out what
you intend to do about my brother," he announced.

The lieutenant sighed but did not move from his
position in the doorway. He stared at Matthew

thoughtfully before answering in a tone reserved for reprimanding school children. "It is not what I intend to do *about* your brother, but rather what I intend to do *to* your brother, isn't it?"

Matthew met his gaze with an intent look. "No," he answered evenly. "You're quite mistaken in that."

For an instant, there was a spark in the Britisher's eyes but it was quickly extinguished. With a bored sigh, the officer leaned against the door in an indolent manner. "My dear man," he replied, "your brother is suspected of participating in armed warfare against British troops. I need not tell you what the punishment for such a crime might be."

"He's a suspect only," Matthew insisted.

Scott smirked and shook his head. "I dare say your brother lost his leg falling off a horse? That he and his confederates disappeared to go on a fox hunt?" He arched his eyebrows and stared at Matthew with a bemused expression. "Come now, dear lad, you and I both know the facts, don't we?" He straightened and pulled on the cuff of his sleeve, obviously wanting to dismiss the talk. "The punishment is clearly stated, and if I have anything to do about it I shall carry it out."

"He's just a boy," Matthew pointed out. "And he's an invalid for the rest of his life. Any punishment you have will be nothing to what he has suffered already."

"Oh really?" Again there was that bemused smile. "Do you consider hanging to be nothing?"

Matthew caught his breath for a moment. He had expected such a statement but was nonetheless unprepared for its bluntness. "What good would it do to hang a cripple?"

"It will teach a lesson," Scott retorted with such

savage intensity that Matthew was taken aback. "Do you think England can let such insurrection take place without punishment? One or two hangings is all it will take to strangle this insanity, believe me!"

"For God's sake, Scott," Matthew shot back, raising his voice to match the officer's. "Do you think that hanging an invalid will teach anything? He will become a martyr, that's all. You'll infuriate more people than you already have."

"Your brother has committed a crime against England, sir," Scott answered, stepping forward and butting his face close to Matthew's. "And I intend to do everything in my power to carry out the punishment."

"If you want someone to hang, sir," Matthew replied coldly, "then hang me. You have wanted me under the noose, so take me."

Scott eyed Matthew with interest and suspicion. "Very noble, very noble indeed, Mr. Bell. Believe me, I would dearly love the opportunity. But unfortunately, you have done nothing to warrant hanging. Or not yet, I should say. One of these days you'll make a slip and I will be there to catch you." He stepped back to close the door but Matthew followed and placed a foot to block the closure.

"Scott! I am warning you. You'll not hang my brother!"

The Britisher stiffened. "I shall not be talked to in that tone of voice. Get out of my house, sir!" Scott's voice was a low menacing snarl.

"Not until we've settled this," Matthew answered tightly. He was only conscious of Louisa hesitantly approaching in the background.

"I have nothing to say to you," Scott replied. The man jumped as his wife touched his arm. "This insolent rebel is just leaving," he said, glancing at her before he turned back to Matthew.

"I'm not leaving until I get an answer from you," Matthew responded stubbornly.

"You'll get no answer from me!" Scott barked, shaking Louisa's hand from his arm and stepping forward. "I'll see you in hell before I give you an answer. And I'll see both you and your brother hang!"

"No!" Louisa's small cry cut through the air, leaving both men speechless.

Scott snapped his head around to look at his wife. "What's that?" he asked incredulously.

Matthew saw the fear in Louisa's eyes as she looked from her husband to him. Quickly, Matthew stepped forward and spun the officer around by his shoulder. "We haven't finished," he said bluntly.

Scott was flabbergasted. He shot one fleeting look of warning at his wife before turning his wrath on Matthew. "I'll give you an answer you might recognize!" The officer turned and went to a hallway stand where his sword and scabbard lay. With a flourish, he bared the blade and turned to Matthew.

Matthew drew a deep breath, his eyes darting from the silver tip of the blade to the officer's face. Scott seemed more assured of his position now that he held the sword in his hand and Matthew had no doubt that he would use the weapon. Scott's face was openly taunting now, and his knees were slightly bent as though he would thrust the blade forward.

Matthew began to crouch forward on the balls of his feet, carefully watching the movement of the sword. With a move that surprised the officer, Matthew dodged to the right, then lunged forward and struck the sword away with a heavy blow of his right arm upon Scott's crooked elbow.

Scott bellowed as the sword dropped to the floor.

Matthew twisted once more as the officer reached out to grab for his wrist. Again his powerful right arm beat down, first on the officer's right shoulder, then the left. As the Britisher sank to the carpeted hallway floor, Matthew sent his fist into his paling face.

"Oh my God!" Louisa cried out and knelt to touch her husband's still form. "What have you done to him?"

Matthew stared down at the body, only just beginning to be aware of what he had done. It seemed unreal. He'd had no idea that he was capable of such a thing.

"Oh, Matthew," she said, her voice hushed with fear as she turned and stared at him. "You surely will be in trouble now."

"Aye," he agreed. "I guess I have given your husband reason enough to come after me now."

"But you can't let him imprison you, Matthew," she warned. "You have no idea what a British prison is like!"

He studied her without speaking, trying to clear his head. She was right. He had heard enough tales of men being chained on harbor ships where they rotted to skeletons that were thrown into the sea. No, he had no want for that type of an end to his life.

Louisa got up and came to his side and pushed him to the door. "You have got to get away," she begged. "You don't know Fitchley. He doesn't have any proof against your brother—I know that for a fact. He was only trying to harass you and scare the other patriots. But you! Fitchley will hunt you down until he finds you, believe me. Please go quickly before he wakes up!"

Matthew moved slowly to the door. "But what about you?" he asked, looking at the unconscious officer on the floor. "He won't harm you?"

Louisia shook her head. "No, don't worry about me," she answered, still struggling to get him through the door. "You must leave, leave Wethersfield. Fitchley won't rest until he has found you!"

Matthew stumbled across the porch and down the steps under her pushing hands.

"Oh, go, my pet," Louisa whispered. "I shall think of you, Matthew Bell!" Her hand squeezed his tightly before she whirled and fled back to the house.

Matthew slowly mounted his horse and then sat staring at the road in front of him. What had he done? The things that had just occurred seemed like a blurred dreamlike sequence of events. He was not quite sure whether they had actually happened.

He closed his eyes and took a deep breath. Lord, give me strength! Savagely, he spurred his horse down the road.

10

"Y OU SHOULD HAVE knocked his head off!" Mark had exclaimed after Matthew recounted his tale.

None of the other Bells in the family room shared Mark's reaction. Deborah and Robert Bell sat on the couch, watching listlessly as Matthew hurriedly packed a few belongings. His face was grim and set, when he hefted his bag and walked outside, followed by the rest of his family. He hated goodbyes and this one was going to be especially difficult.

"Do be careful, Matthew." Deborah approached him as he finished strapping the leather thongs of his saddle. "No sooner does one come home than the other goes."

"It is best this way, dear sister," Matthew answered, taking a deep breath and finally turning to her with a gentle smile. "Scott will not bother you too much. He'll undoubtedly come here in search of me. Tell him I have gone to Boston, and perhaps he will follow. At any rate, he should leave you alone shortly." He glanced towards the house, where Mark was leaning against the doorframe watching them. "I shall stay in Hartford until I know you are all safe. If Scott does do anything to Mark, be sure to send word to me as soon as possible. But I'm certain you won't have to."

Deborah leaned forward and kissed his cheek. "God be with you, Matthew. Please forgive me, but I cannot cry as I did for Mark when he went away. I know somehow that you will return."

Matthew took her hands and held them tightly in his grasp. "I don't know where this road will lead me but I shall not disappoint you. I'm only sorry that I leave charge of this family to you. Perhaps in time I shall be able to make it up to you."

"I shall hear no such talk," she said, wiping away the tears that sprang to her eyes. "We are a family, Matthew Bell, and there's no thought of repaying such things." She sniffed back her tears and tried a brave smile up at him. "And don't you worry about us. The Bells are a hardy lot. All of us, dear brother, especially you."

Matthew kissed her lightly on the brow and turned to his father, who stood patiently to one side. The old man shuffled forward and placed a hand on Matthew's shoulder. "God grant you a speedy return, my son," he said in a shaking voice. "Our love goes with you, know that!" The old man hung his head and shook it slowly back and forth. Suddenly he looked up at Matthew with moist eyes. "What can a father say to his eldest by now? No one expected you ever to leave, especially myself. I am not prepared for such a thing."

"You don't have to say anything, Father," Matthew said gently. "I know what is in your heart—what is in all your hearts—and that is enough." His own emotions were beginning to break through his composure, and so he spun about and mounted his horse. Before spurring off, he looked down at the three of them and touched his fingers to his hat. "I shall be back, don't worry."

His horse carried him out of Wethersfield at a hurried pace as he started his short journey. Hartford had been the first place he had thought of for his destination, and it still seemed a logical choice. It was close enough to Wethersfield so that he could be of some use if his family needed him. And because it was a rebel town, he would be safe from Scott while he collected his thoughts about his future. The thought of joining up with the new Continental Army had even occurred to him, with some prompting from Mark. And the idea was becoming less and less repugnant to him, although there were still questions in the back of his mind.

Matthew rode into Hartford at dusk. It was quite a different scene than when he had last visited the town. The haze of smoke from many campfires lay heavily along the banks of the wide river, where men wandered about among the scattering of small tents. There was the noise of laughter from men and women, of singing, and a fiddle here and there. Matthew made his approach slowly, stopping when he came to a makeshift barrier across the road. A handful of bedraggled men, bearded and unkempt, came forward curiously to inspect the newcomer.

"You New Yorker or Rhode Islander?" a voice asked, as though naming off some vile disease.

Matthew shook his head and looked about for a familiar face. "From Wethersfield," he answered guardedly.

The man nearest him gave a contemptuous snort and said, "Then you want down river a piece. That's where Connecticut people is." He looked up at Matthew to scrutinize him. "You ain't one of them new officers we been hearing about?"

Matthew smiled. "Me? An officer? Hardly."

The man eyed the horse, then looked back to Matthew. "You won't be needing that horse then. Only them officers is doing the riding. The rest of us walk." The man strolled around Matthew and the horse. "You'll do better selling the animal. Give you a good price for it."

"If you're not an officer, then what use will you have for it?" Matthew asked curiously.

"To eat, naturally," came the quick answer. "With all of us here, food is a mite scarce. We're eating anything that moves."

Startled, Matthew stared at the man and then glanced at his companions. Beneath all the brown leather and homespun cottons were men who regarded him with mistrust, hunger, suspicion. Except for the fact that they were from different states, they were all basically from the same molds—farmers, tradesmen, merchants, probably other coopers. And under normal conditions these men were probably jovial, friendly, helpful. But now it was every man for himself, the survival of the fittest as they were massed together, struggling to live off of whatever they could scavenge.

"I'm sure your offer is more than generous," Matthew responded to the guard. "But I think I will keep my horse—at least until I have reached my destination."

The man eyed Matthew carefully, measuring him as he fingered the long musket held loosely in his hand. It flashed through Matthew's mind that had it been darker the man might have tried to unhorse him.

"I'm obliged for the directions," Matthew said and touched the brim of his hat as he spurred forward, grateful to get away but now wary of possible dangers.

By the time he found the Connecticut crowd, it was dark and campfires spotted the rivershore as far as the eye could see.

"Hale?" The man who walked at his side was a printer from the northern part of the state and had volunteered to show Matthew around the camp. "Never heard of him. But then there's a heap of people hereabouts. It's a certainty a name will be difficult to remember."

"He's an officer," Matthew said, leading his horse, careful to keep from stepping on the forms that sprawled about in every which way and manner.

"Hell," came the slow drawl. "They's don't know their heads from their asses." The man cast a quick look over at Matthew and grinned. "Not that they're all bad. Jus' some of 'em don't know their places yet." He led Matthew to a large tent, one of the largest Matthew had ever seen. "We bring all the new ones here—sort of get-acquainted time, y'might say. But I got a tent off to the side. You're welcome to share with me if you have the likin'."

Matthew regarded the man and held out his hand

uncertainly. "I'm obliged to you. My name's Matthew Bell."

The man wiped his palm and then clasped Matthew's hand.

"Giles Austin," he volunteered, then was suddenly shy. "Well, I guess you're wanting to be on your own, Matthew Bell."

"No," Matthew answered with a reassuring smile. "It wasn't any forwardness on your part that caused my hesitation." Matthew wondered whether he should confide in the man. What harm could be done? "I'm still not sure whether I am joining your army, that's all."

"What other reason you got for being here?"

Matthew shrugged. "I want to do something—but I'm not sure this army life is for me."

The man smiled, exposing a few missing back teeth. "It ain't all that bad. So far, we all been having a fair amount of fun. Beats plowing fields—and we get paid a good amount." Giles looked about into the darkness, listening to the laughter and singing that filtered through the night. "So far, it ain't been bad. You should give it a try, boy." Without waiting for a reply, Giles Austin disappeared into the evening.

The following morning, Matthew woke with a start from a deep sleep. He lifted his head and looked around at the huddled forms on the floor of the tent, then gathered his things and crawled out into the fresh air, crisp from heavy dew, quiet from a yet unwakened camp. He was not surprised that his horse had disappeared. He cursed the fact that he hadn't taken some precaution, but somehow it really didn't seem that important anymore.

Matthew made his way down to the shore of the

river, threading his way among the tents and bodies. Now that it was light, he realized he had overestimated the size of the encampment. There were not as many men as he had imagined.

As he shaved by the water's edge, he was aware that the camp was coming to life behind him. The sound of voices, the smell of campfires, crackling with fresh wood, the aroma of coffee and food filtered down to him.

Men's voices approached and when Matthew glanced over his shoulder he was momentarily surprised to see that the men coming down to the water's edge were stark naked. They laughed among themselves as they splashed each other at the river's edge and then dove in. Matthew was suddenly conscious of the houses not too far off in the distance, certainly within easy eyesight of this horseplay. But if the men in the river cared, they certainly gave little indication. They carried on with their bathing amid much laughter and joking.

Two men in long blue coats and swords at their sides came striding down to the river's edge and pointed to the group. "You men will have to stop this," one of them shouted out. "We have been receiving complaints from local residents about nude bathing."

The men laughed and looked around to see if any of the villagers had gathered. "Well, we sure in hell ain't going to take a bath with our clothes on, now are we?" The burly man who had spoken cocked his head in a challenging look at the two officers. "Besides," he added, "we're not taking orders from villagers—nor from just anyone else either."

One of the naked men stepped forward, hands on

hips. "Is it true that some goddamn Southern farmer was appointed commander in chief?"

The two officers stiffened and glanced at each other. "We understand General Washington was an outstanding officer in the French and Indian War."

Matthew edged forward to listen at mention of the name. Deborah's beau, John Langley Hunter, had often spoken of Washington, and always with great respect.

"He's still a Virginian farmer!" one of the bathers cried out.

"We're not going to have no stranger lead us," another answered indignantly. " 'Specially no farmer from the south!"

"What's got them so riled?" Giles Austin's deep voice startled Matthew and he spun around to face the man.

"They've been talking about General Washington," Matthew explained. "They're expecting him to come through here."

Giles nodded and fell in beside Matthew as they walked back to the camp. "Coming from New York, we heard. Going to get them Britishers out of Boston once and for all."

They walked through the camp together, Giles nodding to a few of his friends and then suddenly stopping at a tent and beckoning Matthew to follow him in. Inside was a uniformed man seated at a table, his attention on the papers spread out in front of him. Matthew shot Giles a questioning look but it went unacknowledged.

"I got you a new recruit," Giles said without any formality. The man glanced up and inspected Matthew with a tired sigh. He thumbed through a stack of papers, pulling out a long, printed form and pushing it toward Matthew. "Can you read?" he asked. When Matthew nodded, he gestured toward the paper. "Read it and sign at the bottom."

Matthew scowled but took the quill which was handed him. He read the document slowly. "Sixty dollars?" he asked incredulously.

"A year, plus your bonus, plus a supply of clothing, plus provisions," the officer explained. It was obvious he had said those words too often to suit his purpose.

"Can't beat that at home," Giles said.

"Where can I get my clothes?" Matthew asked hesitantly.

"Supplies haven't been issued to us yet," the officer replied with another sigh, "but you'll get them soon enough."

Matthew hesitated with the quill over the dotted line. It was a most important decision and he had really wanted more time to think about it. "C'mon, boy," Giles urged. "The sooner you get your name on his list, the sooner you can start earning that sixty dollars."

Matthew sighed, then signed his name to the document. "Is that all there is to it?" he asked.

Giles slapped him on the back and spun him around before the officer could answer. "That's it," Giles announced. "You're now a recruit in the Continental Army. How does it feel?"

Matthew grinned and allowed himself to be propelled outside and back among the tents. "I guess I don't feel much different."

"Oh, you'll like it here," Giles answered and stopped before a small lean-to made of burlap and cotton. "And here's home." He grabbed Matthew's things and tossed them into a corner. "And that's about all there is to it. Once in a while some bastard will be taking us up to the meadow to march us around, but mostly it's drinking and playing cards."

The next three days found Matthew wandering about the camp wondering whether he had made the right decision. He was relieved not to have heard from his family; that meant that Scott had left them alone. But his own course was still not clear. The army was far from what he had imagined it to be. And not a night had passed when there hadn't been fights among the unruly soldiers. Last night he had witnessed a knifing that had almost led to a small rebellion between a group from Delaware and a group from Maryland.

Matthew had tried to locate Nathan Hale and had even gone into Hartford to the house where they had first met the schoolteacher, but the man was nowhere to be found. Disappointed, Matthew had returned to camp and sought out Giles's company. He found the printer leaning against a tree, watching the scene unfold before them.

"We got us a new general," Giles reported. "Come riding in this afternoon with a whole caboodle of other muckamucks."

"What's he like?" Matthew asked curiously.

"I got to admit he looked the part, once he was pointed out. Y'know how some men ride a horse like they got the world between their legs and they know just the right way to turn it? That's the impression this one gave." He hesitated and gave a snort. "Of course, he's got to match up to the test, I reckon."

"Test?"

Giles shrugged. "Look about you, lad. You ever see such a ragtag sackful of odds and ends as all these people?" Giles waved a hand to include all the tents and wandering soldiers. "And each one will be testing,

seeing just how much the general will let them get
away with. You can rest assured of that."

"You think he can do it?" Matthew asked.

Giles pursed his lips and then slowly shook his
head. "Hell no," came the answer. "I reckon no one
could. Consider it. You put a whole bunch of different
people from all them different states together, ain't no
way in hell anyone can make them pee in the right
direction."

Matthew grinned, thinking of all the fights he had
already witnessed in the camp. "I guess I don't envy
him the responsibility," he commented.

"No, I reckon hardly anyone would want that responsibility. That's another count against him. Only a
damn Southern dirt farmer would be crazy enough
to accept the job."

Matthew turned to eye his friend seriously. "I don't
know," he answered. "I've heard good things about
Washington from someone who served under him. I'd
like to meet him and see what kind of a man would
accept that kind of a job."

"You should probably see him anyway," Giles said.
"I heard he passed through your town on the way
here."

"Wethersfield?" Matthew asked excitedly.

Giles nodded. "That's what I heard."

11

WHERE you think you're going?" The soldier raised his musket and blocked Matthew's way.

"I want to see General Washington." Matthew gazed up the long path to the white structure where he had been told the new commander in chief was staying. There were several other militiamen along the porch railing, talking idly among themselves, but none seemed to fit the description Giles had given of the new general.

The guard smirked. "You and half the country," he remarked. "Everyone lookin' for favors."

"I understand he just came through Wethersfield. That's where I'm from," Matthew started to explain. He hesitated for a moment, suddenly realizing how absurd he must seem, but his concern for his family overrode his embarrassment. "When I left Wethersfield, the British soldiers were giving my family a difficult time. I was wondering whether the British were still in the town, now that the general has passed through."

The guard sighed, set the stock of his gun alongside his shoe and leaned upon the gun in a lackadaisical manner, a slight smile of disdain across his lips as he looked at Matthew. "Lad, the general is up to his ass with all sorts of problems. That's why I'm here, to make sure them problems don't get above his belt buckle." He glanced at some men approaching and straightened. "Now stand aside while I tend to these here."

"Ya'll can't go in there!" he barked out when he saw that the men were bent on entering the premises. One smiled patiently and came forward.

"That gentleman there," the newcomer explained, pointing to an older white-haired man, "is General Philip Schuyler."

"He could be George the Third for all I care," the guard replied, still unimpressed. "You got any proof he's who you say he is?"

"My dear sir," the man said indignantly. "I am General Schulyer's aide-de-camp, and these others are his ranking officers. The general is here to meet with General Washington."

The guard inspected the captain and the rest of the company. Finally, the guard nodded grudgingly. "You can go in I guess," he said, eying the group with reservation as they made their way up the path onto the porch and finally inside the home. With a sigh he turned back to Matthew. "Can't win 'em all the time," he said with a grin. "Ain't no way in heaven nor hell to tell who's who around here. I hear that one guard wouldn't even let Washington pass because he didn't know who he was. But then there's some that still don't fancy no Virginian telling 'em what to do."

"There's no way I can get to see him?" Matthew asked anxiously.

"Just don't give up, do ye?" the man answered with a grin. He stepped closer to Matthew. "Now, I ain't givin' away any military secrets, but I hear tell the general takes his constitutional at dusk. Likes to go around and see how the rest of us are living, y'know what I mean?" He winked at Matthew. "Now, I ain't guarding him while he's walking around, so I can't rightly stop you from bumping into the man, can I?"

Matthew laughed and grasped the guard's elbow with a tight squeeze. "God bless you, sir," he said in appreciation. "And God go with you."

The man was embarrassed and backed off. "We're all in this together, lad," he answered soberly. "We've got to help each other out best way we can if we want to do this thing right. At least, that's the way I'm looking at it."

The evening shadows found Matthew positioned across the street from the white house. The guard he had spoken to had been replaced by another. The street was quiet, and Matthew enjoyed the solitude of the early evening. His day had been spent practicing marching with a large group of fellow Connecticut recruits. The excitement of being in the army had already paled for many of the men, and most of them found marching much to their dislike. Perhaps things would change now that Washington was here, but Matthew suspected that soldiering was not for him. True, he had signed the recruiting papers, but no one seemed to feel obligated to live up to their promises. Already, several of the farmers planned on staying

only another three or four weeks before returning to
their farms to start spring planting.

As Matthew sat beside the large maple, keeping a
careful lookout on the house, his mind wandered to
the possibilities that lay ahead of him. If Washington
assured him that Scott was no longer stationed in
Wethersfield, Matthew could most likely return home
and pick up where he had left off. From what he
could see, there were plenty of recruits for the army.
More and more troops were arriving near Boston each
day, and rumor had it that men from the frontiers of
western New York, Pennsylvania and even the South
were expected. In Matthew's mind, one man more or
less would not win or lose a war.

The figure that emerged from the house across the
street was extremely tall and impressive-looking in
his long blue cloak, buff-colored knee breeches and
blue jacket. He wore no hat and the white wig em-
phasized a handsome face that at the moment was set
in a serious expression.

Matthew stood up and brushed the dirt from his
pants as he watched the man talk to the sentry for a
moment, smile and then walk on towards the river
and the encampments.

They had gone several blocks, Washington taking
long strides on one side of the street and Matthew
following at a short distance across the way. Matthew
had just made up his mind to approach Washington
when the man suddenly stopped and turned to gaze
over at Matthew curiously. His hand came out from
beneath the cloak and beckoned for Matthew to approach.

"You follow me, young man?" The voice had a
gentleness to it.

Matthew nodded as he crossed the street. "I only

wanted to talk to you, General," he answered, whipping his hat off his head. "I'm sorry, sir. I know how busy you have been, all the problems you must have, all the people you have been seeing, and you must be tired. I don't want to intrude on your privacy," Matthew said apologetically.

Washington eyed Matthew for a long moment, his face slowly relaxing, showing a weariness that he had kept hidden until now. "I appreciate your concern for me, young man. Unfortunately, this walk is not entirely a matter of pleasure, as you seem to think. I take these walks to think out all that has happened during the day. And there has been quite a lot occurring these past few days," he concluded grimly.

"I can well imagine, General. And it is no small task to take charge of an army which has never experienced command."

"You speak wisely, my lad." Washington looked at Matthew with new curiosity. "You're not one of my young officers, are you?"

Matthew smiled and shook his head. "I am a new recruit. Matthew Bell from Wethersfield—a town that's not far from here. I understand you spent the night there."

"Ah yes!" Washington nodded.

"That's one of the reasons I wanted to talk to you, sir," Matthew continued. "I was wondering if you could tell me whether the British commandant is still in my town."

The general took in Matthew's intent look, wondering to himself what lay behind the young man's concern. "Almost every British troop in the north here has withdrawn to Boston," he answered at last. "Considering the fact that my new army is being formed in this territory, I imagine any British uniform would be most unsafe at this moment. If I were in your shoes, I would feel it safe to assume your commandant has left Wethersfield."

Matthew smiled and relaxed. It was what he wanted to hear and now it seemed he could breathe easier.

"You mentioned you had a *couple* of things to talk to me about," Washington said as they approached the broad field that was filled with the army encampment.

Matthew was now even more embarrassed. "Sir, I hope you won't think I'm presuming, but I believe we have a friend in common."

When Washington stopped and turned to Matthew with an encouraging look, Matthew told him of his sister's friendship with John Langley Hunter and was rewarded with a laugh of pleasure from the officer.

They spent more than an hour in easy conversation, and when they parted Matthew was surprised to find that Washington had taken him on as a messenger within the camp, an assignment which relieved him of some of the marching practice. And so Matthew put off returning to Wethersfield for a time. The thought was always in the back of his mind, but his frequent conversations with Washington over the next few weeks made him waver. It was as if their talks had somehow opened a whole new world to him, and he was reluctant to close the door on it. But the meaning of that new world did not become evident to Matthew until one evening when he and Washington stood on a high knoll overlooking the encampment.

They stood side by side and watched the scene slowly fade with the approaching darkness. Men scurried about, preparing campfires and making ready for another evening of rollicking music, dancing and storytelling.

"It is not what one could call a disciplined army, is it?" Washington said wryly. "But it is a start. If only they will bear with me a while more, it is a start for all of us." He paused and looked at Matthew speculatively before continuing. "Pardon, my friend, if I'm being too inquisitive, but I sometimes sense that you are not happy here, that you want to be gone."

Matthew turned to Washington in surprise and then gave a slow nod. "If what you say about Wethersfield is true, sir, then it means I am able to return . . ." He trailed off, embarrassed and confused by the subject.

Washington let out a soft "ah" and turned to stare down at the distant camp. "So you feel you must return."

"It is not that I *must* return," Matthew explained hastily, "or that I am unsympathetic to the rebel cause or unwilling to help fight for its ideals, sir. To be truthful, I find that army life is not suited to me, nor I to it. I cannot tolerate all this marching about and brandishing arms in drills," he said, waving his arm to include the scene in front of them. "It seems such a waste of time, and I had my fill of it under Wethersfield's British commandant. If I return to my home and the work I know, perhaps I'll be able to find some way to better serve the cause," Matthew concluded, but he felt curiously little confidence in his solution.

Washington finally turned to him and stared with wide-set eyes that bore into Matthew with full intensity. "I need men such as you, Matthew. I need a great many men. We cannot win this fight if we do not have a larger army. You have a head on your shoulders, and that is a rarity." He shook his head disbelievingly. "I swear, I still cannot understand you New Englanders. You have strange habits, strange language and strange traits. But then I imagine my ways are just as out of place to you." He studied Matthew intently, wondering how far he should indulge this young man he had become attached to in so short a period. But his independence and intelligence were traits that could be put to use in other ways, the officer reasoned, and there was little doubt of his loyalty. "Right now those soldiers below us are hellions, more intent on enjoying their holiday than on training for what might lay ahead of them. When the time comes, though, they'll serve with all the strength they have. But I need brains as well as brawn in the army. Suppose I could offer you another way to help us—to help *yourself* fight for our liberty."

Matthew glanced at him with a look that was both startled and hopeful. "How?"

"I've been recruiting certain men in secret, unbeknownst to even my closest friends. These people are working for me and for me alone, in espionage against the enemy. And believe me, a spy performs one of the most vital jobs I can think of in an army."

"And that is what you want me to do?" Matthew asked curiously.

Washington smiled but his face quickly turned solemn. "They're keeping me informed about the Tories, both civilian and military groups. But it is not as easy a task as you might think, Matthew. For one thing, in most cases, you would have to pass yourself off as a Loyalist. The better you can infiltrate yourself into the British network, the more valuable your information. I would expect you to win their confidence so that you have easy access to knowledge of their movements, their whereabouts and their preparations."

"And then I am to report to you?"

"Correct. Needless to say, it is a most risky occupation. If discovered, you would undoubtedly be hanged as a spy. And as a supposed Tory sympathizer, your family and friends would probably cut off their association with you."

"You mean I couldn't let my family know?"

"You would not be allowed to let anyone know. It would be for your own good, believe me. The fewer people who know your true affiliation, the safer you will be."

Matthew was shaken by the suggestion, yet knew he was enticed by the offer. "It does sound interesting," he murmured.

Washington placed a hand on his shoulder and stared at him with a piercing look. "It is not an easy task, nor one to be taken lightly, young man. The information you bring to me could very well shift the balance of the war. You will have to live in close association with the enemy without betraying yourself or your true feelings, and you will have to cross their lines and our lines without getting caught in order to get me the information. It is a dangerous sport, so consider your decision carefully." He hesitated. "If it is any consolation to you, I would never have mentioned this had I not thought you were capable of handling the part."

Matthew flushed. "I must admit, I am intrigued by all you have said."

"It is not a glamorous role," the general warned. "You will never receive the accolades that some of my confederates are so concerned with, and you will probably be shot at by your own countrymen. But I assure you that I, for one, shall know of your valuable contribution. And of course you will be paid for your services. Not much, I admit, but it should be sufficient. This will be coming out of my own pocket so that no one will be able to identify you."

"And you want me to be with you in Boston?"

"No. For now, I already have more than enough spies in Boston. I'm sending you into a hotbed of Tory sympathizers, I'm afraid," Washington answered gravely. "Once we've driven the British from Boston, their only recourse will be New York City. I want you to go there as soon as possible and get embedded in the Tory network. By the time I return from Boston, you should have enough information and statistics to help me."

The shine in Matthew's eyes gave the general the only answer he needed. Washington grasped his hand in a firm handshake, saying, "That's it, then. After tonight we shall see each other only in secret and you shall become a fervent Tory." Washington carefully inspected Matthew's face for a reaction. "And may God have mercy on your soul if you are caught by either side."

12

Mᴀᴛᴛʜᴇᴡ!" Deborah sprang down the front steps and into his arms almost before he had dismounted. They laughed, embraced, laughed again and pulled back to look at each other before another powerful embrace. "Oh, Matthew, has it been only a month? It seems so much longer!"

Matthew drew back and grinned down at his sister. It felt good to be home, even if only for a short stay. He looked about anxiously for Mark and his father as she led him back into the house.

"They're in the barn," Deborah explained, pushing him down into a chair and looking him over as a schoolmarm would à mischievous child. "But first I want you all to myself. You look none the worse for wear, Matthew Bell. Thank God for that!"

"None the worse for wear, am I?" Matthew exclaimed in feigned surprise. "I have never felt better and am as fit as a fiddle, and all you can say is that I'm none the worse for wear?"

"You know what I mean," she responded with a warm smile. "We've been so worried about you. And it *is* good to have you back."

"But only for a day or two, I'm afraid," Matthew answered with a sigh. "I'm sorry but I have not come back to stay."

She frowned and pulled back. "Not to stay? You mean you're off to war once again?"

"I stopped to make sure you were all right before going to New York," he answered, hoping she wouldn't press for further information. Matthew was tempted to tell his sister; she would be able to keep the secret. But he had made a solemn promise to General Washington that he would not divulge his mission to a soul, that he would not even hint what his purpose might be. "I am bound there in a fortnight."

"New York! I have heard the sisters Deane tell stories of things that go on in that city. It is a nest of harlots, for one thing."

Matthew grinned. "And maybe that is why I am so eager to go there."

Deborah shook her head, a small smile at the corners of her mouth. But her tone was thoughtful as she added, "More importantly, it is a Tory fortress."

"It's no Tory fortress, Deborah," Matthew answered, trying to appear calm. "And there is no need to fear for my safety."

"I don't see why you have to go to New York, that's all." She backed away to watch him carefully. "It's a strange place to go if you're still running away from the British. Or is it something else?"

Matthew took her question as a means to change the

subject. "Speaking of the British, is Scott still in Wethersfield?"

"He came here just after you left," she responded, knowing it best to answer his question before pursuing her own. "There were a few bad words said by all of us but the next day he and his people disappeared. I guess they got word the new commander in chief and his staff were coming through Wethersfield."

"I know," Matthew answered. "I've even met General Washington and he's every bit as impressive as John Langley made him out to be. He's the one who told me Scott might have left."

"So you see," she answered brightly, taking a chair across from him. "You can stay here now. We're all safe."

Matthew knew he could not evade his sister's persistent questioning without giving her some explanation, but there was so little he could tell her. "I cannot stay—and I cannot tell you the whys and wherefores, dear sister. So it is useless for you to try to pry information out of me."

Deborah stared at him with unblinking eyes, her face betraying a frown of worry and concern. "Is it that serious, Matthew?" she finally asked.

"I cannot divulge anything to anyone, including you. You will have to believe that it is the best way, for all of us."

"But New York," she said slowly, giving him a quizzical look. "I don't understand, Matthew. That's where all the British are."

"The British are in Boston," he corrected. "On ships. New York has only a handful of loyalists."

"Oh, of course," Deborah responded derisively, "merely the governor, the mayor and most of the population!"

"I shall be safe, I assure you," Matthew declared. "But I must have your cooperation to assure my safety. You must help me with Mark and Father. They mustn't ask me too many questions."

"But—"

He raised a hand to silence her. "No buts," he insisted. "Help me. I promise you I shall be safe. Just trust me."

"I want to trust you, Matthew," she answered, tears forming in her eyes. "I do trust you, but I worry."

He rose and went to sit beside her. "Don't worry," he said reassuringly. "Whatever I do, whatever you hear I have done or am doing, just trust that I know what is going on."

"Oh, Matthew," she cried softly, "you make it sound as if you're about to do something terrible."

He held her to him, waiting for her stifled sobs to subside. He was glad now that he hadn't told her his mission, for she would be all the more worried. He sighed and pushed away to look down at her. "I shall be seeing you every once in awhile. It's not that I'm going away forever." He tried to smile to encourage her. "Come on. Let's go find Mark and Father. And help me, Deborah help me keep this from them. It will be much easier on all of us."

She hesitated, but when he poked her playfully with a finger she managed a smile and a nod of her head. "I shouldn't give in to you so easily," she finally said. "Now I'm going to worry about all sorts of things happening to you."

"Just think of me with all those harlots." He laughed and ducked as she swung out at him.

13

MATTHEW could never have imagined the conges-gestion and bustle of humanity that he en-countered on Manhattan Island. There were blocks of brick buildings as far as the eye could see. It hardly seemed possible that people could choose to crowd so closely together on such a small plot of ground when there were lush green pastures and quiet solitude only a few miles north.

Matthew looked about him, giving his horse a rest from the long ride and giving himself a chance to get his bearings. From now on, he would have to be a loyalist, a Tory sympathizer. General Washington had given him a few helpful hints, a few facts, a few names, but the rest would be up to his wits and his imagination. Would it be that easy to conceal his beliefs and take on those of the opposition? For a brief moment, Matthew wondered whether the wisest thing to do would be to turn about and abort the mission.

He straightened his back and sighed. Well, it was now or never. He would at least give it a try. No, he corrected himself, sitting still taller. He would give it his best effort. And maybe, just maybe, he would find out his full measure.

It was the general's idea that he should stick to what he knew best. "The fewer lies you have to tell, the less likely you are to forget and make a slip. Do what you do best, coopering. Use your real name and town when you have to give your background. You might get away with telling them that you left Wethersfield due to difference of opinions. You don't even have to say you're a loyalist or that you're not a patriot. Let them draw their own conclusions if you can. A suggestion, a hint, a facial expression or even a slight nod of the head allows people to think whatever they want to think. But take your time. We're in no hurry to use your services. I would rather you take your time and establish yourself firmly in their good graces. It's a mistake to try to hurry these things— sometimes a fatal mistake."

And so Matthew took his time. Washington had been generous in supplying him with a heavy purse which was tied around his waist inside his shirt. His first days were spent observing, listening and watching, trying to adapt to the mood of the city, to match the movements and conversation of the New Yorkers, to be as unobtrusive as possible.

"Ya want to look closer to the waterfront, boy," the saloonkeeper said as he set a plate of clams before Matthew. "There's a couple of them barrelmakers down there might be hiring. But as you're probably already finding out, these aren't good times around here. Not with them damn rebels acting up so. Every week is bringing in more of them troublemakers by the acre," the man continued. "They're disrupting business, that's what they're doing!"

It took several more days before he found a cooper who would even talk to him. "So you say you're a cooper?" The big man of German descent walked slowly around Matthew, eyeing him carefully.

"Aye," Matthew replied. "My father and his father before him have all been in the trade."

The man pulled in his chin and looked sternly at Matthew. "I'm not hiring your father, lad. I need someone to hew a sharp stave and hoop a head true to line. You think you can do that?"

"I'll pit my barrel against any," Matthew answered confidently.

"Oh ho!" The man beamed, amused at Matthew's aggressiveness. "I have a master from the old country. You think you can match skills with the likes of Albert Hilden?"

"Give me the oak and I shall show you ready enough!"

Gunther Mahler shook his head and smiled at Matthew. "In time, me boy, in time." He gestured for Matthew to follow him and led the way through one barn to another. "You shall work your way to that position," Mahler answered. "One of my coopers is thinking about returning to his homeland. If he goes, I shall need someone to replace him. If he stays—" Mahler shrugged. "If he stays I might still need you to fire and stack the barrels."

Matthew nodded eagerly. He knew jobs were scarce in New York and was grateful that he had this opportunity to plant himself in any kind of a position.

The remainder of the day was spent locating a

suitable lodging within walking distance of the cooperage. The streets were lined with saloons and small obscure hotels to accommodate the crews of the ships that had once frequented the harbor. The number of signs advertising rooms for rent indicated the dire hardship these places were having due to the lack of shipping.

"Come along." The young woman at the door beckoned to him as he studied the sign in the window. "For less than any place yon can find, I'll give you the captain's room itself. No finer place in New York, I can guarantee." She took Matthew's arm and ushered him into the building and down the hall. "All the conveniences a man will ever want." She unlocked a door and gestured for Matthew to enter.

It was a large room. Its window looked out into a small lane littered with crates and debris, but it let in a bit of sun. The furnishings consisted of more than the usual bed and chamber pot. A small dresser with white marble top was against one wall, and an oval mirror, flecked and distorted, adorned the adjoining wall. A sturdy rocker was set in the corner next to the bed, which was covered with a slightly threadbare but clean down comforter.

"If you want, for a slight fee, you can have your meals with me," the woman coaxed, eyeing Matthew carefully. She had a pretty face and lively dark eyes, Matthew noticed. He judged her to be his own age or a year or so older.

"Your offer is most generous ma'am," Matthew responded, looking about the room that was to become his home. "And I shall be most happy to accept your hospitality for the meals."

His answer brought a laugh of relief from the woman. "You are a fine gentleman," she exclaimed, "and you shall not regret staying here." With the last, her eyes met his and her manner suddenly became subdued, wary, as she hastily added, "My husband will be happy of your company, I expect, when he's home. Like most of the others around here, he's a seaman. Comes and goes, one never knows when."

"Your husband," he said, turning away from her and busying himself with his knapsack. "He's on a British warship?"

"Oh, no," she said, watching as he put his things into the dresser drawers. "He sails on a privateer," she answered nonchalantly.

Matthew grinned. "Aren't you afraid that the British will catch him?"

She shrugged and absently inspected her fingernails. "They haven't been caught yet," she answered. "Besides, most of the British boats have sailed to Boston. His ship is safe."

"But is he safe here in New York?" Matthew asked curiously. "I mean, it is still a British city."

"You are new, aren't you? Why his Lordship Governor Tryon himself buys from privateers. We supply most of New York, in fact."

Matthew hesitated, wondering just how far he could continue without her getting suspicious of all his questions. "Aren't you afraid the Tories will arrest your husband?"

She looked up at Matthew with a tired sigh. "I don't care a whit who's a Tory or who's a Son of Liberty. Just because we're privateers doesn't mean we're loyal or disloyal. We became privateers only so we wouldn't have to pay those damn taxes. That doesn't mean we want to overthrow His Majesty." She suddenly eyed Matthew. "And what about you? Are you a Tory?"

Well, there it was, thought Matthew. It was the first time anyone had asked him directly. It was his first step into the new life. "I'm not even sure what that is anymore," Matthew responded putting on a troubled expression. "Where I come from they're all patriots. All of my family is. That's one reason I left and came here."

"I understand," she murmured. "I know just how you feel, when you have one idea and all the rest have other ideas. Just doesn't work out, does it?"

"It wasn't easy leaving my friends and my family," Matthew admitted.

She got up and smiled. "Well, you came to the right town. There's lots of Tories and you'll make lots of friends, you'll see."

"Do you know many Tories?" he asked.

She laughed, throwing back her head. "Oh, la! Do I know many Tories?" Again she laughed and shook her head in amusement. "Well," she answered, in control once more, "I must admit I knew a great many more than I do now. I was courted by some of the most influential men in New York, would you believe it? Me, Martha Dundee, actually in Grace Manor?"

"That comes as no surprise to me," Matthew answered. "And I bet you can still go there."

She laughed. "Well, maybe I can at that, although it might have to be through the back door."

"I'll tell you what," Matthew said grandly. "The next time I'm invited to Grace Manor, I shall take you on my arm."

Martha Dundee curtsied before him. "Oh la, Mr. Bell," she cooed, "you are a most gallant gentleman."

He bowed in return, and then they both laughed. "I'm glad you've decided to stay here, Matthew Bell," she said, and reached out to touch his arm. "You're very good company."

"Well, thank you, maa'm," he answered, bowing low at the waist. "You are a most charming hostess, Mrs. Dundee."

She smiled, suddenly shy, and started for the door. "My goodness! If I'm to have supper ready for my new guest, I'd better start preparing." She turned at the open door and looked over at him. "You're a good man, Matthew Bell, I can tell. Most of the men who come here—well, they're not the gentleman you are."

Matthew watched her retreat down the hall to her front room apartment. She was certainly like none of the women of Wethersfield. By turns tough, wary, or open and gay, but always with a slight edge of sadness under it all . . . But then New York was a harsh environment, he reminded himself, and Martha Dundee was much on her own with a husband who was often at sea. Perhaps, he suddenly realized, she was even more on her own than she would have him believe. He gave a short laugh, wondering what Deborah would think of what he guessed was his landlady's former profession. Knowing his sister, she'd probably decide to ignore it and invite Martha to tea.

14

THE FALL MONTHS in New York were a disappointment to Matthew. For one thing he missed the
bright reds, oranges and yellows of the trees.
There were maples scattered about the city, boasting
some of the coloring that marked the season, but nothing compared to the New England countryside that
Matthew had been raised in.

The wind that whipped out of the Atlantic and
across Long Island to blast the river frontage had a
bite to it that was far worse than the interior winds.
After three months in New York, Matthew was beginning to wonder why anyone in his right mind
would suffer the kind of weather he was experiencing.
Walking the chill streets to and from work was an
ordeal that dispelled any thought of settling perma-
nently in this locale.

"It is the ocean dampness," Colin Page explained as he watched Matthew huddle over the small open hearth in the barn where they stacked barrels for Mr. Mahler. Colin, two years younger than Matthew, had taken a great liking to the newcomer.

"You are used to this wind," Matthew said between chattering teeth.

Colin laughed. "You will be too soon enough."

"You New Yorkers are a hard lot," Matthew said, ribbing him good-naturedly. "We gentle New Englanders are not used to such harshness."

"Harshness!" Colin exclaimed. "Don't tell me about harshness! My family and I have spent a winter in your New England, and we'll never do it again."

Colin Page came from a well-to-do Tory family. His father, John Page, was a deputy on the mayor's Harbor Commission; Lydia Ramsack Page, his mother, was the daughter of one of the original families of Manhattan and had been a frequent visitor to the court in England; Colin's sister, Coleen, was almost engaged, according to Colin, to Major Winslow Whitehead, aide to General Gates himself.

"With your upbringing," Matthew had declared some weeks ago, "why are you working here?"

Colin's face turned sour. "It's sort of a punishment," he explained. "My father thinks all this will bring some sense to me."

"Has it?"

Colin shrugged and whittled at a slab of wood with his sharp cutting blade. "I know that I don't want to do this for the rest of my life," he answered. "I hope you don't mind me saying that."

Matthew smiled reassuringly at the boy. "Believe me, I wouldn't want the kind of life you've been raised to live any more than you would want my kind of life."

"But you seem so sure of yourself," Colin said with admiration.

Matthew raised his eyebrows and laughed. "I'm just older. It comes with age."

"Don't make fun of me, Matthew," Colin objected. "You are different from anyone I know."

Matthew inspected the youth out of the corner of his eye. The boy was gazing at the shavings that fell to his feet, his mind lost in his hopes and fears. Colin had been given everything he'd ever wanted in life. He might easily have been proud and spoiled, but Matthew saw that there was a serious side to the boy that had also been cultivated.

In the days that followed, Matthew had made a point of trying to get closer to Colin Page. If the stories were true, Colin's family knew many high-positioned Britishers whose information could be most highly prized by Washington. But the closer Matthew got to Colin, the more difficult it was for him. He was beginning to take a genuine liking to the boy and was bothered that he was using him only to infiltrate the Tories. It was therefore ironic that both his friendship with Colin and his loyalty to Washington should be tested in a single event.

It was the last week of October, after an especially grueling day. The two of them decided to indulge their earnings in some mugs of ale at the corner saloon.

"To His Majesty." Colin lifted the mug in front of him and grinned at Matthew. It had been a customary salute on such occasions in the past, but on this evening their toast was noticed by a group of men seated at the adjoining table.

"Goddamn loyalist!" one of the men growled aloud.

Colin made a move to stand but Matthew reached out and grabbed his arm, warning the boy with his eyes to calm down.

"Look at them two lobsterbacks," the man continued, encouraged by the laughter of his friends. "They're drinking to ole Georgie who's been putting the screws to us."

"Keep calm," Matthew said softly to Colin. "They're drunk."

"They're rebels—in our town," Colin said between clenched teeth. "Damn rebels stirring up more filth!"

"What're you saying?" One of the men staggered to his feet and came to lean over their table. "You too chicken-livered to say anything to me aloud, you cowardly redback? You ain't got the guts to face me?"

Colin stood up and glared at the man. "You're a goddamn rebel lookin' for trouble, that's what you are. How'd you get into this city anyway? Through the sewer like all your other four-footed friends?"

"Colin, sit down," Matthew warned. He yanked him down just as a chair sailed across the table, nearly hitting Colin's head.

"Goddamn traitors!" Colin screamed and went charging headfirst into the man who had thrown the chair. The two crashed onto the ground as the others quickly scurried out of the way.

Matthew let out a moan and got up to make his way through the quickly formed crowd. "Colin!" He started to reach down to pull the boy away when a hand reached out to stop him.

"Leave him be," one of the man's companions growled. "He's got it coming to him."

"He's just a lad," Matthew answered, and shoved the arm away roughly.

"He's a damned Tory," the man snarled and drew back his arm to swing.

Matthew had been ready for him. He ducked the blow and drove his fist into the man's stomach, waited until the form doubled up in agony and then clenched both fists together and smashed down across the man's back. He felt strangely elated, the blood pounding fiercely inside him as he watched the man slide to the floor.

"Tory!" The biting pain that buried itself into the side of his head nearly toppled Matthew to the ground. He spun around dizzily in time to see the fist strike again.

Matthew reeled, his hands reaching out to steady himself, finding the jacket of his attacker and desperately hanging on as further blows rained on his back. "Goddamn Tory!" a voice boomed in his ear as he was thrown backward and caught by another man. He tried to lift his arms but they were pinned. A sudden blow to his stomach knocked the air from his lungs. He coughed, nearly retching the ale he had just drunk. He was blacking out, he realized, gasping in vain for air. Oh God, he cried out to himself. There was yelling and screaming all around him and more blows came down on him as he sank to his knees.

He tried to raise himself but the blows against his bruised body kept him down. His head reeled, and then everything went black.

When he came to, he was dimly aware that he was being dragged across the floor, that it suddenly became cold and dark. Hands dropped him and he lay there, breathing painfully, waiting to make sure that he was being left alone. Suddenly a great weight was thrown on him and he groaned as his ribs were jabbed by a boot.

"Get outta this town, Tory," a voice snarled, followed by another sharp-toed kick into his side. "This is only the beginning if we catch you again."

There was laughter as the group made its way back into the saloon. Somewhere a woman's voice shrilled raucously, then faded away. All of a sudden it was very quiet.

As he lay in the street face down, the pain began to weave its way through each fiber of Matthew's body. The hurt became more intense as his mind cleared, the cold stung more across his wet face. He tried to rise but it felt as though a great weight was pressing down on him. He waited a second longer, regaining his breath, keeping his eyes tightly closed and gritting his teeth against the cold and pain. It was then that he realized the weight on his back must be Colin. He slowly turned on his side and eased the boy down upon his legs.

"Colin!"

The boy was unconscious, but still alive. Even in the darkness Matthew could see the battered face, bruised and already beginning to swell from the beating. Carefully, Matthew eased his legs from underneath Colin's form and kneeled in the street to inspect both of them for more serious injury.

"Oh, Colin," Matthew whispered, choking on swelling tears. His hands trembled and he suddenly looked up at the closed door of the saloon. "You damn bastards!" he screamed. "You goddamn bastards!"

He didn't know why he cried at first, but he let the tears come and the reasons came with them. He cried because they had beat up a young boy, because it had been a gang of bullies against two unarmed men. He cried because those bullies were patriots, fighting for the same cause he was. But most of all he was crying because, for the first time, he knew how it felt to be truly alone.

"C'mon, boy," Matthew finally murmured as Colin began to revive. "We'll take you to my place. It's closer."

The two struggled down the lonely streets, taking time out every once in a while to lean against a building and rest. Matthew half-dragged, half-carried the boy, wincing at every sore movement. He became angrier with every step, and the angrier he became the more determined he was. When he reached the front door of Martha Dundee's small apartment, he booted the front door open with such strength that one of the lower door panels splintered apart.

"Matthew!" Martha was at her door immediately, at first ready to do battle with some drunken neighbor. But upon seeing the two battered men she uttered a small cry of alarm and beckoned them into her room. "Put him on the couch," she ordered, darting to her small kitchen for water and a cloth.

Matthew gently laid Colin on the couch and then collapsed on an adjoining stuffed chair. She took a long look at him to make sure that he was all right and then turned to the boy. "Glory be," she muttered, "what have you gotten yourself into now?"

"Sons of Liberty," Matthew responded with a bitter bite to his words.

"Oh, la," she exclaimed without stopping her gentle washing of Colin's face. "They're all about now. I hear they burned down a house only a couple of blocks from here. It's not going to be safe for any of us, Matthew."

"Don't you worry, Martha," Matthew responded, wearily closing his eyes. "I'll make sure no harm comes to you."

"Just as you took care of this young lad? No thank you, kind sir. I think I'll take care of my own self."

"I guess I didn't do such a good job at that, did I?" Matthew smiled weakly and opened his eyes a crack to watch her caring for Colin. "How is he?"

"He shall not be as handsome a lad for quite a while, I'm afraid," she answered. "He took a fair beating, but nothing serious as far as I can see. Who is he?"

"We work together at Mahler's," Matthew answered.

"He is a fine boy though, isn't he?" she said musingly.

"And a good one," Matthew said. He stifled a groan as he shifted in his chair, preparing to get up. "I had better get him to his home."

"He's in no condition to be moved about, Matthew Bell," she protested. "He shall stay the night here, where I can keep a good watch on him."

Matthew sighed. In these weeks at her place he had come to know Martha quite well, and they bantered almost as brother and sister. His landlady was both street-wise and generous-hearted—and exceptionally stubborn.

"I'm far too tired to argue with you, Martha," he finally responded, and rose to his feet dizzily. "If you need me you know where I'll be."

When he had disappeared behind his own door, she turned and stared at Colin, a faint smile on her lips as she went over and laid a gentle hand against his cheek.

15

MATTHEW AWAKENED in the morning when he rolled onto his side and an excruciating pain shot through his spine. He rolled back over, moaning, and then lay still, letting his swollen eyes adjust to the light.

The room was bitterly cold as he pushed off the coverlet and swung his feet onto the bare floor. He rose, steadying himself on the bedpost, feeling worse than he had ever felt in his life. Feebly he shuffled over to the mirror.

Even without the flecked distortions of the ancient mirror, the image that stared back at him could not have been more horrible. His hand gently traced the innumerable bumps and bruises and small cuts along his lips and around his eyes. He looked like some nightmarish creature.

Dressing with slow, painful movements, he knew that working at Mr. Mahler's was out of the question today, and Colin Page was undoubtedly in even worse condition.

"How is he?" Matthew asked when Martha opened the door to his soft knock.

She placed a finger to her lips and beckoned him to enter. "He's resting nicely," she whispered, leading the way to the bedroom door and allowing Matthew a look.

The boy was propped in bed, against a couple of cushions. His naked chest was covered to the shoulders with a heavy quilt that was one of Martha's prize possessions.

"You got him to bed, I see," Matthew commented as he sat at the table and accepted her mug of hot tea.

"He woke shortly after you left, so it was no trouble getting him into the next room."

Matthew smiled openly and pressed his hand appreciatively on top of hers. "You are a good woman, Martha Dundee."

"I'm not sure my motives are as pure as you'd have them," she said laughingly. She glanced at the door to the bedroom and added in a gentler tone, "I must declare to you, dear Matthew, I am attracted to the boy."

"*Boy* is correct," Matthew reminded her. "Don't you forget it either."

She laughed good-naturedly and started to prepare his breakfast. "I suppose you think you can protect him from a woman better than you protected him from a gang of bullies?"

"I judge by your talk, Martha," Matthew responded in a serious tone, "that you have set your cap for

Colin. I doubt whether your husband would appreciate your goal."

"Oh posh," Martha responded with a shake of her head. "You know as well as I that I have no husband. The man I live with is at sea most of the time, and I'm certain that he has women in other ports. He'd consider it no loss if I were to find someone else."

Matthew studied her with apprehension. "He is no match for you, Martha," Matthew responded gently. "I am your friend—I hope you know that, and that you won't take my advice amiss. But I see you thinking about Colin Page and I don't think it will work out, no matter how much I care about the two of you. You are miles apart from each other, and that's no good."

"But maybe it is," Martha responded. She came and sat across the table from him, holding his hands in hers and looking deeply into his eyes. "Maybe it's only natural for two people who are so far apart to be drawn together, like a sponge and water."

Matthew shook his head sadly. "You're dreaming, Martha. Perhaps you're hungry to find someone to love, someone to care for you and help you and be with you. But Colin is a boy who has had very little responsibility. He still has a loose head on his shoulders—and he's been brought up in a different world from yours or mine."

"Oh, Matthew," she said and kissed his hands. "Please don't discourage me now. You can't imagine the types I have associated with. You have been the first decent person I ever met, and I love you like a brother. But when I saw that lad in there my heart burst—I could feel it. I stayed awake all night just staring at him, not even touching him." She grabbed Matthew's hands and held them to her cheek, which was beginning to dampen with tears. "Don't tell me I cannot even try. I would be so good for him and he for me."

Matthew sighed and stroked her silken hair. "I cannot tell you not to try," he answered. "I can only warn you it could be very rough for both of you. And these are bad times for anyone. It will not be easy."

"It's never been easy for me, Matthew," Martha answered tearfully, "it's never been easy. But I've got to try, I must try and get out of this existence."

Matthew looked at her tear-streaked face and sighed. Gently, he started to wipe the tears away. "I guess I know how you feel. Of course you've got to give it a try. That's what life's all about, isn't it?" He gave her a smile to encourage her.

"Oh, Matthew, you are truly a fine friend. I'll take good care of him and I'll—"

"Whoa now," he laughed. "You're going a bit too fast. For one thing, I've still got to take him back to his own home—"

"Oh, Matthew, let him stay a bit longer."

He shook his head. "Don't you worry, I shall invite him over as often as I can. From there on it will have to be up to you. *And* to him."

"Oh, he'll like me," Martha insisted, rising and straightening herself. "I'll see to that."

"I'm sure you will," Matthew said grinning. "Now, you prepare our breakfast and I'll attempt to wake your victim and bring him to the table."

Colin's eyes were half-open as Matthew softly stepped to the bedside. "Is this your home?" he asked weakly, squinting up at Matthew.

"It is where I stay," Matthew responded.

"There was a woman—"

Matthew nodded and sat on the bed next to Colin. "Her name is Martha Dundee. She's the landlady. A finer lady you will not find," he added. He studied Colin's face more intently. "And how do you feel? Are you up to coming into the kitchen to eat something warm?"

Colin nodded and then winced in pain. "It feels as though the roof fell on top of me." He regarded Matthew through swollen eyes. "Do I look as bad as you?"

Matthew laughed and pulled back the covers. "Worse! Come, Martha is preparing food for us. I think that's the best thing for you right now."

Martha let out a laugh as Matthew pulled a reluctant Colin into the kitchen. Dressed in one of her dressing gowns, he did look a pathetic sight.

Colin stared down at his long, bare feet and drew the gown closer to his body in embarrassment. "It is all we could find that I could fit into," he stammered.

Both Matthew and Martha laughed as they pulled the hesitant youth to a chair. "Don't you worry," Matthew said as he gently assisted Colin to the table. "As soon as you've eaten, I'll be taking you home."

"You've both been most kind to me," Colin said, his eyes lingering on Martha. "I shan't ever be able to repay you."

"Repay?" Martha turned to face him with a stern look. "And who do you think you owe?" Her eyes met Colin's and held for a moment before she flushed and glanced away. "You certainly don't owe your friend here anything. Some bodyguard he turned out to be. And as for me—" She suddenly turned her back to them and busied herself at the stove. "Well, I had nothing better to do."

"I shan't forget your friendship," Colin murmured. Then, conscious of Matthew at his side, he quickly turned to his friend. "Nor shall I forget yours, Matthew. You took a beating because of me."

Matthew shrugged. "They called us both Tories."

"The bastards!" Colin looked over at Martha. "Excuse me, ma'am."

"I've heard and used worse language," Martha responded with a smile. "They *were* bastards! And my name is not ma'am. It's Martha."

"Martha!" Colin repeated, shyly returning her smile.

After they had eaten and dressed and bid their adieus to Martha, the two men headed for Colin's home on the other side of the island, close to the Hudson River. No sooner had they left the house than Colin began singing praises of the girl, concluding with: "And I think she likes me!"

Matthew smiled patiently. "That should come as no surprise to you, lad. You're a fine specimen of a young man."

"You speak as though I were considerably younger than you," Colin complained. "I am but a few years younger than you, but I feel that you treat me like a boy."

Matthew looked over at Colin. "I'm sorry you feel that way, for it is not true. Perhaps I see a bit of my younger brother in you, but I consider you a good friend and an equal."

"We are more than equal, Matthew," Colin stated soberly. "We are comrades now. We have fought and suffered side by side, and that makes us comrades."

Matthew laughed and slapped Colin good-naturedly on the back, instantly regretting his action as the boy winced in obvious pain. "I am sorry," he said, "but you are right, we are indeed soldiers in arms. Although I'm afraid it is one tale I shan't repeat too often."

"We shall be prepared for them the next time," Colin

said stoutly. "These rabble-rousers can't come into our city and tell us what to do!"

Colin's home was a large, grey-stone Dutch structure that shared a common wall with an adjoining home of similar architecture. A stone-columned iron fence faced the front.

"I dare say all of Wethersfield could live in such a grand place," Matthew murmured as he stopped to view the home.

Colin laughed and pulled Matthew to the front door. "Come in and meet my parents," he urged. "I want them to meet you, too."

"Young man, where have you been?" A tall silver-haired gentleman descended the stairs that curved down into the immense hallway. As he approached, his stern features softened to concern. "Good lord, Colin, what happened?"

"We were set upon by a mob of patriots, Father," the youth explained, proud of his battle scars.

"Let me see." John Page came closer and carefully inspected Colin's face. "It looks like you took the worst of it, but I see you survived." Before the boy could reply, the elder Page turned to study Matthew.

"This is my friend, who saved me," Colin quickly explained, stepping to Matthew's side. "He works with me at Mr. Mahler's."

"Ah, yes," John Page answered, stiffening slightly in a stranger's presence. "I believe you did mention something about your friend. Michael Bell, is it not?"

"Matthew Bell, sir," Matthew corrected and thrust out his hand.

"So you saved my boy's life, did you?" the father said, his eyes taking in the bruises Matthew had suffered.

"I am afraid Colin exaggerates. We were both set upon by the same group."

John Page shook his head. "I have heard these riffraff have come into our city. Tell me where this was and I shall have soldiers sent at once."

"I don't think it would do much good now, sir," Matthew said, speaking before Colin could reply. "Knowing that this is a Tory town, I'm sure they would protect themselves by moving on to another area of New York."

"You're probably right," Colin's father agreed. "But I shall make a recommendation to the governor that he increase our patrols of the city streets."

"Oh, Colin!" A woman's voice broke into their conversation, and the men stepped aside to make way for a lady quickly descending the staircase. She was a strikingly beautiful woman, her aristocratic features framed by upswept silver hair that cascaded into curls. "We were so worried when you didn't return last night," she scolded, looking first at Colin, then over at Matthew. "Look at you! You are a mess!"

Colin grinned and drew her close to the others. "Mother, I'd like you to meet my friend, Matthew Bell. I spent the night at his place."

Her glance at him was of bare approval. "I trust that you weren't the cause of my son's disfigurement."

"No, ma'am," Matthew answered uncomfortably. Before he could continue, Colin spoke up.

"We were both attacked by rebels, Mother," Colin explained. "If it hadn't been for Matthew, I might very well have been thrown into the river and left to die."

It was obvious that Lydia Ramsack Page was used to Colin's exaggerations. "Then we are in your debt, young man," she announced coolly, turning to inspect Matthew from head to foot.

"No, ma'am," Matthew answered. "I consider Colin my friend. My friends do not owe me, nor I them."

His answer struck a chord, for she regarded him more kindly. "Perhaps some tea would be appropriate." She turned and raised her hand. From out of a rear corner, as though a silent bell had rung, there appeared a man-servant.

"George," Mrs. Page announced, "tea for us. And please be so kind as to tell Colin's sister that he has returned."

"According to Winslow," John Page said as they seated themselves in the living room, "the city will be cleared of these rebels before winter sets in."

Colin leaned closer to Matthew. "Winslow," he whispered, "is Coleen's fiancé, a major in the army."

"Major Winslow Whitehead," Colin's father explained for Matthew's benefit, "is one of General Gates's aides. If anyone should know, it would be he."

Matthew smiled and made note of this fact. Luck was with him to have found a gateway to such an important link to British activities. "That must mean Boston will be secured before long."

John Page turned to face Matthew, obviously pleased that he had an audience for a political discussion. "I hear that it is only a matter of time before British troops disembark to drive off that rebel band. Can you imagine," he said with a sympathetic smile, "a bunch of farmers, being led by a man who has held no rank higher than colonel in the Indian wars, thinking they can stop the combined leadership of such mighty men as Clinton, Burgoyne and Howe?" He gave a polite laugh. "The colonies have had small uprisings since their beginnings. This one too will soon be past. I'm only sorry that you and my son received such abuse."

Matthew tried to shrug off the misadventure. "I've seen far worse," he answered. "I have a brother who got his leg shot off."

"Really?" John Page turned back to Matthew with mild curiosity. "He saw battle?"

"Against my wishes," Matthew added truthfully. "In July at Boston." He looked at Colin's parents with an apologetic look. "He was fighting for the patriots."

Mr. Page let out a long, "Ah yes," and studied Matthrew intently. "I've heard that families have split over the issues. Is that why you left Connecticut?"

Matthew nodded. "I thought I would be more useful here in New York."

Colin's father shook his head. "And look what it brought you. Those barbarians follow you here and beat you up, eh?" He shook his head again in sadness. "These dissidents cause harm and destruction, and we peaceful citizens must bear their foolishness. Frankly, I think the king has been too patient. Those mob leaders in Philadelphia should be collected and locked up. That would put an end to these disloyal riffraff."

"I often wish I were able to help," Matthew said. "At times I feel so useless at the cooperage."

"I daresay I can sympathize with you," John Page answered. "You seem to be a bright lad. Perhaps I can put in a good word for you with Major Whitehead. Or better yet, perhaps Coleen could introduce you to her major." The father looked up and beamed beyond Matthew. "And speaking of Coleen, here she is."

Matthew rose quickly and turned to find himself staring at the most beautiful creature he had ever laid eyes upon. Coleen Page had the same fine features as her mother, outlined in a golden mane that flowed around her face like wisps of corn silk. She had a full figure and moved gracefully as she ran to engulf Colin in a tight embrace.

"Let me look at you," Coleen exclaimed, pulling away and staring intently into her brother's face. "Oh, my heavens, you look a fright."

Colin grinned and then pulled his sister over to Matthew's side. "I want you to meet my friend," he announced. "Matthew, this is my sister Coleen."

Matthew bowed, trying not to let his face betray his inner thoughts. "I am honored," he said.

"You're as dreadful-looking as Colin," she exclaimed. Her hand went to her mouth. "Oh, dear, I didn't mean it the way it sounds."

Matthew smiled. "But I do look dreadful," he answered. "You do not have to apologize."

"But that was rude of me." She took a more studious look over his face and then met his eyes.

"He's quite a handsome brute under all those bruises," Colin said. "And he's my best friend."

Coleen was amused at her brother. "Well, best friend," she said to Matthew, "thank you for bringing my brother home again."

Matthew bowed, not knowing how to respond. "I should be returning to my own home," he said as he turned to the mother and father. "It was an honor to meet you both. Thank you for your courtesy."

Colin's mother came up to Matthew and took his hand in hers. "We're truly grateful that you took care of our Colin. If there is anything we can do to repay you, please let us know."

"Yes," John Page echoed. "And I shall be sure to speak to Winslow about your desire to fight the rebels."

"You are all most kind," Matthew answered, starting to back away. He turned to Coleen Page. "It has been a pleasure meeting you, Miss Page."

"Maybe we will see each other again," she answered.

As the front door closed behind Matthew, he took a deep breath. Maybe we will see each other again. . . . Her words rang in his ears over and over again. He was going to make sure that he and Coleen Page met again, if it meant moving heaven and hell.

16

MATTHEW STARED up at the ceiling of his bedroom, hands locked behind his head as he lay on his iron-framed bed. He was fully dressed in his best brown suit, his shirt freshly laundered and ironed by Martha for this special Christmas occasion.

Time had gone quickly, and one more week would bring a new year—seventy-six. He had hurried through his dressing far too eagerly and now, as he waited for the appropriate time to leave, he thought about the past months. He and Colin had grown to be fast friends, and through that friendship, Colin had encountered Martha.

For Matthew, his acquaintance with Colin Page led him to his goal. Colin's father, his mother and Coleen's fiance, Major Whitehead, were all valuable contributors to information on the British movements. His conscience plagued him, however, for using their friendship for his spying activities.

And then there was Coleen Page. Cool, distant, reserved and beautiful Coleen. He sometimes wondered if his interest in her had been guessed by Major Whitehead, who at times regarded him with a look of skepticism and had asked unusually pointed questions about his background and views. But not even that could keep Matthew away. And if he was using his friendship with Colin to see the boy's sister, Colin was equally eager to see Martha Dundee during his visits to Matthew.

"I do believe Colin likes me," Martha had admitted last night as she and Matthew spent the late evening hours washing and ironing his things in her room.

Matthew smiled as he relaxed in one of her chairs. "I *know* he likes you Martha," he stated. "The boy is infatuated with you."

"No," she answered stubbornly, "I don't mean infatuation. I mean I think he really *does* like me—as a woman.'"

"And that's one of the problems," he answered gently, not wanting to be cruel. "You are a woman— and he's merely a lad."

"I'm not that much older than he," she answered. "There are only four or five years difference. Why is it that a man can marry a woman who's younger, but a woman cannot marry a man who's younger?"

Matthew laughed. "There's no ruling that says such a thing, Martha. It's just that the man provides for the woman, and has to be strong and knowing to take proper care of her."

"Colin already has lots of money to take good care of me," Martha answered lightly. "I would make him a very good wife."

Matthew studied Martha without her noticing. She was a beautiful woman, but there was a soft glow to her face that hadn't been there before Colin entered her life.

There was a timid knock at his bedroom door and Matthew woke from his daydreaming with a start.

"It's almost time for you to leave," Martha said quietly, eying his handsome figure with motherly thoroughness when he opened the door. "You strike a handsome figure, Matthew Bell," she smiled bravely up at him. There was no doubt that she was hurt by the fact that she had not been invited to the Page's Christmas dinner.

"Thanks to you," he responded, not knowing how to ease her sorrow. "You take good care of me." He hesitated, then took her hand and smiled. "I was going to save this until tonight when I returned." He reached over to the top of the dresser and handed her a small box wrapped in lavender paper. "Please open it," he said softly.

"For me?" Martha whispered, inspecting the small box on all sides. "This is for me?" Quickly her fingers ripped open the package and pulled out a white silk handkerchief trimmed with delicate white lace.

"I never know what to get a woman," Matthew explained shyly, "but my sister said a woman can always use a handkerchief."

Martha looked up at him and kissed him gently on the cheek. "It is the most beautiful thing I have. I shall always cherish it, dearest Matthew." Then she became solemn. "But this is not fair. I did not get you anything for Christmas."

He laughed and hugged her. "The best Christmas present you can give me is your smile, your happiness and your friendship. I really mean that."

"You are a dear man," Martha whispered, touching him tenderly on the face. "And now you make me feel all the worse, for I did get something for Colin."

"That is the way it should be," Matthew answered. "Besides, I have all that I need."

"Please tell him," Martha urged, as she helped him on with his greatcoat. "Please tell him I have something for him, that he can come by any time and pick it up—any time at all."

He smiled down at her. "I shall tell him the first chance I have," he promised as he opened the door to the wintery evening.

It was one of the first things he did manage to convey to Colin. "Please let me stay the night with you, Matthew," Colin urged, as he guided Matthew into the living room. "I must see her tonight."

Before Matthew could reply, he was greeted by Colin's mother and father, who came forward with outstretched hands. "Matthew," Lydia Page said sweetly, "how nice you could partake in our Christmas celebration."

"It is most kind of you, ma'am." Matthew bowed politely. "Since I have no family now, I'm afraid my Christmas would have been very bleak. Your generosity warms me greatly."

"Colin informs me that Mahler might be laying men off this winter," John Page said, draping an arm over Matthew's shoulders and guiding him into a corner sofa. "His business is in trouble too?"

Matthew nodded. "With the rebels coming into New York now, almost everybody is closing up shop."

John Page let out a soft oath. "We're being outnumbered and there's not a damn thing we can do about it."

"The British garrison surely will protect us," Matthew prompted, but Page had turned his attention to the door.

Coleen was entering the room, escorting a tall, blond man in full dress scarlet.

"Ah, yes," John Page said, rising to his feet and beckoning the newcomers to come forward.

There was a click of heels and the officer gave a slight bow as he acknowledged Matthew. "Master Bell," he said in a clipped accent.

He then turned his attention wholly to his prospective father-in-law, but Matthew saw his beseeching look to Coleen when John Page began to question him about action being taken against the rebels.

"Oh, Father," the girl responded, coming forward and coupling her arm with Whitehead's, "we all vowed there would be no discussion of politics or rebellions today. You promised."

The elder Page scowled in disappointment. "Very well," he answered grudgingly, "we shall save our talk until our brandy. However, there is one small matter which I must discuss with your major, I'm afraid. It will only take a moment." Before there was any objection, her father took hold of the officer's sleeve and propelled him into the study.

Coleen shook her head and smiled. "My father cannot stand not knowing what is going on," she explained, turning to face Matthew. "I'm afraid you're stuck with me," she said after glancing over to notice that Colin and her mother were talking to each other.

"I cannot think of a more pleasurable fate," Matthew said.

She gave him a quick troubled look as she spread her skirt neatly over the settee's cushions. "Thank you," she answered softly, looking at him with an expression in her eyes that was impossible to identify.

"Is there something wrong?" he finally asked, becoming uncomfortable under her silent scrutiny.

She shook her head. "I'm sorry," she answered quickly, a slight red coming to her cheeks. "I was staring, and that was rude of me. Oh dear," she moaned, "I always seem to be doing or saying the wrong things, don't I?"

Her remark eased his discomfort and he laughed softly. "You are honest with your feelings," he replied. "There can be little harm in being honest with each other."

Their eyes met and locked. She had the most delicate green eyes that seemed to probe into his inner depths and aroused him so that his breath was taken away.

"My honesty," she finally sighed, being the first to look away, "has sometimes gotten me into trouble, I'm afraid."

"I don't see how it could," Matthew answered, glancing at the study door, hoping it would never open. "Are you honest with your major?"

Her eyes darted to his and she pursed her lips in thought. "I've tried to be," she answered softly.

"Has he been honest with you?" There was no stopping his questions, it seemed.

Again her eyes lifted to his, this time with a troubled expression. "Military men sometimes have a difficult time with honesty. Their work makes it so." Her words came haltingly, and she looked away from Matthew with an unhappy expression.

"Anyone who deals with wars has to deal with the ugly side of life," Matthew said comfortingly.

"And you, Mr. Matthew Bell," she said soberly, "have you ever dealt with the ugly side of life?"

"These are war times. We all have to deal with the

ugly side of life now, whether we want to or not. Colin and I experienced some of that ugliness a couple of months ago."

"And what have you two been talking about?" Colin's voice broke the silence that had followed Matthew's remark. He settled on the settee next to his sister, scooping her dress aside.

Matthew drew in a deep breath and leaned back in his chair, conscious that Coleen was red-faced and flustered that her brother had interrupted them.

"Our famous fight against the patriots," Matthew replied with a smile. "We must have been a sight when we showed up here with all our bruises and scars."

"You should see the scar across his back," Colin volunteered.

"That wasn't from the fight," Matthew corrected. "It's a scar from long ago," he explained when Coleen raised her eyebrows questioningly.

"It nearly cost him his life," Colin stated.

Matthew shook his head and smiled at Coleen apologetically. "Not half as glorious as it sounds, I'm afraid. Some barrels came down on top of me." He turned to Colin with a severe look. "What are you trying to make me out to be?"

Colin shrugged. "She could have been impressed."

"Impressed?" Coleen gave her brother an amused look. "Why must I be impressed with your friend, Colin?"

The boy shrugged and wouldn't meet her eyes. "I don't know," he finally answered. "I guess I just want him to be your friend, too."

Coleen sighed and took a quick glance at Matthew. "I'm sure Matthew doesn't need you to sing his praises."

Matthew laughed. "If I do anything worth praising, I shall be sure to contact you to lead the chorus. But I appreciate your trying to get me in your sister's good graces." He glanced quickly at Coleen to see what her reaction was, but the girl's attention had been caught by her father and fiance reentering the room. Matthew drew in a deep sigh and turned away as Coleen rose and went to them.

"What I want to know is why you're allowing this riff-raff into our city?" John Page stood by the fireplace, studying the amber liquid in his large snifter as Colin, Matthew and Major Whitehead settled themselves in nearby chairs in the study. The dinner had been ample, the talk light and easy, and now, well-satisfied, the men had retired to the study for drinks and smokes.

"I'm afraid there's not much we can do to stop them," the officer replied between puffs as he lit his large cigar. "Every available man we have has been sent to either Charleston or Boston. Our small garrison here cannot afford an open conflict with any mob."

"But aren't you doing anything?" the elder Page asked, indignantly.

The major, uncomfortable under the direct questioning, took a deep breath and sighed slowly. "With winter set in, there's nothing anybody can do—at least not outwardly. But I assure you, there are things happening all the time. Our spies inform us that most of the renegade army has disbanded and gone home. This Washington has only a handful of men, no way of stopping our ships from entering Boston harbor come springtime. We predict that things will calm down no later than June.

"June?" Matthew asked. "That late?"

The major shrugged. "Of course there are other

things in the making, just in case. Governor Tryon, for instance, is organizing a counter-rebellion. The people of New York are tired of these mobs and their disruption and it's time they rise and get rid of the rabble themselves."

"That's what I say," Matthew remarked. In a thoughtful tone he added, "How does one become part of Governor Tryon's counter-rebellion?"

Major Whitehead raised his eyebrows and took a quick look at his host.

"You see?" John Page said with a smile. "I told you our Matthew was willing to assist you."

"Yes, I want to help," Matthew answered seriously. "I want to do anything I can to help end this war." So Page had spoken to Whitehead after all, Matthew thought. No doubt it was that, rather than jealousy, that was behind the skeptical looks and questions that Whitehead had directed toward him over the last months. Whitehead had been sizing him up.

The major leaned forward and rested his glass on his crossed knee. "Yet you told me yourself that your family is sympathetic to the other side."

"I'm afraid so," Matthew answered, keeping his face expressionless.

"Do you have many friends in the Continental Army?" came the next question.

Matthew guardedly nodded his head, wondering what was coming.

There was a long pause before Whitehead continued. "Mr. Page states that you are a fervent loyalist."

Matthew chose his words carefully. "To be honest with you, I did enlist in the Continental Army. I thought it was the right thing to do, and my family and friends had enlisted. But I found that kind of life wasn't for me and, as you know, I left."

"Wise of you, son," John Page commented, lifting his snifter in a salute to Matthew. "Most wise of you."

Major Whitehead rose and stepped to the fireplace beside the elder Page to stare a long moment into the flames. Slowly he turned about and faced Matthew.

"How would you like to return to your town, to your family and friends?" he asked.

Matthew stared at him uncertainly, then glanced at Colin and Mr. Page. "No, sir," he answered, "I can't. I left because of my beliefs, and my beliefs haven't changed."

The major smiled and shook his head. "No, I don't mean to return as a rebel, but as one of us." He allowed time for it to sink in. "You heard me mention our spy network? How would you like to become part of it?" He smiled at the look of genuine astonishment on Matthew's face, and quickly continued. "You would be a perfect spy for us. You could go back to your town declaring that you've changed your mind, that you are a rebel. Since they're your family and friends, they would want to believe you. We'll try to set you up so that you'll have direct contact with some of our agents on Washington's staff."

"Washington's staff!" Matthew exclaimed, and immediately wondered if he had overreacted.

But Major Whitehead only grinned. "Yes, we have men right under that Virginian's nose. I trust that with you there, we'll be able to set our plans in action right away."

Matthew's head fairly spun with the impact of Whitehead's words. Luck was with him, it seemed, but things were going too fast. "A spy," he said heavily, coming to his feet. "I don't know . . ."

"From what I've seen of you," the major responded, "I'm sure you can handle it. I'll see you in my office first thing next week to brief you on the details."

John Page came over to Matthew and placed a fatherly arm around his shoulders. "We'll be proud of you, boy," he boomed and grinned his endorsement.

Colin grabbed Matthew's hand and shook it energetically. "Isn't this exciting?" he exclaimed, continuing to pump Matthew's hand.

17

Traveling to Boston in mid-January was a grueling journey. Matthew would have preferred to wait until the March thaws, but Major Whitehead needed up-to-date information on Washington's movements.

"There are four things we wish to know," the major had stated, pacing back and forth in his office. "As you might have heard by now, we have defeated the rebel force in Canada. We need to know Washington's plans on what he's going to do with the remainder of that ragtail army."

The officer drew in a deep breath and looked out his window upon the wide harbor that spread out in front of the barracks. "We also need to know Washington's spring campaign. My spies think the rebels are attempting to bring guns down from Ticonderoga," he said, turning to a map on the wall and tracing a line from the small black dot on Lake Champlain down to Boston. "They're foolish to think they can drag cannon such a distance in the dead of winter," he said, frowning as he once again faced Matthew. "But it's best we make sure. If the rebels get control of the harbor, our troops will not be able to land. You can imagine the consequences."

The British officer paced the floor a moment more. Matthew watched him carefully, still in wonderment that he was actually inside the enemy's fortress. At any moment he expected someone to fling open the door and come in to point a finger at him, ending it all.

"Thirdly," Whitehead continued, "we have another rumor that Charles Lee might be coming to New York with his troops."

"Lee?" Matthew asked incredulously. Everyone had heard of the famous military brain who was Washington's confidant.

"Yes, I know," Whitehead said grimly. "Washington's ablest man assigned here to New York."

Matthew made mental note of his instructions, all the time wondering just how Washington was going to receive the news that he was to be a spy for the British. To Matthew's thinking, the new position was a godsend, enabling him far easier access to British movements. "You said there were four things, sir?"

The last assignment was apparently the most crucial, for it was obvious that Whitehead was deliberating about divulging it to Matthew. He studied Matthew intently, weighing his decision.

Matthew decided to help the officer along. "Perhaps," he suggested, "if you have doubts about my allegiance, you had best not tell me, sir. I know you are trusting me with important information and that I am new. If I were in your shoes, I too would hesitate."

It was perhaps the suggestion that the two of them could possibly be alike that made Whitehead react quickly. "No," he answered gruffly. To him, hesitation was a sign of weakness. "No, I was merely thinking what course of action to take."

"Of course, sir."

"The fourth task concerns a highly dangerous secret." The major sat on the front edge of the desk and leaned closer to Matthew in confidence. "As I told you last week at the Pages', there is a movement already in the making to start a counter-revolution against the rebels. Governor Tryon and Mayor Matthews have already enlisted the aid of several prominent citizens—including the Pages, by the way—to spread the word and enlist not only every loyalist but every dissatisfied citizen in the country. We have been finding that there are quite a few rebels who have become disaffected." He hesitated and straightened, speaking with more gravity now. "There are men within the ranks of Washington's army whom we have approached and enlisted in our cause. It is most important that we keep an open line of communication with these men so that, when the time comes, we can overthrow the leaders of this rebellion quickly and efficiently. I have contact with some very high officials in the ranks already. I want you to open a new one for me—or re-open, as it happens."

Whitehead went to the other side of his desk and began to shuffle through his papers. Suddenly, he looked up and stared at Matthew. "Your contact is with one of our most important agents. He's a sergeant on Washington's private staff."

Matthew was impressed, both that the British had managed to infiltrate so close to Washington and that he was being informed of such a valuable secret.

"One of the reasons we have picked you, Mr. Bell," the major continued, "is that our agent is from the same town as you."

"Wethersfield?" Matthew asked, his stomach suddenly knotting.

"Yes. Thomas Hickney. Do you know him?"

"Only from when we were training in the militia," he answered, trying to remember all he could about the man. "But he was one of the first to leave. I thought he was a patriot."

Major Whitehead smiled knowingly. "He was at first, but now he's one of ours."

As far as Matthew knew, there was no way Hickney could betray him. He felt a bit easier. "And you want me to contact him?"

The major nodded. "Since you're both from the same town, it would be natural for you two to get together. Hickney is most important to us and has access to valuable information. We'll be using you as a contact, going back and forth. You can use going home as an excuse for leaving New York—or whatever else seems a reasonable explanation."

"You've thought everything out most clearly," Matthew commented.

"Thank you." Whitehead bowed slightly with a small smile of satisfaction. "But you must remember that we've been in this war business for centuries and are quite confident in our abilities. You've volunteered in a most worthy cause and I'm sure His Majesty will reward you handsomely—as he does all his loyal subjects."

"I shall do my best, sir," Matthew promised, rising to stretch out a hand. "The most important thing is that the right side wins."

"You're so right," the major answered, standing behind his desk to clutch Matthew's hand. "You're so right. We shall crush this rebellion once and for all, thanks to dedicated citizens such as you."

Matthew managed to stifle a smile at the major's words and manner. "We're only trying to do our best to end all of this," he said solemnly, wondering if he sounded as pompous as Whitehead did. There were times he enjoyed his role and the chance to deceive the likes of Whitehead.

He had told Mahler and the Pages that he had urgent family business to attend to. The Pages had volunteered to pay the expense of traveling by coach but Matthew had declined their offer. It was easier for him to travel from one camp to the other alone, without having the worry of explaining himself to fellow travelers. Besides, the long ride, even in the shivering cold, would give him plenty of time to think.

His thoughts often went to Coleen during the journey. She brought warmth and sunshine to his soul even though none of these feelings were encouraged by her. Most of the time, it seemed he hardly existed in her eyes. Of course, it was only natural that her attention would be on the major, although Matthew sometimes felt there was something amiss between the two. It wasn't only that the major was so frustratingly formal. Matthew's brash questions to her on Christmas Eve had revealed that something was troubling her, and it had seemed that she was on the verge of confiding in him when Colin had interrupted. But perhaps it was all his imagination, he chided himself, and her timid glances and sudden smiles in his direction were no more than polite acknowledgment of his presence.

He couldn't quite bring himself to discuss it with Colin. And in any event, the lad was very absorbed in his own love affair with Martha. The two were a joyous and handsome couple, but as of yet Colin had made no attempt to bring Martha out into the open. It was beginning to strain their relationship, a fact that was of some concern to Matthew. He would have to take the boy aside when he got back to New York and tell him how distraught Martha was at not being introduced to his family. . . .

Matthew would have been tempted to veer from his route and visit Wethersfield, but the information he had received from Whitehead was crucial to Washington, and he had set a true course toward Boston.

They had arranged their signals well. Matthew huddled against the fence of Washington's magnificent headquarters until the general took his usual evening stroll, this time with a small group of aides. They had exchanged glances quickly, without so much as a nod of the head, and for a brief moment Matthew wondered whether his leader had recognized him. But when the group had stopped outside a small saloon, Washington waved the others away and beckoned Matthew to follow him into the darkened room.

"I did not expect to see you this soon," the older man said as he slid into a booth and turned to Matthew. His face was haggard and there was a sadness about him. He sighed and managed a slight smile when he saw Matthew's look of concern. "I'm afraid my health has been a bit off lately. I'm not used to your harsh winters. But tell me, you must have important news to have traveled in this cold."

Matthew eagerly recounted his progress in New York, his contact with the Pages and finally his assignments for Major Whitehead. When finished, he leaned back, waiting for the tall Virginian's response.

"You have done most well, Matthew," came the slow, soft response. "In such short a time, most remarkably well. I don't know of either Page or Whitehead, but as an officer on Gage's staff Whitehead would indeed have access to valuable information. Gage has been replaced by Howe and that might alter the picture a bit, but it is an excellent start. My only worry," Washington warned, "is that you are in even more jeopardy as a double agent. One slip and your life will be worthless. You are playing two roles now, not just one."

Matthew nodded. "I shall be careful. But it is you I'm concerned about. Whitehead says there are many in your ranks ready to strike against you."

Washington smiled wearily and leaned back in his seat. "I've been aware of that for a long time. There are those in Congress and other governmental positions who oppose me as commander in chief. But there are also a great many in the ranks who want to go home, who are not happy with various orders I've had to give out. I suppose by now there are those who are disillusioned with the rebellion and perhaps have even forgotten the cause we're fighting for." He sighed and looked about at the forms crouched over mugs and desultory conversations. "That's one of the hardships of the winter campaigns. Nothing to do but wait out the cold. Idleness too often breeds ill will in an army . . . When the time is right, we shall tend to your Sergeant Hickney," Washington said, turning his gaze back to Matthew. "Whitehead would be too suspicious, I'm afraid, if Hickney were arrested right after you arrived here."

"Of course," Matthew agreed. "How do you want me to use my new role?"

"We shall give the British information they want to hear, information that will not give you any difficulty. For one thing, the major is correct about the cannon from Ticonderoga. I've sent General Knox there to see if there's a way to bring them down here. No one knows yet whether the feat is possible. But just between you and me, Knox can do it, if anyone can. But we need not tell your major that." There was a twinkle in his eye, for he too enjoyed playing with the British, but his face turned suddenly serious as he went on. "We lost our campaign in Canada—your major was correct on that. It was a gamble I thought would work, and it didn't. We lost a great many men, I regret to say. I suspect General Arnold is bringing the rest down Champlain and the Hudson. I'm expecting word on them at any minute." He sighed and thought what to do. "I guess that's another question mark to give to Major Whitehead. No, tell him you heard that what is left of the army is stranded somewhere between Fort Crown Point and Canada. Tell him no one knows for sure where they are in this weather. We might as well let them think we have fewer than expected."

"What shall I tell him about Hickney?" Matthew asked.

"Ah, yes. You'd better meet with Sergeant Hickney. The name is familiar, so I must have met him. Get his confidence and see what else you can find out. But take no chances. We have plenty of time to deal with Hickney and his friends. As for Governor Tryon and

Mayor Matthews, I've long suspected that they're loyalists. The news comes as no surprise to me—although it is useful."

"And General Lee?" Matthew asked.

Washington smiled. "As a matter of fact, Lee should be in New York by now with his troops. For your information, Charles is there to start setting up fortifications to defend the city against the British."

"You've started to attack New York?" Matthew asked aghast, thinking of his friends.

The general shook his head and smiled patiently. "No. New York is a divided city—half loyalist, half rebel. Whoever gets there first has possession of it. Since the British are off the coast of Boston waiting to pounce on me, I thought it was a good opportunity to lay claim to New York."

"But will there be fighting?"

"My orders are most strict. Charles is merely to start fortifications to defend the city if and when the British give up on Boston. Their only other goal has to be New York. I want to be there first."

"What shall I tell Major Whitehead?"

Washington laughed. "I don't think you'll have to tell him anything. He's probably watching Charles this very minute."

"Does General Lee know about me?" Matthew asked.

"No one does, and we shall leave it that way. You've become too valuable for me to risk revealing your identity, even to someone as trusted as Charles. If I have assessed the British correctly, New York will become their next port and I'll need every bit of information about their plans you can find."

"But what about Boston?"

"If the guns arrive from Ticonderoga, the British have lost Boston harbor. If they don't arrive, then I'm afraid we might have lost here. At any rate, come spring, you'll meet with me in New York—one way or another."

18

THE CABIN was made from logs cut nearby. Stumps of trees pocked the landscape, their uneven shapes covered with new snow. The room was small and uneven, a halfhearted affair, built as temporary shelter from the wind and snow rather than as permanent housing.

A man sat huddled in one corner, a heavy brown blanket thrown over his shoulders, a blue and gray striped scarf wrapped over his tricorn and covering his ears and half his bearded face. He beckoned Matthew to hurry in and pull the canvas across the doorway.

"This had better be good, lad," he growled, distrust in his eyes as he inspected Matthew carefully.

"You do recognize me, don't you?" Matthew asked guardedly.

The man cocked his head to one side, "Aye, you're Robert Bell's oldest," he answered. "You take me out'a good betting game just to say hello?"

"I come from Major Whitehead," Matthew said slowly, watching to see how the man would react.

Hickney inspected Matthew with new curiosity. "Whitehead, eh?" he muttered. "How do I know? The last I seen of you, you weren't exactly bosom buddies with Scott—though you may have been with his wife," Hickney added with a leer.

Matthew managed to cover his surprise at mention of Louisa.

"Scott and I were not the best of friends," he said wryly, deciding it was safest to acknowledge his affair with the lieutenant's wife.

Hickney gave a short laugh, then suddenly stopped smiling and leaned forward. "And how did you get in with Whitehead?"

"Same as you," Matthew answered calmly. "I enlisted with the rebels but became disillusioned. Went to New York hoping I'd be of some help there and met Whitehead. When he found you and I were from the same town, he asked me to be your contact. Wouldn't arouse anyone's suspicions if we were seen together, he said."

Hickney studied Matthew intently. "You got anything else to show me 'sides your word?"

Matthew sat down on the bare floor and pulled off his left boot. He drew out a piece of paper and handed it silently to Hickney.

The man read the document slowly, every once in a while looking over the paper at Matthew. "All right then," he said, folding the paper and handing it back. "So you're from the major. What's 'e want now?"

"Nothing immediately. Only an update on what you're doing," Matthew answered, trying not to show his relief at having won the man's trust. "I shall be your contact from now on."

"Wondered who'd be taking ol' Riley's place," Hickney sneered. "They caught him, y'know?" He wiped at his nose with his sleeve, then grinned and continued. "Yep, caught the ol' geezer up to no good and hanged him 'fore he could make peace with his maker. General Greene was madder than a hornet for that hanging. I wouldn't be here if them boys hadn't been so quick with the rope. Ya can bet your last cent on that!"

"How did he get caught?" Matthew asked.

There was a sly smile and the man winked and nodded to Matthew's boot. "They found a piece of paper on him—almost like the one you're carrying."

When Matthew instinctively pulled his leg under him, the sergeant laughed and pointed at him. "That's why I never carry no papers on me. I'm not going to have no mob stretch my neck."

Matthew made a note to himself that one of the first things he was going to do once he left the cabin was destroy his British papers. He would have to take his chances on getting through British lines by his wits.

As it was, there was no need of explaining his travels. The ride back to New York was uneventful. He encountered no soldiers, and the country inns and eating places seemed content to assume he was on their side—whichever side that was.

Matthew noticed the difference in the city as soon as he came upon the first streets. The trees which had once lined the avenues had been felled and dragged away. Matthew could not believe his eyes.

The grey houses seemed so exposed, and the stumps were blights in the snow.

He looked around and saw that there were still visible tracks where horses had dragged the logs toward the Hudson. Curious, Matthew followed the route, noting that all the streets had been stripped of their trees.

As he approached the Hudson frontage, there was more activity. Men hurried about or met in groups in the streets. These were obviously not New Yorkers. They wore the coarse brown jackets and greatcoats of the Sons of Liberty, and Lee's troops had arrived, he realized with a small thrill.

Ahead, the broad expanse above the river was now a breastwork of logs piled high and braced. Snow had been piled into emplacements for future cannon and musket fire. Tents had been erected in some semblance of a military encampment.

"Hey you!" a voice boomed out.

Matthew twisted in the saddle and waited as a group of blue-coated guardsmen approached.

"Where's your command?" The group surrounded him and looked up with suspicious eyes.

"Captain Hale's Connecticut brigade," Matthew answered with the first thing that cropped in his head.

There was an exchange of glances and one of the men reached out to grab the bridle of Matthew's mount. "There ain't no Connecticut brigade hereabouts," he snarled. "They're all around Boston area."

"We were," Matthew answered calmly. "We just rode in from there. We're to help General Lee."

With the mention of their commander's name, there were a few doubtful shrugs and an exchange of glances. "How come you're not in uniform?" someone asked.

"I've been visiting with friends," Matthew answered, knowing even as he spoke that the explanation was a poor one. He suddenly had that same feeling of aloneness that had struck him the night he had had to fight with Lake against the rebels, against his own side.

"Henry," one of the men barked out, "you and Jonathan take this bloke wherever he's going. Stick close to him 'til he gets there." The man looked up at Matthew. "I don't trust him and his cocky smile. If he can't find where's he going, then bring him back here." He leaned toward Matthew and snarled, "There's too many goddamn New York Tories spying on us. You be one of them, Johnny, and we'll hang you up where you can see everything we're doing."

The others laughed, all eying Matthew with suspicion. Two men came forward, grabbing the bridle on either side and led Matthew off toward the houses. "You tell us where to go," the one called Henry called over his shoulder, then turned to his companion and grinned. It was obvious they both believed this was going to be a wild goose chase.

Matthew contemplated what his next move should be. If he took them to Mahler's or to Martha's he might only get his friends in trouble. It seemed foolhardy to try to get them to go all the way down to the Battery where he might find Major Whitehead; he doubted these men would travel that far and he wasn't even sure of locating Whitehead for his protection. His only alternative was to get as close to the center of the Tory populace as he could. Surely he would receive some kind of assistance in that neighborhood, and with luck he could make his way to the Page residence and hide out there.

"Down this street," Matthew finally said. It was a

small avenue he was familiar with, only blocks from where the Page family lived. "That house, over there." He headed them toward a brick building halfway down the street. "You can go up there and see for yourselves."

Henry eyed the white steps and front door warily.

"I assure you, this is where my friends live," Matthew said, trying to appear confident and unconcerned.

The two guards looked at each other. "Okay," Henry said, handing the reins to his friend, "but you stay put." He turned and trudged up the stairs to knock on the door.

Not daring to breathe, Matthew watched the curtained door for some sign of movement, hoping there would be a long enough delay.

"Well, perhaps no one is home," Matthew said, and started to dismount. "Maybe I'd better go up there and see."

"You stay there," Jonathan snarled. Just then the front door opened, and the guard turned to see what his friend had found. Matthew took the opportunity to move. His boot shot out savagely against the guard's face, sending him flat on his back. With a heave, Matthew was back in the saddle, reining his mount around.

"Stop!" Both Henry and Jonathan ran out into the street in pursuit. "Stop him! Traitor!"

Matthew rounded the end of the street only to pull up short. A group of militia was chopping down a tree, but they stopped and turned as they heard the approaching commotion. Quickly, Matthew pulled in the horse and raced down another street. Behind him he could hear the shouting. Ahead, only a few people bothered to turn their heads at his approach and at the commotion he was stirring. He knew he had to stay away from the waterfront where the militia was camped. His only recourse was to double back and try to seek asylum at the Page's home.

He found the alley he was looking for. Pulling up short, Matthew quickly dismounted and pulled open the small barn door. "Hyiah!" He slapped the horse inside and shut the door. As he gasped for air, he heard the yells of his pursuers and made a dash to the Pages' back gate, praying he hadn't been seen.

As Matthew bounded up the path to the back door, he slipped on the ice, falling flat on his back, hard enough so that he was winded.

"There he is! Catch the scoundrel!"

Before he could regain his feet, they were upon him, knocking the breath from him.

"Hang him right here," Henry shouted. "The bastard is a spy." He was roughly collared and dragged to his feet, and hands reached out to strike at his face and body. Matthew tried to duck the blows but they seemed to come from every direction at once.

"Hold on there!" a voice boomed out. Suddenly, it became very quiet. Matthew found his footing and struggled out of the clutches of those around him.

"You men are trespassing on my property!" John Page's voice was loud, imperious. Matthew looked up to the porch and saw the man standing with pistol in each hand. "That man is a friend. Let him be."

"Goddamn Tory," one of the men growled.

"Yes, he's a Tory," the elder Page answered proudly. "But damned? We'll see who is damned soon enough!"

Matthew took the silence as his chance to escape. He dodged out of the pocket of men and grabbed at the porch railing as he mounted the steps.

"It's all right, boy," John Page said. "You're in safe hands now." He waved the pistol at the group. "Now begone with all of you. Begone!"

The one named Henry stepped forward and brandished a finger at both Page and Matthew. "You two are marked men," he snarled. "You can sleep on it, if you can. But you're both marked!"

"It will be all of you who will be the marked men," John Page replied, undaunted by the threat.

There were some low curses and grumbling among the group but slowly they walked out of the yard, every once in a while casting scowling glances back at the two men.

"Are you all right, son?" John Page asked, looking at Matthew's bleeding face. Mr. Page helped him up the stairs and into the kitchen, where his wife and daughter were waiting. Coleen came forward and took Matthew's arm to lead him to a chair.

"I'm afraid," Matthew said, grinning crookedly, "that every time we meet I have bloodied up my face."

Coleen's expression remained serious as she wiped the blood from his cheek with a wet cloth. "Your face is not going to be as handsome if you keep this up."

"Believe me," he answered, grimacing with every touch, "none of this is my wish." He looked around, suddenly concerned. "Where's Colin?"

"He's at the shop," Lydia Page answered, handing her daughter some salve to apply to his cuts.

"It's not going to be safe for him," Matthew answered. "It's not going to be safe for any of you from now on. I'm afraid I've brought you trouble."

John Page sighed and leaned against a counter. "It hasn't been safe here since Lee arrived. His damnable troops marched in and took over everything except the Battery. There's a group of us meeting with General Lee to complain about the behavior of his troops towards the civilian population."

"I thought that would be the duty of Mayor Matthews or Governor Tryon," Matthew said.

John Page shook his head. "A ticklish matter," he answered soberly, "a very ticklish matter. Lee, Matthews and Tryon seem to be on the best of terms. The general has been their guest on numerous occasions, I'm told, and a few of us are beginning to think they cannot bring up the subject with their guest. We think it is in our best interest if we talk with General Lee rather than expect the mayor or governor to get results."

"You sound so disgruntled by all of this," Coleen chided.

"And why not?" Page answered hotly. "It is my family that I worry about, not the game of politics."

"We'll be all right, Father," Coleen answered.

Page began to pace the floor uneasily. "There was a time when we thought we might have had the protection of British troops. But now that Major Whitehead has gone—"

"Gone?" Matthew glanced to Coleen.

"He received his orders to go to Charleston," she replied, shrugging and continuing to apply salve to Matthew's open wounds.

Stunned, Matthew didn't know how to reply. Whitehead's departure left him with no one to report to—and with little or no access to information for Washington.

"I can imagine how sorry you must be . . ." Coleen's voice was low enough so that only he would hear. When he glanced at her in surprise, her expression was enigmatic and she quickly turned away.

Matthew studied her profile, his heart beating wildly. Perhaps she knew he was a spy for Whitehead and her remark was no more than a sympathetic response to his supposed disappointment. That was the most logical explanation he told himself. Otherwise, if she had seen through him, it meant either the worst or the best—that she knew he was a double agent . . . or that she knew he was in love with her.

19

THEY WERE ALL seated at the Page dining table, listening to John Page recount his visit to Charles Lee. Colin had taken a seat next to Matthew, exuberant that his friend had returned, and Coleen sat across from them. At the end of the table, Lydia Page had noted Coleen's furtive glance at Matthew and Matthew's quick and appreciative inspection of her daughter. She smiled to herself. It would not matter terribly who won the hand of her daughter. Major Whitehead came from one of the more prominent English families and held a high position, but being the wife of a British soldier would have its disadvantages. Matthew Bell, on the other hand, had no position, but he did have looks, warmth and intelligence, and might easily make something of himself. Much, she had decided, depended upon the outcome of the friction between

England and the colonies. She had decided to wait until all was over before putting any pressure upon Coleen.

"He's undoubtedly the most disgusting individual I've ever met," John Page was saying, still smoldering with anger. "The man is uncouth, ungentlemanly, and certainly lacks any breeding."

"He's supposed to be the finest general they have," Matthew answered, surprised at the report he was hearing. He had not expected such a picture of a man with such high prestige.

"He may be a military genius," Page conceded, "but he's sorely lacking in common courtesy. For one thing," he explained, leaning forward, "we had to wait over an hour before he would see us. We were told he had to take his dogs for a walk. Can you imagine that? Dogs before us?"

Colin grinned. "It's probably his way of trying to insult you."

"Insult me?" his father answered indignantly. "To meet the man is insult enough. He spent more time cuddling up to two damned creatures than he did talking with us. And to add to this insult, he never donned his jacket! I swear he must have slept in his clothes." John Page shuddered as he recalled General Lee.

"You didn't get what you requested?" Matthew asked.

"I doubt it. Lee said his men's behavior was only *prankish!* You see, this is the type we have to deal with. No wonder the king can't get anywhere with them!"

"Then we're not safe?" Lydia Page asked from the far end of the table.

"I'm afraid, my dear," was the sober reply, "that no one is safe as long as these rebels are around. We'll have to stay together, certainly never go out alone. Matthew, you're certainly welcome to stay here with us for your own safety."

Matthew could barely keep from looking at Coleen to see what her reaction might be. But as he was about to accept the invitation, Colin leaned forward.

"There's no need of that, Father," the boy answered. "I shall stay with Matthew when he goes home."

The color drained from Matthew's face as he turned to gaze at his friend.

"It's much closer to Mahler's from your place," Colin said, grinning. "It will be safer if we go to work from there.

John Page frowned but slowly nodded. "Perhaps that's the wisest thing. But we shall expect the two of you here on the weekends when there is no work."

Matthew could hardly restrain his anger with Colin. But then how would the boy know? He had never told anyone of his feelings for Coleen.

Whatever ill feelings John Page had from his visit to Charles Lee, the group must have left some impression. The Tory families of New York were left virtually unmolested for the next couple of months as activities subsided along the entrenchments of the Hudson River. The April rains brought a standstill to activity, the militia huddling under their tents or lean-tos, content to gamble or to visit the brothels that had sprung up along the waterfront upon their arrival.

Life seemed to have come almost to a standstill for Matthew. Most of his time was spent in his room, alone, when he wasn't at work or with Martha and Colin. His visits with the Pages were almost always devoted to exchanging tales with the elder Page or playing games with Colin. He was conscious of Coleen in the background or across the table at dinner time, but rarely did either have a chance to discuss anything more than how wet it was outside.

Then, in late April, Major Whiteheead appeared at the Pages' front door. Matthew's heart sank when he saw Coleen throw herself into the officer's arms.

"We're delighted with your safe return," Matthew announced as Whitehead was welcomed around. "I was afraid we wouldn't meet again."

Whitehead was more than delighted to see Matthew there. He bowed stiffly to the Pages and Coleen. "You must pardon me," he said soberly. "I did not realize Mr. Bell was here. I must have a few words with him, if you don't mind."

Matthew's stomach churned uneasily as the major led him to the study. "I tried to reach you upon my return, but you had left," he explained.

"I know," Whitehead answered. "It was not your fault. My orders came so quickly I was unable to get word to you. However, we now have most of the information you went after." He sighed and went to the window to look out. "You have probably heard by now that we failed at Boston."

"No," Matthew gasped.

"I don't know how he did it, but Washington got his cannon and we couldn't land." He smashed a fist into his palm. "Unbelievable luck!"

"What's going to happen now?" Matthew asked, knowing the answer full well.

Whitehead turned around, leaning against the window sill with both hands behind him. "We'll be taking over New York, of course." He stared at Matthew for a long moment. "Did you happen to make contact with Sergeant Hickney?"

Whitehead smiled when Matthew nodded. "Good,"

he answered. "We want you to reach him again. Tonight, if you can."

Matthew sighed. It would be a dreadful ride in the rainy weather. But it had to be done. "Whatever you say," he answered. "I can pack my bag and be ready tonight."

Whitehead smiled. "There's no need of that. Hickney is here in New York."

"Here? In New York?" Matthew asked, hoping the major could not see the elation he felt.

"Washington has just moved his camp here to New York. As a spy, you should have found that out," Whitehead said, shaking his head disapprovingly. "In any event, you are to look up Hickney and tell him to go ahead with our plans."

"Go ahead?" Matthew blinked his astonishment.

"Either Washington is getting lucky or we have underestimated him greatly. Whatever, we certainly cannot have New York become another Boston. We're going to strike now with everything we have. But before we do, we want disruption in the ranks and elsewhere. Mayor Matthews and Governor Tryon will be doing their part. Hickney will spread the word to his group and we'll do the rest."

"I shall relay your orders," Matthew promised.

"Good." Whitehead nodded and stood up, straightening his red tunic. "Before I forget it, I brought a Captain DeWitt with me from Charleston. Captain DeWitt was my counterpart in the South, you might say. If I am not around, you shall make your contact with him. And now," he said with a weary sigh, "shall we join my fiancee and her family?"

It had not been difficult to give his signal to the tall blue-caped figure. Matthew had been especially careful that no one had followed him, and he was in a section of town where no one was likely to recognize him.

"So . . ." Washington sighed heavily as he leaned back against the high wooden booth and shut his eyes in thought. "Hickney is to start his work, is he?"

"I'm to meet with him after this talk," Matthew explained in a low whisper. He waited while Washington thought it out.

"So you shall," the general finally answered. "You've done good work, Matthew. I'm proud of you. But you're in an even more dangerous position than before. I cannot allow Hickney or the others to do their deed—but if I act on your information, your British friends will almost certainly suspect you." Washington opened his eyes and stared heavily at Matthew. "For your own protection, I shall place a warrant out for your arrest when we do the same for Hickney and the others. Branding you as a deserter and traitor to our army should satisfy your British friends." Washington looked up at Matthew with a frown. "Unfortunately, you will be thought of as a traitor by your family and by your country—at least for the time being. Can you live with that for a while?"

"I'm not happy this has to be done," Matthew admitted, "but if it's the only means of helping you, then so be it."

Washington regarded him with an even deeper frown. "It will also mean that we probably won't be able to meet like this again. You'll have to find some other way to get information to me, my friend. You'd be gambling too much being so close to my troops."

"I understand," Matthew answered, saddened with the news. He would miss his meetings with the man he had come to admire so much, and he suddenly felt more alone than ever.

They were both quiet for a moment with their own thoughts. Finally Washington leaned forward. "In case I should want to get hold of you, is there anyone you trust who I could send?"

Matthew thought but slowly shook his head. "There's no one I know—" Then he stopped. "I can only think of one. He is or was a captain in the Connecticut regiment. Captain Nathan Hale. He knows me and he can be trusted, I'm sure."

Washington nodded. "Nathan Hale, I shall remember that name. If I have need of you, I'll try to send Captain Hale." He paused and looked up at Matthew with a concerned glance. "You've been a powerful ally, Matthew Bell. We are indebted to you. I regret I have to send you back to such a dangerous situation."

"I think I'll be safe, sir," Matthew answered. "I've found a Tory family who have taken to me. And if I do say so myself, I'm so convincing a Tory that General Lee's men have me on their hate list."

Washington smiled. "Ah, yes, Charles Lee. A most unpredictable friend but my right arm. He's done an excellent job preparing New York for our battle."

"Then you think there will be a confrontation?"

Washington's answer was so long in coming that for a second Matthew wondered if the man had heard him. "I'm afraid, Matthew," he finally answered in a tired voice, "that the people are getting tired of England's delaying tactics to our demands. And it may not be only a matter of fighting for our rights, but of fighting for complete independence. But we might be getting ahead of ourselves," he said, suddenly speaking more briskly. "A step at a time. Hunt up your

Sergeant Hickney and give him Whitehead's orders. I'll wait a few days before placing him and the others under arrest. That should be ample time for you to prepare yourself. Remember, you'll be a marked man and you'll have to be twice as careful if you're to continue your business. It will not do to have to arrest you."

Matthew grinned. "I understand. I'll go into hiding as soon as you publish my name. With luck, this might even put me in a stronger position with the Tories."

"Be careful, lad," Washington answered gravely. "Don't underestimate your enemies."

20

THE KNOCK on his door was timid. Certainly it wasn't Martha, who usually sang out his name, or Colin, who always announced his arrival with a loud, energetic rapping.

Curious, Matthew got out of bed and slipped into his robe as he went to open the door.

"Coleen!"

In the early July weather she wore a dress of the finest cotton, its flowered skirt made of yards of material gathered around her small waist and the bodice accented by a dark rose-colored vest with lace trim.

"May I come in?" she asked, coloring under his appreciative look. Her eyes quickly darted about, inspecting his small room as she talked. "I had Colin drive me here. He's with his lady friend now."

"Oh?" Matthew raised an eyebrow. "So you know?"

"He just told me, as we came down here. Now I know why he's spent so much time with you. Or should I say with *her*," Coleen added with a grimace.

"Don't be angry with either one of them," Matthew answered. "They're very much in love."

"Love?" Coleen eyed him skeptically. "Are you sure it's love?"

Matthew felt his face flush with rising anger. "Martha is a most gentle and sweet girl," he said, "not at all like the others."

"Oh?" Coleen said quietly. "So she *is* a prostitute?"

Matthew silently cursed himself for his blunder. "She was," he admitted, "but she hasn't been for some time. What matters is that she is devoted to Colin—and Colin to her. I see nothing wrong with their being together."

"You don't?" she asked. Coleen took a deep breath to regain her composure and sat stiffly on the edge of the rocker. "And since when is it your place to decide what is good for Colin?"

"I do not wish to get into an argument with you, Coleen," Matthew replied. "And it is not my place—or anyone else's—to tell Colin what he can or can't do. He's his own man now and has his own choices to make."

"But you encouraged it!"

"Not at first—but finally, yes. I saw two people very much in love."

"Even knowing what type of woman she is?" Coleen asked.

"Even knowing what her background was, yes," Matthew admitted. "There are a great many important people whose backgrounds have not been entirely paved with great deeds and lily-white innocence.

People change. You have only to meet Martha and you too will like her."

"I doubt that," Coleen charged.

Matthew cocked his head. "You should not condemn so quickly, Coleen. Colin fell in love with Martha because she is a sweet, sensitive and loving woman. Her past is finished. They're both willing to forgive and forget the things life sometimes requires of us—that ugly side of life that you and I once discussed," he said pointedly. "Why can't you? Surely you should know about love."

Coleen's head snapped up. "Yes, I know about love, Mr. Bell," she answered angrily. "And I know loving someone beneath your class is not—"

"Beneath your class?" Matthew interrupted. "Who's talking about position and class? That's not love, Coleen Page. Maybe that's one of the things wrong with your—" Matthew stopped, a pained expression on his face as he turned his back to stare out the window.

There was a moment of silence. Then Coleen rose to her feet and straightened her dress self-consciously. "Maybe this is not the time or place to discuss this," she murmured, head downcast. "It is not the reason I came here."

Matthew drew in a deep breath, trying to will away the pain of knowing how hopeless his love was. "I'm sorry if I have been rude to you," he said, his tone subdued as he turned from the window.

She smiled, and there was a warmth in her eyes that eased the tension in the room. "I really didn't come here to reprimand you about Colin," she remarked. Then her eyes suddenly turned serious. "I came to warn you."

"Warn me?"

She nodded. "Winslow—Major Whitehead—sent me a message saying that your name has appeared on an arrest warrant from the rebel force."

"My name?" Matthew asked, feigning surprise and concern. So Coleen had known all along . . . "But why my name? Surely they haven't found out that I'm a spy!"

"They must have," Coleen confided. "Winslow said there were names of many prominent persons, including the mayor and the governor. Winslow also wanted me to tell you that the name Hickney was on the list too, whatever that means."

"It means that Washington must have found out about the plot," Matthew said with a frown.

"Are you in danger?" she asked anxiously.

"I'm afraid I must go into hiding."

Coleen came forward and touched his arm reassuringly. "You can stay at our house."

Matthew was tempted, for it would bring him closer to her. But he shook his head sadly. "No. There are too many who know of my friendship with your family, and they might be watching. I'll have to stop going to Mahler's too," he added. "It will be best if it looks as if I've simply disappeared."

"But where will you be?"

"I think I'm safe here. There's only you, Colin and Martha who know where I live."

"And Colin can bring you supplies or whatever you need," she offered, pleased with the solution.

"Will you come?" Matthew asked quietly.

She stared down at her hands, then slowly looked up at him with wide eyes. "I don't know," she replied hesitantly. "I shall try, once in a while."

"I shall miss you, Coleen . . ."

Her eyes stayed on his a moment before she looked away in sudden confusion and turned to take her leave.

At the door she looked back at him with questioning eyes. "There was no need of saying that," she said softly. She paused as if weighing more to say. Then, with a shy smile, she opened the door and was gone.

"Matthew! Matthew!" It was the next day that Colin burst into his room. "Come and see!" he urged, tossing him a shirt. "Martha is getting ready too."

Colin half-dragged them outside to make their way toward the river front. The street was alive with people hurrying out of their houses and excitedly heading in the same direction.

"Hurry," Colin urged.

"This had better be good, Matthew," Martha called out. She was laughing at Colin and was excited by the commotion.

Only Matthew was apprehensive about the scene unfolding before him. He had been out of the house daily, but usually in the early morning or late evening when few people were about. For the first time he was fearful of a cry of recognition and capture.

"Look, Matthew, look!" Colin pointed to the left, toward the tip of the city, where the Hudson poured out into the larger harbor. It was as if a wooden bridge had been built at the entrance to the harbor. Hundreds of masted ships lay at anchor. It was the British navy at its mightiest, waiting for God only knew what.

"They're here!" Colin exclaimed. "Can you imagine that, Matthew? They're finally here!"

Matthew pulled the boy closer and told him to keep his voice down. "We're right in the middle of the rebel crowd," he reminded Colin. He looked around to see if anyone had taken notice of Colin's outburst, but all were engrossed in the distant scene. "We'd better get back before we're spotted," he warned. He hoped Colin would attribute his solemn attitude to his fear of being recognized and not to any concern about the presence of the British force. Washington was undoubtedly aware of the situation, but could anyone hope to defeat all those ships?

"You won't have to worry too much longer," Colin answered. He was in high spirits and clutched at Martha excitedly. "We'll be rid of these rebels once and for all, now."

"It certainly looks that way," Matthew answered soberly.

"But you should be happy, Matthew," Colin remarked, noting Matthew's downcast look. "You'll be free again."

Matthew drew in a deep breath. He knew he had to keep his guise, but the strength of the British forces worried him. "I was only thinking that these rebels are not going to leave without a fight."

"Don't worry about that," Colin replied. "The rebel guns are no match for us. There's no way they can stop those ships." He turned and hugged Martha. "Aren't you happy too, my love?"

Martha grinned and hugged Colin back. "I'm happy whenever you are. I just want the fighting to end so we can all go about our business."

"Amen to that," Matthew replied.

Matthew watched the calendar as each day ticked away. By the eighth day of July there was still no movement from the British ships. The crowds along the river had dwindled down to a few curious bystanders who had nothing better to do, and the militia had reverted to a minimum watch.

Every day it had been the same question—why didn't the British troops land? With every loud noise from outside Matthew's window, he expected to hear cannon and musket fire and yelling. However, the noise that finally ended the waiting was not of fighting but of people cheering with merriment.

Curiously, Matthew went to the door where Martha was already standing and peering down the street.

"What's going on?"

"I don't exactly know," she answered, half-afraid of exposing herself to whatever was slowly approaching.

As the crowd began to filter into view, they saw that it was comprised mostly of militia, mixed with a few patriotic New Yorkers, drunken doxies and camp followers. This was not a trouble-seeking crowd, but one waving banners and flags and drinking toasts to anyone and everyone who appeared at doors and windows.

Confident that they meant no harm, Martha stepped out onto the stone landing and down the steps. "I'll find out what's happening," she said over her shoulder.

Matthew stepped back into the hallway and partially closed the door; there was no point in taking foolish chances. As he watched Martha approach the crowd, he tried to guess the reason for the gaiety. It puzzled him that the patriots had found something to celebrate while the British warships were in the harbor. For a moment he wondered whether the fleet had left, just as they had left Boston. That would be too good to be true.

Martha hurriedly entered the hallway and closed the door behind her, leaning against it as she tried to catch her breath.

"What is it?" Matthew asked anxiously.

"The rebels' Congress has declared independence," she said, still panting. "Apparently, a few days ago their Continental Congress wrote up a document saying they were no longer a part of England—just like that!"

So it had come to that after all, Matthew thought, just as Washington and so many others had predicted. "We've got to get out of here," he said at last. "Get your things together, just what you can carry."

Martha reached out and grabbed him as he was about to return to his room. "What do you mean?" she asked. "Why do we have to get away?"

"Because you're—we're not part of them," Matthew explained heavily. "Don't you see, Martha? This is now rebel land—rebel property."

"Will they harm us?"

"Not if we get out of here. Right now they're celebrating—it's a good opportunity for us to get away. But as soon as the celebration is over, you can rest assured they'll be after every Tory they know of."

"The Pages . . ." Martha murmured.

"I know. We'll go there and collect them too."

It did not take long for either one of them to pack their bags and leave. They took the back paths, skirting the crowds. When they had to join the parade they pasted on smiles and cheered along with the rest of them until they were safely away. Fortunately, the mobs were too absorbed in their merrymaking to notice anyone with suitcases. Their attention was drawn to any sign, notice or statue that hinted of George III or any past association with England. With the toppling of each royal statue, there rose a loud cheer that echoed down streets and gathered in a fresh crowd of enthusiasts.

"Hurry! Come in!" John Page waved the two inside and bolted the door securely. "You've heard?"

Matthew nodded and looked about for the others.

"They're packing," Mr. Page announced, returning to his study and rummaging through some papers in his desk. "I see you two have the same idea. Dreadful, that's what it is. Positively dreadful!"

"It isn't going to be safe for any of us," Matthew remarked, casting a nervous look toward the open door and up the stairs. He was tempted to introduce Martha, but decided that this was not the time. Let the Pages assume Martha was with him, if need be.

"We're all getting out of New York," Mr. Page explained as he shoved papers into a small leather valise. "We'd heard the rebels might do this and we made plans."

"Plans?" Matthew asked curiously.

"The British Force has relocated to Staten Island. It should be safe for us there until they get these bloody heathens out of our city once and for all."

"Martha!" Colin appeared at the top of the stairs with both hands filled. He bounded down and took the girl in his arms.

John Page arched his eyebrows and turned to Matthew in surprise, but Matthew only shrugged. It was up to Colin now.

"What is this?" Mr. Page demanded.

Colin's face sobered and he took a deep breath before he spoke. "Father, this is Martha Dundee. She and I—we're engaged."

"What?" his father exploded.

Martha turned to Colin in surprise and then her smile spread wide with happiness.

"Yes, Father," Colin admitted, drawing himself straight. "Martha is my fiancee."

John Page was speechless. He glared at the couple and then turned to Matthew in disbelief.

"I know this comes as a shock to you, sir," Matthew

responded quickly, "but this is not the time to discuss the matter. I shouldn't have to warn you how dangerous our situation is. We should make way for Staten Island as soon as possible."

"Yes, you're quite right," John Page answered. "As for you, young sir," he said, angrily facing his son, "we shall take this up immediately upon our arrival at the island."

"Yes, sir," Colin replied solemnly. He waited until his father stormed up the stairs and then turned to Martha and grinned. "That was my father, by the way."

Martha laughed and threw her arms about his neck. "I thought it might be," she answered gaily. "I just wish I'd had a chance to tell him how much I love his son."

Matthew shook his head and smiled in spite of himself, forgetting for a moment the danger that lay ahead.

21

T HE EAST RIVER front was already crowded with anxious families clamoring to find boat passage.

A few still kept a vigilant eye towards the city, where smoke began to billow high from the fires set by what now was a cheering mob of patriots.

"They've gone crazy," John Page had muttered as he guided their wagon through the streets. Matthew and Colin rode horseback close to the wagon, their hands near their waists where they had tucked pistols under their shirts.

Several times Matthew had gone ahead to speak to groups who blocked their way. His nonchalant manner and genuine interest in their celebration was often enough to allow them through.

"My family," Matthew had explained once, nodding toward the wagon. "We've come from Philadelphia to help celebrate!" He would smile along with the rebels as he watched the destruction unfold before his eyes. He was almost caught up with the spirit, but he was only too conscious of the role he was playing and of his concern for the Page family.

"Utter destruction," Mr. Page muttered in disgust, watching helplessly as familiar landmarks were destroyed. Everything that depicted England, the king, Parliament and Tory was being torn down or burned. At first the patriots had left the Tory families alone, but as the mob grew, so did the hunger for complete obliteration of anything British.

"There's no stopping them now," Matthew admitted, beginning to worry that they might not find space aboard a boat.

Tory families were desperate to get away, forgetting their homes and possessions, now only worried for their lives. As a result, the waterfronts were packed with screaming and terrified people.

"There's nothing available," John Page announced as he came back from the wharf to those waiting patiently by the wagon. For the first time, he was losing some of his dignity and self-assurance.

"Oh, my God," Lydia Page murmured and buried her face in Coleen's shoulder.

Matthew looked around in desperation. "We'll head down toward the Battery," he suggested, motioning for Colin to mount up. "Perhaps there are still some British troops down there."

"That's one of the first places the mob will attack," John Page said as Matthew helped him into the carriage.

"It's all we've got," Matthew answered. "Stay close to us and try not to look panicked."

They made their way along the river streets. Most of the mobs were still toward the middle of the city, but Matthew's small party could not avoid the crazed and desperate clamor of the frightened loyalists who were trying to escape. At every pier, Matthew would make them stop while he went ahead to inquire about passage. To their left, the river was filled with all kinds of small boats making their way toward the harbor and Staten Island. Aboard, silent groups of survivors stared back at New York, watching the disappearance of their homes and their pasts.

The closer Matthew and the Pages got to the tip of Manhattan, the more crowded it became with desperate people. Matthew was beginning to think it was no use when Martha beckoned to him.

"I might know of a place," she said, speaking so that only he would hear. "I know the shipping master—he might be able to find us something."

Matthew reached out to squeeze her hand, knowing that her decision had not been easily made. He nodded his understanding and mounted up, following her directions as he led them down the street, breaking a path for the wagon.

Hands reached up several times to stop him, but Matthew kicked out savagely. "Make way!" he shouted down. "Official business, official business!" His words had the desired effect on both Tory and Patriot, and they were more or less left unmolested.

"Over there!" Martha shouted out, pointing to a large dock and boating facility.

They stopped in front of a heavy iron gate that was guarded by several men brandishing large clubs. An angry crowd stood before the gate begging admission, but their pleas fell on deaf ears. Matthew dismounted and helped Martha alight from the carriage. "Doesn't look like there's much hope here either," he muttered to her as they stepped forward.

"Let me see," she whispered, flashing him a determined look before she turned and smiled her prettiest at one of the men behind the gate. "Good sir," she said lightly, "could you tell Mr. Mallory that Martha Dundee would like to see him?"

"He ain't talking to no one," came the gruff reply. The man wouldn't even look down at her.

"If you asked him, I wager he would say differently," Martha continued, not a bit discouraged by the reply.

The guard finally glanced down, giving her one quick sweep of his eyes. "He ain't got time for you," was the only answer.

"Please, sir," Martha said, "you shall be richly rewarded if you will only tell Mr. Mallory that I am here."

This time he looked at her with careful appraisal and then sighed. As he started back to a small shack, Martha called out again. "The name is Martha, Martha Dundee." Then she quickly turned to Matthew. "How much money do we have?"

Matthew shrugged and strode back to the buggy to ask John Page.

Page looked about him to make sure no one was within earshot. "I've brought everything we have," he answered, and shoved a small leather bag into Matthew's hand. "I've got three more of these."

Matthew hefted the bag in his hand, wondering if it would be enough. "Do you think this will buy us passage?" he asked when he returned to Martha.

She only took a quick glance at the gold. "I don't know," she answered. "Put some in your pocket just in case we can save some. A few coins should do for the guard."

A small spectacled man waddled up to the gate behind the returning guard and stared through the bars. "Martha? Martha, is that you?"

"Hello, Steven," Martha cooed and leaned up against the gate. "I knew you would be able to help us."

Steven Mallory looked at her smiling face and then stepped back, shaking his head. "Oh, no," he said. "Not you, too?"

"Come, Steven," she coaxed, still smiling. "Certainly you're not going to say no to me—not after all we've been through."

Matthew took a quick look back at the wagon to make sure Colin and his family were out of hearing. He could see the boy was worried enough, just from watching Martha, but at least Colin couldn't hear what was going on. That would have hurt Martha as much as anyone.

The little man took a quick look at Matthew, then at the far wagon. "I only got one boat left," he groaned and bit his lip in frustration.

"But that's all we need," Martha answered. "You'll have your boat back before nightfall." She waited for his answer and then added, "There's money in it for you. We can pay." She nodded to Matthew and he took the leather pouch out of his pocket.

Mallory's eyes fixed on the bag. "I don't know," he answered hesitantly. "I got my orders never to let all the boats out."

He had one hand closed tightly around a bar of the gate, and Martha brought her hand up to cover his. "For old times' sake? For your little Martha?"

Mallory let out a resigned sigh and motioned to

the guards. Matthew beckoned to the Pages as the man stepped aside and the guards opened the gate for them. There was a loud outcry from behind as the crowd tried to follow, but the gate was quickly closed and the guards again took up their positions.

Matthew tossed a couple of gold coins to the guard and walked on quickly, before there could be any objection to the amount of payment. Mallory was waiting for him with outstretched hand. When Matthew pressed the money into the man's hand, Mallory hefted the bag and frowned.

"This is all we've got," Matthew explained, and dug into his pocket to hand over the few coins he had taken from the bag.

Mallory looked him over carefully, then glanced back at the Pages, taking a good look at their packages to see if there might be anything he could use. "We've only had time to pack our clothing," Matthew explained, hoping the answer would satisfy the man.

Seeing the shipping master's hesitation, Martha grimaced at Matthew and then stepped over to Mallory with a knowing smile to whisper something into his ear.

Mallory's face brightened and he grinned. Without a word he waved them into the large wooden boating facility. At the dock was a small one-masted skiff, rolling gently with the lapping of the waves. "Come on, jump in," he commanded and began to untie the mooring lines.

"What was all that about?" Colin asked, standing close to Martha, after he boarded the skiff.

"Martha did a splendid job," Matthew broke in, seeing her embarassment. "If it hadn't been for her, we'd never have gotten a boat, that's for sure." He looked around to make sure the Pages had heard, but they were absorbed in settling themselves among their belongings on the small boat.

As the boat swung out into the light and onto the river, they were saddened by the sight that met them. In one boat after another were people who were making a silent journey, watching their homes and all that was familiar to them fade into the distance as they crossed the river. The only noise was a soft rumble that floated out from the city, the noise almost lost in the swell of the waves lapping at the sides of the boats.

Lydia Page sat alongside her husband, weeping softly, her head buried in his shoulder. John Page looked sternly ahead, every once in a while casting a furtive glance toward the shore as the tip of the island came into view. Colin held Martha, he too silent as they watched the familiar sights pass from view. Coleen sat next to Matthew, her hands twisting her handkerchief as she stared at the city passing by in the distance.

Matthew watched each one with sadness. He felt for their loss. They seemed so exposed and vulnerable. They had been wrenched from their home and deprived of position, wealth and respectability, of almost everything but themselves. But there was a tough side to these people too, and somehow he had little doubt that they would survive.

"Father, look!" Coleen stood up and pointed to the docks. The boat began to rock with her sudden movement and Matthew reached up to steady her and bring her back down. "No," she yelled out, fighting to get away from his clutch. "Look there!"

Matthew stopped his struggle and turned to look, There were two red-coated figures kneeling behind crates at the end of the dock that adjoined British headquarters on Manhattan. A large crowd had gathered at the other end of the dock, and puffs of white smoke billowed into the air as the two forces exchanged gunfire.

"It's Winslow!" Coleen exclaimed.

"By God, it *is* Whitehead," John Page muttered as he leaned forward to examine the two small figures more carefully.

Matthew looked around the area. Far out into the harbor, two row boats filled with the remainder of the British garrison in New York were headed toward the flotilla of British ships in the distance.

"They left them behind," John Page exclaimed. "Those bloody soldiers left Whitehead behind!"

"They didn't have room," Colin quietly observed.

"Papa," Coleen moaned and leaned out to clutch her father. "We can't leave them there!"

Mr. Page turned to Mallory, who stood at the helm of the boat. "Can't we go over there?" he asked.

The little man shook his head. "Not if we don't want our heads shot off, we don't," he answered. "'Sides, we don't have no more room."

"My good man," John Page admonished, "certainly you're not going to pass them by. They'll be at the mercy of that crowd."

Mallory shot the elder Page a look of disdain. "That's not what you paid me for. Ain't enough money in the world to make me go close to that ruckus."

Coleen moaned aloud, her eyes never leaving the two pathetic figures on the dock.

Matthew glanced from Coleen to her father. She caught his look and took his hands in hers. "Please, Matthew," she begged, her eyes moist now. "Please do something! We can't let them die that way!"

Matthew squeezed his eyes shut, for her look was

more than he could stand. With a sigh he turned to Mallory. "Take us over there," he commanded. He took the pistol from his waistband, sticking the barrel directly under the man's nose.

"That's not what you paid me for!" Mallory stammered.

"It's your life we're talking about, Mallory. How much is that worth to you?"

Mallory took a quick look into Matthew's face and saw the determination. With a small groan of defeat, he turned the rudder toward the dock.

By the time they had reached the end of the pier, the passengers had made their readjustments to accommodate the two officers. Squeezed tightly to each other, they waited anxiously as the two men struggled down the small wooden ladder at the end of the dock.

"Off!" Matthew shouted as Whitehead's boot touched the boat.

Colin pushed and Mallory whipped the sail about to catch the wind. "Duck down, everyone!" Colin shouted and they all bent forward.

There was loud yelling and a couple of shots were fired behind them, and then it was quiet. Slowly, the group straightened up and peered back at the crowd of patriots who watched helplessly as the boat sailed beyond their muskets' range.

Coleen blushed as she realized that she had been clutching Matthew's hand. Drawing her hand from his, she turned her attention to her fiance, who had just settled himself next to his fellow officer.

"I must say," Whitehead announced calmly, "your timing was almost perfect."

"You have Matthew to thank for that," Colin announced, grinning from ear to ear now that the excitement was over.

The major raised an eyebrow and stared across the small confines of the boat at Matthew. "Well, our gratitude, Mr. Bell, for saving us." He placed a hand on the knee of the other officer, a man a few years his senior, thick-set from good living, but blondly handsome and with a look of keen intelligence.

"I'd like to introduce my colleague," Whitehead announced, smiling first at the officer, then turning to those in the boat. "Captain Magnus DeWitt."

As the introductions were made, Matthew studied the newcomer carefully. So this was Whitehead's spy from the South. More like a spy-master, if one could judge by a certain coolness that Matthew sensed behind the man's easy demeanor. Suddenly Matthew realized that he had heard the name of Magnus De-Witt long before he'd come to New York. Where and when he couldn't recall, but he would work at it. Some day he would remember.

22

W HAT HAD BEEN an idyllic summer retreat for New York's affluent now resembled a jousting field of the days of yore. Brightly colored banners and streamers waved in the gentle harbor breeze amid rows upon rows of tents erected by the British army.

Staten Island had been taken over by the military. The heavy war ships anchored close by sported fancy gold and scarlet flags, indicating clearly that the high command was present. The docks were filled with soldiers who stood gawking at the lost souls who climbed out of the boats that arrived from Manhattan.

Matthew had never seen so many red-coated men. Wave upon wave, extending as far as the eye could see across the open fields—this military encampment staggered the imagination. Matthew could not help but compare this scene with the clutter and disarray of the patriot's military encampment outside Hartford.

"You people wait here," Major Whitehead ordered as he appraised the scene at the dock. "DeWitt and I will try to find lodging for you."

"Have you ever seen such force?" Colin gasped, staying close to Matthew. "They'll make quick work of those rebels in New York!"

Before Matthew could respond, John Page beckoned to them. "Stay close to the women," he murmured, keeping his voice low so that the women wouldn't hear. "I'm going to look up some friends of ours who have a house here. I'm sure they'll take care of us until this thing blows over."

Colin and Matthew moved over to the three women, who stood watching over their luggage.

"I don't like the way those soldiers are looking at us," Mrs. Page said indignantly.

"Oh, Mother," Colin said with a smile. "They've probably been on those ships for months and haven't seen a woman in a long time."

"That's just what I'm afraid of," his mother replied. "They're leering at us like blithering idiots."

"It's all right, Mother," Coleen answered and placed an arm protectively around Mrs. Page. "Winslow will be back soon and we'll be away."

Winslow . . . Matthew turned his back to the two women. Now that they were deep in the major's domain he felt farther away from this beautiful girl than ever.

There was no use moping about it, he told himself. What would be best would be for him to keep his eyes and ears open. What better opportunity could

he have than to have been placed in the middle of
British headquarters? If he played his hand right, he
would be able to hear news that would be helpful
to Washington.

"What are those men saying?" Lydia Page asked,
turning away from a group of green-coated men who
were obviously pointing at them and laughing.

"They're speaking some foreign language," Colin
said, glaring at the soldiers.

"It's German," Matthew answered. "I recognize
some of the words. I've heard the British hired some
Hessian mercenaries to fight."

"They're horrid men," Lydia Page answered, turning her back to them only to find herself confronted
by a group of grenadiers who began to whistle their
appreciation of such a beautiful woman.

Colin placed a protective arm around Martha and
his sister, pulling them closer together.

Matthew glared at the soldiers and then noted that
other civilian parties were having similar problems.
Many of the soldiers had begun boldly to step forward and make advances to the women. His opinion
of the English troops was making a fast reversal, and
he found himself remembering the rumors that most
of the recruits of the English armies were misfits and
derelicts who were shanghaied into service or allowed
to substitute military duty for prison sentences.

As he inspected the men more closely, he found
they were indeed a dangerous-looking group, unin-
hibited and coarse when not watched over by the
officers. Matthew was somewhat relieved when he
spotted Major Whitehead and Captain DeWitt threading their way back to the wharves.

"I regret to report that every inn and boarding

house has been taken. I put in a request for rooms at the officers' quarters but only families are permitted." He turned to Coleen with a sad smile. "I'm sorry," he said.

Coleen reached out and touched his arm. "I know you've done your best," she replied. "Father has gone in search of some friends. I'm sure we'll find a place."

"It's most unfortunate, madame," Captain DeWitt announced in his soft southern voice. "But with the entire British army camped on Staten Island and now everyone from New York coming here, I'm afraid that things will become quite desperate for everyone fairly soon."

"The captain does not wish to frighten you," Whitehead spoke up quickly, "but with so many people, food and lodging will be hard to come by."

"Surely this won't last long," Lydia Page exclaimed. "I mean, these troops will be put into action to get back our homes, won't they?"

"Most assuredly, madame," DeWitt answered with a confident smile. "The major and I have an immediate meeting with the general staff to make such preparations."

"You mean you're going to attack New York?" Matthew asked.

"Ah, one step at a time," Whitehead answered, "one step at a time. Unfortunately, neither one of us knows exactly what General Howe has planned, but I assure you we shall all be wintering in New York."

"Wintering?" Lydia Page gasped. "I hope it shall be before winter."

Whitehead smiled patiently. "Only an expression, madame," he explained. "By August the military has to begin thinking of quartering its troops for the winter. I assure you, we shall be back in your fair city long before then."

"If there's anything I can do to be of service," Matthew said, "please let me know. I'll become restless without something to do on this island."

Whitehead nodded. "We appreciate your offer, Mr. Bell, and we shall undoubtedly be using you. But for the time being, I'd be relieved if you would see to the care of Coleen—and her family."

Matthew bowed slightly, covering a smile. The officer's condescending manner had long since ceased to affect him, but Whitehead's blindness to Matthew's feelings about Coleen was an unending source of amazement.

"You might begin by doing something about those men," Lydia Page remarked, nodding toward the Hessians.

"You must pardon some of the soldiers," DeWitt apologized. "They lack a gentleman's manners, but as fighters they're of great value."

"Will we be safe, Winslow?" Coleen asked, her face pale as she looked up at him.

"My dear," Whitehead said impatiently, "no one can guarantee anything in these times. If I were able to be at your side, of course you would be safe. But I cannot; I have things I must do. Besides, you have your brother and father to look after you—and of course Mr. Bell."

Coleen glanced over at her brother, then at Matthew, and tried to smile in gratitude. "Of course," she murmured.

"Now, that's a good girl," the officer said lightly and stepped back. "I'm afraid Captain DeWitt and I must be off for our meeting with the general staff."

Coleen nodded but kept her eyes downcast. The

major hesitated, not knowing quite what to do, then finally gave a small shrug, clicked his heels and bowed stiffly. "I shall keep in touch with you," he said. He bowed again and the two officers disappeared into the crowd of soldiers.

The small group was silent with whatever heavy thoughts were running through their heads. Martha looked around at each one, then caught Matthew's look and shrugged her shoulders. "I'm sure everything will work out fine," she announced, putting on a cheerful front. "Of course," Matthew added and stepped closer to Coleen. "Your father will find a place to stay."

Coleen looked up at him and gave a faint smile. "Thank you . . ."

Matthew could see the hurt in her eyes at Whitehead's uncaring attitude. He could feel the great sadness she was feeling, the emptiness that he wished he could fill. He smiled encouragingly. "I care for you," he said softly, and then added, "I care for all of you. I'll make sure that nothing happens to any of you."

"Oh, Matthew!" Mrs. Page sighed. "You've been most kind to us—and helpful. You're truly a dear and we appreciate all you've done." She stepped toward him and placed a gentle kiss against his cheek.

There was a loud burst of crude remarks from the soldiers watching, and Matthew whipped around to confront them. "There are ladies present, you animals!" he barked out at them.

There was some snickering from the group. "Lookee 'ere," one burst out, "we got ourselves a brave 'un!"

"Y'watch the way you talk to us, bloke," another one called out, "or you'll get what'll be coming to ya!"

Matthew took a step forward, but Coleen grabbed his sleeve and pulled him back. "No," she warned, "no, Matthew." She pulled at him until he reluctantly backed toward her, the soldiers still taunting him.

"They're not worth it," Coleen whispered, trying to turn him around to face her. "We're not listening to their words."

"They're scum!" Matthew muttered, glaring over his shoulder at the laughing men.

She took his arm in and pulled him closer to her. He could feel the softness of her body, smell the sweetness of her perfume, and all at once everything surrounding them seemed unimportant. He turned to look down at her.

"You should not have to suffer such things," he insisted softly.

She smiled her appreciation and squeezed his arm. "You're too good to us, Matthew," she answered. A twinkle suddenly appeared in her eyes. "Our gallant knight!"

"I would have helped him, too," Colin spoke up. Always one to come in at the wrong moment, Matthew thought to himself.

Coleen laughed and turned to hug her brother. "Of course. My two gallant knights, then!"

They were in a much better frame of mind then, crowded close together, turning off whatever surrounded them. The continuing arrival of refugees from the city kept the bustle at the wharf at a high pitch. Children screamed and cried in confusion. Women ran about trying to collect their offspring and keep track of what few possessions they had brought with them, while their men wandered aimlessly about, not knowing who to turn to for help.

And amid all this confusion, the British army lay about, watching the spectacle as if it had been put on for their entertainment, not moving, not helping in the plight of the New Yorkers. They were only moved to action if a pretty woman caught their fancy or was left alone, and then the poor woman was overwhelmed by the clamoring of their insults and lewd invitations.

By the time John Page returned to his family, they were all disgusted with the soldiers' behavior.

"I finally found the Waterfords'," the elder Page panted, his face red from exertion. "Their house is full of relatives, but they did say we could have one room. That's all I could find. They also have a barn which they said we could use." He gulped in a mouthful of fresh air, looking dejected with the result of his mission. "You and Coleen should have the room," he said, turning to his wife. "The rest of us can provide for ourselves in the barn."

Colin's head shot up angrily and he placed a protective arm about Martha. "Martha and I shall find a place in the barn."

Mr. Page shot Martha a look of apology and bowed his head.

"No," Coleen suddenly spoke up. "You and Mother should have the room. Martha and I will use one part of the barn and Colin and Matthew another part. We shall all do fine."

"I can't let you," her father protested, but Coleen put up her hand for silence.

"I'll hear no more. It's settled," she said with determination.

Matthew could hardly stifle the smile that came to his lips. Perhaps Providence had not forgotten him

after all. There was no guarantee that sharing a barn
with Coleen would lead their friendship where he
wanted. But if he had his way, it would be a step
in the right direction.

23

With the help of a few nails and boards, Matthew and Colin had managed to build a small private bedroom in the Waterfords' hayloft for the two women, complete with pegs to hang their dresses and boxes to store their other possessions. To Coleen, it was much like camping, and she seemed to enjoy the adventure. Martha was a bit hesitant about being separated from Colin and placed with his sister, but she took it all in stride.

"You and Martha will have to put off your love-making, I'm afraid," Matthew said with a grin as he and Colin finished boarding off the horse stall they had chosen for their bedroom. "I don't think your sister would approve."

"At least it will give them a chance to get better acquainted," Colin answered. He had already lost a couple nights sleep staring at the wooden ceiling where he knew Martha was lying, almost directly above them. So close but so far away.

"I hope it will bring us all closer together," Matthew said in a low voice. He too had lain awake, picturing the beautiful Coleen asleep in the loft.

August came, and with the new warm month came more British troops. General Clinton, smarting from a defeat in the South, sailed into the harbor, bringing more troops to Staten Island. Matthew had watched the row boats come in from the big ships with load after load of soldiers. He had lost count of how many troops were stationed there. All he knew was that the British were preparing for something big, probably their attack on New York. He wondered what defenses Washington was setting up and where the patriotic forces were located. He was sure Washington was aware of the size of the force encamped on Staten Island. What was important now was to find out the battle plan that Howe and his staff must be making, but Matthew had been unsuccessful in placing himself in a position where he might learn something.

He was pondering his situation as he returned to the Waterford farm, slowly walking along what had once been a peaceful country lane, bordered by waist-high stone fences and shaded by an occasional spreading elm. The fields on either side were now filled with groups of soldiers, some lying idly around, some gambling and playing cards, and others walking restlessly among the tents. It was obvious that they were bored by the inactivity. Fights frequently broke out, and as often as not the officers would merely lean back and wait until one or the other antagonist was felled. Then they would beckon to some sentries and march the culprits off to a barn, where they were kept for a restless night to wear off their anger.

Matthew was familiar with the scene, remembering his own enlistment not too long ago, but this British group was far rougher, obviously the dregs of the back streets of London and the British Empire.

As he came down into a small glen, off to one side there came shrieks of female laughter. A line of tents nestled among a small grove of spruces. Clotheslines criss-crossed several trees and various pieces of women's apparel hung out to dry, including white undergarments. Around a smoking campfire three women relaxed, all three in various stages of undress. They were laughing and taunting a line of men who waited patiently in front of two tents. From the rear of one tent, a soldier stepped out, buttoning his pants, his shirt slung over his naked shoulders. In front, one of the men in line opened the flaps and stooped to enter.

"C'mon, sweetie!" One of the women had noticed Matthew and beckoned to him. "Sweetest lovin' you'll find this side of the Atlantic," she called out. "C'mon over and join the crowd!"

Matthew blinked in amazement. He had never seen such an open display of such women. He shook his head and continued on his way.

As the country opened up and the outer perimeter of the tented army passed from view, Matthew began to relax and to enjoy the countryside. He was reminded of his own home and wondered what his father and Mark and Deborah were doing. He would like to go back and visit them. It would be good to go home. Especially if he could take Coleen back with him too.

Matthew stopped and stared at the ground. She was a Tory and he was a Son of Liberty, he reminded himself. Even if she could return his feelings, they would still be enemies. Matthew drew in a sharp breath of air and looked up into the blue sky before walking on at a slower pace. Neither one of them could change what they were. Did that mean Coleen could never, under any circumstances, be his love?

Head downcast, Matthew had come upon the farm without realizing that he had arrived. He stopped short and looked up in surprise at where he was. A group of red-coated men sat on the porch watching him, their muskets braced between their legs. There was something strange about their presence, about the way they broke off their conversation and stared at him. Matthew shot a quick glance toward the barn. From his vantage point, he could see another group of soldiers milling around near the back doors of the barn.

Matthew went cold with the realization that something was drastically wrong. He began to walk toward the barn, quickening his steps when he saw that the men on the porch were not going to interfere.

The soldiers at the barn had crowded together into the doorway, their backs to Matthew. Obviously they were watching something, and as he approached he could hear their laughter. Matthew ran the last few steps.

He grabbed the first man he met and pushed him aside, darting through the rest into the center of the barn floor and glaring angrily at the scene before him.

Colin, his head rolling unconsciously, was being held on his feet by a large stringy-haired Hessian.

Other Hessians had drawn into a circle around Coleen and Martha, who clutched the torn fragments of their dresses close to their bodies.

"Matthew," Coleen called out, her face tear-streaked and ashen from the humiliation she had suffered.

Matthew came forward and drew her into his arms, then reached out to pull Martha close to them. He looked about at the sullen ring of soldiers, his face set hard, eyes blazing a warning.

"Get out of here," he snarled.

There was a shuffling of feet, and a few of the British soldiers glanced at each other uncertainly. The small contingent of Hessians glowered back at Matthew, heads lowered in defiance.

"Go to it, Fritzy boy," a voice called out. "Ya got yourself a larger audience!"

The big man who held Colin grunted and pushed forward. Matthew edged around so that he could face the man, his arms still around Coleen and Martha.

"Get out of here!" he snarled again.

"I vant dem," the big man growled and nodded toward the two women, his eyes narrowed in determination.

"*Ja*," the same voice called out jeeringly, "Ol' Fritzy and his friends want your women, friend. They've already taken on every other woman on this here island." A red-faced leering Britisher stepped forward from the background. "Come on, civvie, you're stopping a free show."

"You scum!" Matthew growled. "Get out of here."

The man grinned. "We're only here to show them Germans a good time. They're here to help us win the war, y'know."

"By raping women? Is that the kind of war you're in?"

The man shrugged. "It's part of it. Another part is watching the likes o' you get knocked about a bit." He cocked his head at the big German. "Go get 'im Fritzy. Then you and your friends can have them women."

The Hessian dropped Colin in a heap on the floor and drew himself up to confront Matthew.

"What's going on in here?" Major Winslow Whitehead pushed his way through the crowd and stood in the center of the ring. "My God, Coleen, what have these brutes done to you?"

"Winslow!" Coleen reached out for him, but he turned to his command. "All of you—get out! Sergeant, collect the names of everyone in here. I shall deal with them later!"

There was an angry murmur among the men as they shuffled out of the barn. When the last man disappeared Whitehead turned to look at Coleen. "My dear," he said stiffly, "you should get something about you!"

Coleen stared up at him in disbelief, then nodded meekly, still in shock from the ordeal.

Matthew stepped into his small room and came back with a sweater and a jacket which he handed to the women. Then he turned to Whitehead. "What kind of men do you have who'd rape innocent women?" he asked savagely.

Whitehead sighed and politely kept his back to the women as they dressed. "I assure you that these men will be dealt with severely. As for the kind of men I have, sir," he answered tightly, "they are fighters and they're tired and bored with this waiting. This thing—" he waved his hand behind him at the women, "is not an uncommon occurrence. It is deplorable, to be sure, but it does happen." Matthew saw the major take a deep breath as he turned to inspect Colin on the floor. "The boy is merely unconscious. Perhaps it was best for him not to have seen."

Matthew stared at the man, staggered at what he was hearing. Here was the man who was engaged to Coleen, and he was talking as though nothing had happened. Whatever respect Matthew might have had for the major disintegrated in that one moment.

"It's a lucky thing I came by," Whitehead said, his tone becoming brisk. "I had come not only to pay my respects to the Pages, but also to talk to you."

Matthew stared at the officer. "You came to see me?"

Whitehead glanced at Coleen as the women self-consciously turned back to face the men. "Ah, I see you two have adjusted." He studied their faces. "I trust," he asked hesitantly, "that we arrived in time?"

Coleen closed her eyes and nodded, reaching out to grab hold of Martha's hand.

"Ah, I'm glad to hear that."

Coleen opened her eyes and stared at the major, then turned to give Matthew a look of helplessness.

Matthew could hardly believe his ears. He wanted to throttle the man for being so callous, but he could only look back into Coleen's eyes, wishing he could place a comforting arm about her shoulders.

"Good," the major said, dismissing the subject. "And now, if you ladies don't mind, I must speak with Matthew about an extremely important matter."

"I'm sorry, Winslow," Coleen answered. Matthew could tell by the glance she gave the officer that something had died within her. "I'm sorry to have inconvenienced you."

She took Martha's arm and before Winslow could

reply the two women disappeared into an adjoining room.

The major stared after them, then turned to Matthew, shaking his head as if in exasperation. "We have a mission," Whitehead said, grasping Matthew across the shoulders and drawing him to the other end of the barn, where it was quiet and darker. "We want you to go across the harbor into Long Island as an advance."

"Advance?" Matthew asked curiously. "Advance to what? I thought we'd be going to New York, not Long Island."

Whitehead smiled. "That's what everyone is thinking," he confided. "Including Washington, we hope. So we're going to come in by the side gate, you might say." He drew Matthew in closer and lowered his voice.

"We want you to head immediately for Gravesend, Flatbush and then Brooklyn Heights. We want to know the enemy's positions and anything else you can find out. You shall report back to me at the point where we drop you off, in seven days. Do you think you can do that?"

Matthew nodded, his mind thinking quickly, his heart beating excitedly. "When will the attack start?"

"I'm not at liberty to say, lad," Whitehead answered, "but it shall not be long. The important thing is that you bring back accurate information in exactly one week's time—no more, no less. Is that clear?"

Matthew nodded again. "When would you like me to start?"

Whitehead looked surprised. "Why now, of course. That's why I came here."

Matthew cast a quick glance at the room where

the women had retreated, wishing he could spend time with Coleen after what she had just been through. But he had no choice. "I'll just pack a few things," he murmured.

"Good," Whitehead answered. "We shall be waiting for you outside."

No sooner had the major disappeared than the far door burst open and Martha came flying out to kneel by Colin's side. "You poor boy," she moaned and cradled his head in her lap.

Matthew stepped to Coleen's side and took both her hands in his. "Are you sure you're all right?" he asked.

She smiled bravely. "Thank you, dear Matthew," she answered. "You always seem to be at hand when it most matters." They held each other's gaze until Matthew stepped back self-consciously.

"I—I have to go," he said.

Her look was one of hurt and surprise. "Go? Where?"

Matthew sighed, wishing he could forget his duties and remain with her, but he fought desire and took a deep breath. "I'll be gone only a short while. In the meantime you take care of yourself." He glanced at Martha and Colin. "All of you take care of yourselves."

Coleen stared up at him with concern in her eyes and lifted her hand to his cheek. "And you, Matthew," she said softly. "You take care of yourself."

24

T HE MAJOR TOOK Matthew's arm in a tight grip and leaned forward in the boat. "Remember. Seven days—be here!"

It was a cold, foggy morning. The short trip across the Narrows from Staten Island to Brooklyn had been in a choppy sea, and Matthew had been only too thankful to disembark. He watched in silence as the officer and his rowers backed into the water and disappeared in the fog.

Seven days . . . Matthew stared at the fog bank in front of him. There was no point in connoitering the American troops; he should head for Washington's camp, where he would be told whatever information the general wanted the British to know. He sat down on the sandy shore and waited for the sun to burn off the haze. No need stumbling around in this kind of weather in foreign countryside. Seven days was ample time.

By mid-morning the sun broke through, unveiling rolling meadows with groves of apple trees. Matthew took his time, keeping within view of the harbor. If he walked long enough he knew he would reach the heights of Brooklyn, directly across the river from the city.

"Halt!" A voice from his right boomed loudly across the silent morning and Matthew stopped in his tracks. "Identify yourself!" The voice came from behind a stone fence that bordered the path. A musket was shoved over the top and aimed at Matthew.

"I live down the road—taking my constitutional," Matthew answered guardedly. He raised his hands to shoulder height. "Who's doing the asking?"

Three men slowly rose from behind the fence, Matthew sighed his relief when he saw that they wore the buff colored jackets of the Continental Army, and he started to lower his hands.

"Keep 'em up there," one of the men barked out as they crawled over the stones and made their way down to Matthew's side. "Let's see some papers."

"I don't have any on me," he answered and smiled apologetically. "But I'm certainly not a redcoat."

"No papers?" The man looked him over carefully. "How in hell we going to know you're telling the truth? How we know you're not a spy?"

For a minute, Matthew's heart seemed to stop its beat and he did his best to remain calm. "If I were a spy, would I be walking in the open like this?" he asked.

There was an exchange of questioning looks. "I dunno," one man finally answered. "Y'better come along with us anyway."

Matthew was unprepared for the scene that spread before them as they finished their climb up the steep hills. On the ridge, as far as he could see, cannons were lined neatly in a row. There must have been over two hundred of them, all facing down upon the broad expanse he had just walked. Behind the cannons, the gunners and soldiers were tented in small rectangular encampments that were small groups of eight or ten. Blue and buff-coated soldiers lay idly about. It was almost the same scene Matthew had witnessed on Staten Island, except for the jacket colors and smaller force.

"Come along." He was pushed to a tent apart from the others. "Colonel—we found his one walking up towards us."

The colonel was a stocky, energetic-looking man. He surveyed Matthew from head to foot, then stepped forward for a closer look.

"Name?"

"Matthew Bell?" He held his breath to see if the colonel would remember that his name had been published several months ago as a traitor.

"Where are you from?" The questions were crisp, the officer's face expressionless.

"Originally from Connecticut, sir," Matthew answered.

Colonel Knowlton reared back his head in interest. "Where abouts?"

"Wethersfield," Matthew answered. "It's near Hartford."

"Anywhere near Haddam or Yale?" the colonel asked quickly.

Matthew started and shook his head, suddenly realizing that the man was trying to trick him into making a slip. "Am I suspected of something, Colonel?" he asked.

"Everyone is suspected," Knowlton answered sharply. "That's one of my responsibilities—catching damned spies and traitors." He spun about to address the group of men around him. "Any of you from Connecticut?" He waited a moment, but there was no response. "Find Hale for me."

"Nathan Hale?" Matthew asked hopefully.

The colonel turned to face him, scowling. "You know Captain Hale?" There was definite disappointment in his question.

It wasn't long before the handsome red-haired schoolteacher clasped Matthew's hand tightly in warm recognition. "I trust your sister is progressing well with her studies?"

Matthew grinned. "The last I heard, she was," he answered. "And I can't begin to tell you how thankful I am that you're here."

Hale smiled and made his introductions. "Colonel Knowlton of Knowlton's Rangers, my commander."

Matthew cocked an eyebrow and bowed stiffly to the officer. "I'm sorry, sir, to have disappointed you. But I'm sure there are plenty of British spies hereabouts."

Hale was still chuckling to himself as he led Matthew back to his tent. "It's lucky for you that I *am* here. The colonel could make an innocent man confess, I'm afraid."

"And you're one of Knowlton's Rangers?"

"Yes, I asked for a transfer."

"It's a dangerous job," Matthew remarked.

Nathan shrugged. "I felt useless waiting for war to come to me. As a Ranger, I can at least go out to it. Besides, it's not as dangerous as one would think."

Matthew stared at the handsome narrow face with admiration. Here was a man who was sacrificing his god-given talents to his beliefs. He knew he could trust Hale, but wondered how much it was fair to reveal to him.

"I have a favor to ask of you, Nathan."

Hale noted the tightness in Matthew's voice, the earnestness in his eyes. "It's important, isn't it?" he asked softly.

"Very. I need to get a message to General Washington."

Nathan studied Matthew's eyes and a slow smile turned his lips upward. "Don't tell me—"

"Please," Matthew interrupted. "All I can tell you is that I need to get word to Washington right away."

"He's here now—at the Heights. Came yesterday from New York but I've heard he's leaving again tomorrow."

"I've got to get word to him now—before he leaves." Matthew leaned forward and lowered his voice. "He knows your name. I think he would see you if you went to him."

"And what is it you want me to tell him?"

"That I must speak with him."

Nathan stared at Matthew, then slowly leaned back, a smile playing on his lips. "My dear Matthew," he answered in a consoling voice, "half the nation wants to talk to him. What makes you think he would take time out to talk to you?"

"He'll meet with me," Matthew answered tightly. He watched Hale's expression turn from disbelief to acceptance. "Washington will see me," Matthew repeated. "All you need to do is find out where."

* * *

The meeting place was the Red Giant's Inn, close to the river.

Washington stood by the fireplace in the vacated back room when Matthew stepped through the door. He was uniformed in the blue coat, golden epaulets and buff-colored breeches of an officer, but there was something almost regal about him, Matthew noted, taking in the stance and demeanor of the six-foot-three commander.

"Your news must be important, Matthew," he said, seating himself at a small wooden table.

"I'm here because I've been sent to spy on your troops," Matthew replied, "but I may also have some helpful information for you."

"Go on," Washington encouraged.

"I've been living on Staten Island," Matthew responded, and then recounted what he knew of the British forces. "I'd guess at a figure of about 35,000 troops," he concluded. "Just before I was dropped here, they were moving troops close to the Narrows."

"All of them?"

"I'd estimate about two thirds—plus most of their cannons."

"And they asked you to spy on our positions?"

Matthew nodded. "I'm to report back in six days—*exactly* six days. And Whitehead indicated that the advance to Long Island is simply a roundabout advance on New York. They plan to take you off guard."

Washington was silent, his fingers drumming on the edge of the table. "The Lord Howes have been making peace overtures," he said at length, his voice rumbling softly through the small room. "But I didn't trust them and now I know I was right. I just received a report that some of their gun ships tried to sail up the Hudson. They're going to do that, you know, and I won't be able to prevent it. I have no navy—the Hudson is too wide to stop them."

There was a long pause before he continued. "For the moment, all I can do is divide my army in half, here and along the Hudson." He sighed heavily and shook his head. "Six days, you say?"

Before Matthew could respond, Washington leaned forward and went on. "All right, then let's give them something to ponder. In six days time—that would be the 19th—I suspect the British will start to land on Long Island. That will give me time to reinforce the militia already here. You can tell your British friends that you found the American forces well fortified on the hills to the east and to the west. We are, and I'm not worried they know about it. There's only one way they can come upon us and that's right up the middle where we shall be waiting for them."

Matthew hesitated. "They have a large force, sir."

Washington looked at him under shaggy greying eyebrows. "Yes, I'm afraid they do. But we shall put up a gallant fight anyhow."

"Will we be able to stop them?"

Washington was quiet, this time his fingers motionless on the smooth wooden surface. "The British will be sending their crack troops led by their finest officers. They outnumber us three to one, they have the cannon, the muskets and ammunition and the discipline for open-field fighting. But we'll give them our best, and that's about all anyone can ask of us."

The words still rang in Matthew's ears as he waited in the apple orchard six days later. He was huddled together, trying to protect himself from the rain that had begun to pelt down. He stared out to the chop-

ping waters, hoping for a glimpse of a boat, but
nothing would dare the waves that this summer storm
was brewing. New England was famous for its rain
and thunder storms, but this one promised to be the
worst Matthew had ever witnessed. The heavens sent
down spectacular spikes of lightning, and the down-
pour was so heavy and the thunder so loud that it
began to seem as if it were God's warning of the
chaos that was about to be unleashed between the
two warring countries.

How long the storm lasted Matthew had no way
of knowing. He was only suddenly conscious that the
pelting of rain upon his shoulders had dissipated and
the noise had suddenly given way to silence. As he
raised his head to look about from his crouched position under the trees, he was conscious of the sweet
smell of freshness, the chirping of midnight insects
as they came out of hiding and finally the bright lights
of the stars above. Matthew drew in a deep breath
and closed his eyes. Sleep at last.

Morning brought an abrupt awakening. For a moment, he sat motionless, his ears cocked for a repeat
of the noise he had heard. Surely it had not been
a dream.

He slowly looked about, then stopped as he glanced
out over the waters. A small armada of barges and
long boats was approaching, with white oars sweeping
across the lapping inlet and pulling them forward. Occasionally, a sharp command drifted across from the
distant vessels.

The soldiers jumped out near the shoreline, wading
into land, muskets and belts held high. There were
red-coated Britishers, green-coated Hessians, grenadiers in blue coats with buttoned-back tails and tow-
ering caps. The more disciplined regiments pulled to-

gether in sharp ranks, bullied by officers who lashed
out with their quirts. Others dragged themselves up
to the green fields nearby and fell to their sides to
watch the spectacle. And on they came!

The invasion of Long Island had started.

25

"Y OUR REPORT was most useful!" Major Whitehead
studied the map on the wall of the meeting
house that the British had established as their
planning room in Gravesend.

Matthew sat on the edge of the highback chair
glancing nervously about the room at the various bat-
tleflags, maps and pictures that had been hastily tacked
to the walls. There had been several other civilian-
dressed men in the room—fellow spies, Matthew
guessed—who had kept in the background until they
were beckoned by the major for a conference over
the maps on the table. But now Matthew and Whitehead were alone.

"So the Americans are well fortified on the hills,"
Whitehead said thoughtfully, turning over the infor-

mation Matthew had given him. "It's obvious they would like us to march right up here!" His fingers outlined a road that led through one of the passes. He turned to survey Matthew. "And you say they have all the passes well guarded?"

"As far as I could determine," Matthew answered, hoping the officer would not ask for too many details about the area.

There was a pause, then Whitehead shrugged his shoulders. "Well, a bit of a nuisance, but no matter. The landing was about perfect." He smiled in deep satisfaction. "I honestly don't see how these rebels can expect to hold us off."

Matthew was left with nothing to do but wait over the next six days. He spent most of his time sitting under one of the trees watching the preparations by the soldiers and keeping an eye on the large grey-stoned house that had been pointed out to him as General Howe's headquarters. Never had he seen so many high-ranking officers assembled in one spot. It was obvious that Britain was wholeheartedly committing its military might to the destruction and takeover of the American field. Matthew had tried several times under various excuses to get near the building, but no one without the proper rank was even allowed near the vicinity. Matthew was just beginning to despair of obtaining more information for Washington when he was summoned to Whitehead's headquarters.

"We're going to attack!" Whitehead paced back and forth in front of the small group of men whom Matthew could now identify as fellow spies. "Hollister and Brighton, you two will accompany General Grant's troops as they take the western column." Whitehead pointed to the left far pass closest to the harbor. "You'll leave two hours before the troops advance. I want you to spot the exact enemy positions and find the best and easiest routes. Johnson and Namarrah will be with the Hessians, who'll take the center position. No need to tell you this is the route the Americans would like us to take. It will be well fortified, so use the utmost precaution.

"Bell and Dudley will be accompanying me and the third wing towards the eastern route—Jamaica Pass. You two will receive further orders from me as we go along," Whitehead said, addressing Matthew and the small wiry fellow standing next to him before turning back to the group. "That's all."

The small man chuckled to himself as they all stepped out into the greying dawn and separated to go their own ways. "Looks like we got the brunt of it this time!"

"Brunt of it?" Matthew asked in surprise.

Dudley snorted. "I been w'the major long enough to know he only goes w'the chosen ones."

By the time the sky began to lighten with the rising sun, Matthew and Dudley were waiting patiently by the stone building, satchels filled with provisions and meager belongings. Inside his waistband, Matthew carried a small flintlock, a gift Whitehead had presented to him in gratitude for his help in their escape from New York.

To his right in an open field, men were quickly assembling in lines. A regiment of Highlanders was already on the road to the east, finishing their preparations under the staccato barks of their sergeants. Nearly a thousand dragoons, decked out in fancy black helmets with flowing feathers, scarlet coats and black thigh boots, were slowly making their way up behind the Highlanders, their swords and fusils clanging in the early morning. And far behind, barely outlined in the faint light, horses were being pulled to the harnesses of cannon.

"Yes," Dudley remarked at his side, "I do believe we're going into the thick of it."

Matthew tried to keep track of all he saw as he walked about, pretending to stretch his limbs. Far off to the west, similar preparations were being made by the other two wings of the invasion.

"Bell! Dudley!" Whitehead stepped out of his headquarters and waited while the two men came up to him. "You two will go ahead of our wing. Behind you will come the Highlanders. We don't want the Americans warned, so you're to capture any civilians you encounter and clear the way for the wing. Here is our destination." He unrolled a map and held it before the two of them. "Our main thrust is Jamaica Pass. We have reason to believe the Americans have left this pass unguarded. As you can see, if we make this advance we will have outflanked the Americans. General Grant and the Hessians will start their diversionary attack tomorrow morning. We should be in position by then above the Americans, so that we can make a surprise attack from the rear before they know what has happened. Any questions?"

Matthew's heart was beating savagely. "How far do you want us to keep ahead?"

Whitehead shrugged. "We don't want any civilians to go into hiding at the sight of the Highlanders. They'll be more apt to make their presence known to innocent-looking early morning strollers, so keep ahead by a good distance."

Matthew stole a quick glance at Dudley. Somehow he would have to find a way to separate himself from the man and warn the Americans.

All during the day Matthew waited for his opportunity. He knew he had some spare time, for it would take the main troop an entire day just to get to the area of the pass. They ran into civilians only occasionally, mostly innocent farmers who were caught going about their work in the fields. All along the way guards of Highlanders were left behind to make sure no one was allowed to make their way to Brooklyn and cry out a warning.

When it was almost dusk Matthew still hadn't had a chance to warn the Americans, and he was beginning to worry. Directly ahead lay the rolling hills that led to the Americans' flanks.

"They must have someone up there waiting for us," Dudley commented as the two stopped to study the terrain. "It's been too easy a shot for us so far."

"Maybe the major's information is false," Matthew agreed, "and they're up there setting up a trap for us right now. Let's see how close we can get."

Dudley hesitated, squinting out at the distant knolls, "T'aint the first time we been tricked," he mumbled, "and that's part of our job I guess."

The two made their way up the hill as cautiously as they could among the trees. It was slow going and there were times when Matthew could hardly contain the urge to run out and cry the alarm. Surely their advance had been noticed by now.

"There's a group of 'em over there," Dudley whispered as they came to the top of the hill. He pulled Matthew to the ground and the two of them made their way on their stomachs through the underbrush. Halfway down the slope were two tents, and there were horses tied nearby. Through the trees Matthew could make out a group of men lounging in the shade, half asleep or idly talking among themselves.

"Rebels!" Dudley whispered, keeping his eyes on the distant group.

Matthew slowly edged back, his hand creeping down to the gun in his belt. "We'd better get back and warn the major," he answered, rising to his feet. Matthew waited until Dudley turned to look back. The man's eyes widened as he saw that Matthew was standing in plain view of the enemy. Then he saw the gun levelled at him.

"What y'trying to do with that thing?" Dudley asked, staring angrily at Matthew.

"I'm sorry," Matthew answered, beckoning Dudley to get up, "but I've got to warn these men."

Dudley stared at him in astonishment. "You're one of them!" he finally muttered, shaking his head in disbelief.

"Go on down!" Matthew pointed the direction with the flintlock, watching the man with caution. "But keep your hands in sight!"

Dudley reluctantly raised both hands shoulder high, muttering under his breath as he made his way down the slope in front of Matthew.

At the sound of their approach the soldiers were on their feet, swinging their muskets toward them. "Who goes there?" one man called out nervously.

Matthew waved a hand over his head. "I'm bringing in a spy," he called out and then waited until he was among them before continuing. "The British will be attacking through this pass tomorrow morning. It's urgent that I get this news to General Washington at once."

The soldiers looked at one another quizzically. "How do we know you're telling the truth?" one of them finally asked.

Dudley shook his head and turned to Matthew.

"Might as well give it up," he said sorrowfully. "It didn't work. They've caught us in our lie."

Matthew looked at him in surprise. "This man is a spy for the British. We've come ahead of the main British thrust which will be coming through this pass."

Again Dudley shook his head sadly and placed a comforting arm around Matthew's shoulder. "I told you it wouldn't work." He then turned to the soldiers. "We were sent to trick you into believing Lord Howe was sending his troops this way." He stopped and cocked his head toward the west. "But I can tell you hear them cannons as well as me. We got here too late. We was supposed to get here this morning before Howe attacked over there."

Matthew listened in shock, hardly believing what the man was trying to do. "Don't you listen to him. Those are Hessian guns and they're only a diversion. Head up that hill and you'll see. You can see Howe's troops coming toward us."

Dudley stepped in front of Matthew to appeal to the soldiers. "I hope you'll go easy with me for telling the truth. What my friend is saying, that's what our commander wants you to think. We were supposed to have convinced you that the whole British army was coming this way. You were supposed to run back to Washington and convince him to bring his troops way over here. But I guess Washington wasn't fooled either. Sounds like a ripe fight going on over there."

The group was silent as they all listened to the dull thud of cannons in the distance.

"Take me to Washington," Matthew exclaimed in frustration. "You can't delay, or it will be too late."

Dudley addressed the soldiers once again, speaking in a slow and easy voice. "Me name's John Dudley— I got me papers here. I got me a small orchard on the other end of the island here. I admit, I got a bit of the Tory blood in me so it weren't too hard to accept their offer to come and try to pull the wool over yer eyes." He fumbled in his coat and extracted some worn papers, which he unfolded and handed to the leader of the group. "Here, you can read me papers."

Dudley stepped back to Matthew's side, glancing up at him with the glimmer of a mocking smile.

"He's a British spy," Matthew said firmly, but he saw by the soldier's face that the documents had been accepted as valid.

"I'm afraid my friend here doesn't carry papers," Dudley said with an innocent air. "My *new* friend, I should say. I hear that's a sure way of telling a spy. Anyone who can't prove who he is has something to hide, they always say!"

A hand flashed out and grabbed Matthew's gun from him. "Wait a minute," Matthew growled as the point of a bayonet jabbed into his back. "Take me to your headquarters and I can have this straightened out!"

The soldier beckoned to two men. "Take them back to General Putnam. He'll know what to do with 'em!"

"What about the British?" Matthew asked as the bayonet jabbed him forward.

Dudley winked at him, then spoke to the soldiers. "Ya might as well wait now until sunup. You know them Britishers never attack during the night. And

I bet from yer looks you had a long day. Get some sleep tonight." As he was pushed forward, he yelled back at the confused group, "Ya won't see any troops through here anyway, though. Mark my word on that!"

The walk to General Putnam's headquarters was painfully slow. Dudley had suddenly developed a limp and every once in a while would drop to the ground to grab at his leg. "It's me gout," he explained as the two guards stood over him. "It's me gout!"

Matthew stood watching the act in fascination. He was furious that the spy had gotten the better of him. He had learned a lesson well today . . .

The movement was so quick that it was over before he quite knew what had happened. One minute, Dudley was bent over his boot, swaying back and forth in pain. In the next instant, he had jumped to his feet with a small derringer in his hand. There was a puff of white smoke, a dull discharge and one of the soldiers gripped his head and fell backwards. The other soldier looked at his companion in horror; before he could turn back to Dudley, the spy had charged forward, grabbing the musket in both hands and wrenching it free. With a savage yell, the spy twisted about in a wide arc and sank the blade deep into the soldier's stomach.

As he pulled the bayonet out, Dudley turned quickly to face Matthew.

"Hold it," he gasped and leveled the gun at Matthew. "Just stand where you're at!"

Before Matthew could do anything, there was a movement at their side and a musket bellowed. The soldier Dudley had shot first had dragged himself to his musket and got his shot off. Dudley screamed and grabbed at his side. He brandished his musket at Matthew, warning him not to move as he hobbled over to the fallen soldier, who was frantically fumbling to reload the rifle.

Dudley stared down at the man, his lips in a snarl, one hand grasping the rifle which was pointed at Matthew, the other squeezing tightly at the red stain spreading at his side. He watched as the guard gallantly pulled the ramrod from the musket, all the time whimpering at what he knew was a futile effort to reload his rifle. He looked up at Dudley, tears of anger in his eyes, and spit at him in contempt.

Dudley gave him a hard kick with his boot. With a savage oath, he pointed the bayonet at the man, waiting to make sure the soldier knew what was coming, and then slowly fell forward, his weight sinking the blade into the soldier's chest.

"No!" Matthew bellowed and threw himself at the spy, his weight carrying them both a few feet to topple over the other guard's still form. "You bastard!" Matthew cried out, rolling over onto his knees end swinging his fist back.

Dudley squirmed onto his back, a savage leer on his face as he stared up at Matthew. In his hand was Matthew's flintlock, which he had pulled from the soldier's belt. "Get the 'ell back from me, or you're as dead as your rebel friends!"

Matthew stared down at the gun in disbelief, then reluctantly backed away.

"We gotta get off this trail," Dudley muttered, clutching at his side which was now slick with blood. "And you gotta help me stop bleeding."

"Go to hell!" Matthew snarled.

Dudley grunted and began to laugh. "When I do,

I'll take you with me. I ain't leavin' this bit of property without a companion. Remember that I'll fire this gun with my last breath, just for the pleasure of it!"

26

"WE'LL REST HERE a bit." Dudley gritted his teeth as Matthew bent and laid him down on the ground. They had climbed the nearest knoll, with the gun thrust deeply into Matthew's side, and they had now come to rest beneath a large elm.

"We're going to watch all the action from up here, lad," Dudley said, glancing about to make sure he had a satisfactory view of the area. He looked over at Matthew, who had dropped to his back breathing heavily. "Didn't think I could do it, did you?" he asked.

Dudley began to laugh, amused by Matthew's sullen look, but the laugh broke off into a heavy cough. "I like that," he finally gasped. "It's one thing to get the better of a soldier or civilian. They don't know any better. But to get the upper hand from a fellow spy—ah, that's true satisfaction."

Matthew remained silent, content to look up into the darkening sky, still somewhat in shock over the brutal slayings he had witnessed. It was the first time he had seen men killed.

"It's going to take more than a whippersnapper like you to get the better of ol' Dudley," the little man laughed. His cough had a rasp to it that caused Matthew to look over. The red stain that Dudley clutched at his side had spread wider now, saturating almost the entire length of the white shirt.

Dudley caught Matthew's glance and looked briefly down at his wound. "Aye, I need aid. But they'll be coming along soon enough." He looked up at the last of the sunset glow. "Come early morn, these hills will be swarming with redcoats."

Matthew eyed the small gun in the man's hand. He had to get away and warn Washington. Even if those remaining five guards at the pass suspected the British movement, they would be no match for the contingent of Highlanders that would be sneaking up on them in the early morning. Once that road block had been cleared, the pass ahead looked clear and unguarded.

Matthew sat up and stared toward the west. Even in the darkness he could pretty well make out the territory. To the left, in the shadow of the hill slopes, small fires sparked the countryside. The Hessians had dug in for the night; far beyond was the faint glow of the far western wing.

Facing them on the dark hills were the campfires along the battlelines of the American army. Matthew realized just how far behind the American lines the British would be if they made it through the pass.

He sighed and cupped his chin in both hands. Sometime tonight, as soon as it got dark enough, he would have to overpower Dudley and make his escape.

"Just stay there, lad!" Matthew froze, the cold hard muzzle pressed against the back of his head as Dudley leaned down to him. "It's getting late and I wouldn't want you getting any ideas about escaping."

Before he realized what had happened, metal cuffs were snapped onto one of his wrists. Matthew turned in surprise, but the muzzle dug sharply into his temple. "Quiet," Dudley said in a harsh whisper. "I ain't weak enough yet not to be able to pull this trigger!" He waited until Matthew stopped resisting, his knee spearing into his prisoner's back. "I ain't done by a long shot," he murmured, yanking Matthew's other hand behind him. The other metal manacle was snapped as Dudley's weight lifted away. "Now you can turn around."

Pulling futilely at the manacles that locked his hands behind him, Matthew wrenched himself around and glared up at Dudley.

The spy pursed his lips and smiled. "I might have use for you, laddie," he said, wearily leaning back against the tree, his hand reaching for his side. "You never throw all your cards away before the whole deck is dealt. Never know what will be handed you." He sighed and closed his eyes for a long moment, then suddenly opened them. "You really a double spy?"

Matthew returned his look expressionlessly, making no reply.

Dudley inspected him from head to foot and slowly shook his head. "You don't look like a spy. That's what fooled me, I think. You don't look like you belong in the business."

Still Matthew remained quiet. He was content to listen, waiting for the right moment, saving what energy and strength he had for whatever lay ahead.

It was an hour or two after midnight when Matthew started to raise his head slightly. Dudley was only a dark form, quiet and unmoving. He hadn't moved for quite some time now; Matthew was sure of it.

Matthew crept forward, pausing with each scrape of pebble, each snap of a twig in the early morning silence. As he neared Dudley he began to make out the man's face. His eyes were closed and his head rested against the tree trunk. Matthew studied the sleeping man, judging how best to overpower him without the use of his manacled hands.

He slowly bent to his knees and lay on his side, bringing his knees up to his chest. He closed his eyes for a second, taking a deep breath, and then pistoned his legs straight out, sending his boots smashing into Dudley's face. As the Britisher toppled over, Matthew twisted about and in desperation threw himself on top of the spy, trying to claw with his confined hands. It was several seconds before he realized that the man was not fighting back.

Matthew hesitantly drew back and looked at Dudley, then pressed his head to the wet chest. There was no sound, no movement. Only a cold damp mass. Dead . . . and he would never know whether Dudley had died during the night or whether the blow to his head had caused his death.

Matthew shook himself free of the thought and twisted about so that his hands could search the pockets. He began to sweat profusely, at first from the strain of the effort, then from the panic of not being able to find the key. He forced the body over and hunted through the back pockets—but still nothing.

Matthew stopped and leaned back, willing himself to be calm. He took several deep breaths. Slowly this time, he told himself. He forced himself not to think of the hour, for every time he did it only enforced the knowledge that morning was quickly approaching. Once again Matthew began his search, and again it was to no avail.

Matthew swallowed back his sudden feeling of helplessness and struggled to his feet. There was no time for self-pity. The dawn was already beginning to lighten the eastern skies and with the morning sun would come the British right wing.

Half-sliding, half-running, Matthew made his way down the knoll to the path below. Several times he lost his balance and skidded onto his face and stomach to slide between rocks and brush. He could taste the sweetness of blood in his mouth but he did not care. His only thought was to get to the American lines. When he finally got to the small path, he glanced about to get his bearings, then set off at a quick pace.

Running with his wrists tied behind him was more wearing than he had anticipated. He had just rounded a bend in the road, eyes half-closed from exhaustion, when he became conscious of the row of men on either side of him. He slowed to a faltering halt. Highlanders!

"'E's our bloody advance!" one of the men called out, and the Britishers gathered around him. "M'God, y'been battered about." They stared at his irons and battered face. "Been lookin' f'r us, I bet!"

Matthew was crestfallen. All he could do was nod at these men who led him to the side of the road and sat him down.

"I bet y'was captured by them bloody rebels we caught last night. Is that it?"

Matthew nodded, trying to clear his mind.

"Where's your friend?"

Matthew glanced up at the concerned faces that stared down at him. "I—we were captured," Matthew said. "We were trying to escape. They got Dudley."

The men shook their heads and touched Matthew's shoulders in sympathy. "It's all right," one of them answered softly. "Y'mark m'word, we'll get even 'fore the day's done. We're attacking them rebels from the rear and we'll squeeze their bloody 'eads together."

"We'll take you back to the aid station—get them irons off you."

For the next couple of days Matthew's mind reeled with the stories that filtered back with the men who lay wounded in the large hospital tent. The Americans had been caught unaware of the trap. Thousands had been killed, very few being able to escape through the British lines to the safety of Brooklyn.

Then came the news that filled the British encampment with excitement and anticipation. The American rebels had been pushed to the brink of the river, the remains of their army gathered together in one final defense. There was laughter and celebration in the back encampments. "His lordship is sending the ships up the river to cannon those bastards from one side— we're going to come up from the other side. We hear the rebel leader Washington is caught with them bastards! It's going to be the end of them blokes once and for all!"

Matthew had closed his eyes in pain at the words. Bad enough that he had failed to warn the patriots of the British attack, but now his countrymen and the man who promised them their dreams, George Washington, faced almost certain death. And Matthew was powerless to avert the catastrophe.

He left the camp early the next morning without notifying anyone of his departure. All he knew was that he had to be away when the British claimed their victory. He could not be around when that news came in. And there was only one place he could safely go to where he could find even the hope of comfort. Staten Island. . . .

Colin sighted him from the porch and ran down the path to greet his friend with a squeeze that almost knocked his breath away.

"It's good to be home again." Matthew managed a smile and looked the boy over.

"And it is home!" Colin agreed heartily, as he grabbed Matthew's arm and led him back to the waiting group.

"Back from the wars, eh?" John Page pumped Matthew's arm. "We've been hearing about your victory!"

Matthew was passed on to Lydia Page, who pressed her lips to his cheek. "Matthew," she said, "we have prayed for your safe return."

Matthew was touched by their openness and already knew he had done the right thing by coming here. He gave Martha a quick kiss on the cheek and finally turned to Coleen.

"Matthew," she murmured, her serious expression slowly changing to a happy grin. She hesitated, and then leaned forward and pecked at his cheek, her lips cool and soft. "Oh Matthew," she exclaimed with a gentle smile, "cut up again!" She shook her head. "Maybe one of these days you'll come to us without a battered face."

Before he could answer, John Page led him to a chair and sat down next to him. "And what do the others think of Howe's lax manner at Brooklyn?" Page asked.

"Howe?"

"Oh come, boy," Mr. Page snorted as he leaned forward in his chair and studied Matthew's eyes. "It's all over. Surely you don't side with Howe?"

Matthew looked at Page in bewilderment. "I don't know what you mean, sir."

"Howe allowed Washington and his army to escape," Page replied indignantly. "It was obvious we had the rebels trapped and cornered. Why didn't he attack instead of allowing the rebels to escape to New York?"

"Escape?" Matthew's heart began to race with excitement. "You mean they made it?"

John Page frowned. "Made it? I'd say they were *allowed* to escape. And I'll wager there are plenty of other responsible citizens perfectly aware that Lord Howe deliberately sat back and did nothing to even try to capture those rebels!"

"I don't believe it," Matthew muttered, finding it difficult to hide his joy in the news.

"None of us do," Page continued. "I was hoping you might have been able to shed some light on the subject." It was clear that he was disapointed. "Well, maybe Winslow can defend his commander's actions."

Matthew's eyes shifted to Coleen. "He hasn't been around?" he asked.

"Good God, no!" John Page answered, unaware that Matthew was still watching Coleen. "These soldiers find their military affairs much more interesting than their romantic affairs, I'm afraid."

Matthew shot him a quick respectful glance, but

John Page had turned his attention to his wife. As he returned his gaze to Coleen, he was surprised to see a slight tinge of color in her cheeks and a silent entreaty as she looked up and met his eyes. Matthew debated the meaning of her look and rose hesitantly to step to her chair. "I would deem it an honor if you would walk by my side, Coleen," he said softly.

"A walk?" she inquired, her cheeks still with a touch of crimson.

Matthew drew in a slow breath and looked out at the countryside. "It's a beautiful day—and it's been a long time since I've allowed myself the pleasure of enjoying beauty."

Coleen's look was steady and thoughtful. She knew it was wrong to take a walk with him when she was betrothed to Winslow. But Matthew was like one of the family, she told herself, and she had sorely missed him during his absence. She smiled and nodded. "I am honored," she replied and raised her hand.

27

T HEY WALKED without saying a word, heads bowed as they followed the path that led them through the pastures to the distant shore. The heat of the afternoon began to cool with the breeze that swept in from the harbor. Matthew took a deep breath and looked around. So peaceful, so quiet.

"You said you had something to tell me?" Coleen found a large, smooth rock and climbed on top, spreading her skirt across her dainty black leather shoes and tucking her knees up close under her chin. Her blonde hair cascaded down across her back and shoulders, glistening in the sun like spun caramel.

Matthew remained standing, even more unsure of himself now that they were alone together. "I don't quite know how to say this," he began. He waited, hoping she might have words of encouragement, but she merely stared out into the blue waves, silent and unmoving.

"It was a while back—when I was over on Long Island," Matthew said, watching her profile. "I told myself that no matter what, I would come back to you and tell you my feelings. I didn't want anything to happen to me without your ever knowing how I feel about you."

He saw her stiffen, but she kept her face averted, still gazing out toward the harbor.

"I knew how I felt the first time I ever laid eyes on you," Matthew continued, half afraid that she would try to stop him, that she wouldn't want to hear it all.

"I realize we have different backgrounds, I realize I have no right to expect anything in return from you, but I do feel there is something between us, Coleen. I feel it every time I look into your eyes." He paused, stepping slightly forward to see more of her face. "But I dare not hope for too much. There would be too much disappointment."

Matthew waited, struggling with his emotions. "Damn it, Coleen," he suddenly burst out, "I love you, girl. No man ever loved a woman more. I just had to let you know."

Coleen dropped her head and stared into her lap. Her face was drawn and sad when she finally looked up at him. "Oh, Matthew," she answered softly, "I was so afraid you would do this to me."

Matthew's eyebrows furrowed questioningly. "I don't understand."

She raised her hands in a helpless gesture. "I'm betrothed, Matthew," she explained, her voice catching in pain. "I'm engaged to Winslow and I cannot break it off!"

Matthew stepped forward and grabbed her cold hands in his. "But there's nothing there," he exclaimed. "I know there isn't. I see the two of you together—and you're just two people. Friends at best, but certainly nothing more!"

"Matthew," she answered softly, "Winslow and I are to be married. It's all arranged."

"Coleen," Matthew moaned, reaching out to her and drawing her against his chest as he fell to his knees. She was soft and firm, smelling of the sweetest substance he had ever known. His lips smothered the top of her head with kisses. "Coleen my dearest," he murmured, "you do not love that man. You cannot marry him."

She shook her head back and forth against him, leaving the dampness of tears on his shirt front. "No, not anymore. But it's too late, Matthew," she whispered, choking back a sob.

They held each other until he slowly stood, reaching down and lifting her off the rock to her feet. Her head came just to his chin, and he bent his face close to hers. "I love you so, Coleen," he murmured. "I would be so good to you."

Her hand came up and touched the side of his face, brushing along his cheekbone as she studied the truth in his eyes. "You're so gentle, Matthew," she said almost wonderingly. "I've never known anyone as gentle as you."

His hand found hers and pressed it against his cheek. Then he bent his head further, bringing his lips closer to hers.

"Oh, Matthew," she whispered and tilted her head, rising to her tiptoes.

Their kiss was gentle, their lips pressing ever so softly in that first moment of touch. Slowly, almost reluctantly, her hands crept up his back until they were behind his neck and pulling him down upon her mouth.

His arms encircled her waist and pressed her to him, and she clung as near as she could, fitting her body tightly to his. They were aware of the warmth of each other's bodies; of her breasts, soft and yielding against his hard chest; of their stomachs, pressing together; of their thighs touching, hers separating slightly in surrender to the hardness that he ground first against her stomach and then down into the vee of her legs.

"Oh, Matthew," Coleen moaned, kissing his face, holding him with both hands, their lips wet, their faces hot.

Matthew smothered his face into her neck. He felt he wanted to fold her inside him, to keep her warm, to absorb her being into every nerve-ending he had, to devour her. He couldn't get enough of her.

They sank to the ground. He leaned over her, supporting himself on one elbow while his hand explored the delicate curves and hollows of her forehead, nose and lips. Her face was flushed with desire, and wet with tears and his kisses. Her neck, smelling of lavender, was warm, soft and pliable. The silken bodice felt cold and rough and his hands sought her softness.

She gasped as his fingers folded over one of her breasts. Her back arched slightly, but as his kisses swept over her neck and ear, she sank her face into his shoulder and her body relaxed, settling back onto the sand.

Never had Matthew known such sensations. Her breast spread firmly under his hand and he could feel her body responding. The hardness of her nipple protruded into the center of his palm and he gently circled his hand, presing softly upon her breast, slightly kneading. Her body arched under him, and he heard her gasp as he rolled his leg over hers and dug gently between her thighs. The firmness between his own legs was straining at his britches, the sensation of rubbing against her almost taking his breath away.

When the small pearl buttons of her bodice refused to unfasten, her cool fingers reached down from his face and helped him. Their kisses never ceased as he spread open her top. Her skin was moist, yet there was a softness to it that no clothmaker could ever match. Her nipple stayed hard under his touch and she began to moan. He struggled down so that his head was even with her breast, then slowly bent his head and took the hardness between his lips. Coleen gave a small stifled cry as her hands came up to clutch his head. His tongue snaked out, licked the tip and then flattened down around the circle. He sucked in the softness, still gently but more urgently now.

Coleen gasped, her body stiffening tightly. "We mustn't!" she whispered, gasping again as his lips moved back to the nipple.

"I love you, Coleen," Matthew moaned, "I want you so." He drew himself up close to her face and kissed her lips hungrily. "Say you feel something for me, Coleen."

Her hands caught his face and pushed him away so that she could see him. Her face was wet and flushed, and her green eyes dark as they searched into his. "Matthew," she whispered. "Oh, Matthew, I can't," she moaned and tossed her head back and forth, closing her eyes so she couldn't watch him. "I can't, Matthew. I'm engaged to another."

"Break it," he demanded. "Break it off—do whatever is done, but call it off."

"I can't," she cried, keeping her face turned from

him. "Our engagement has been published and my parents are counting on it. All my friends—"

"But you, Coleen," Matthew urged. "What about you?"

She took in a long, shuddering breath and looked up at him with glistening eyes. "It is too late."

Matthew stared down at her in frustration, then slowly raised himself to a kneeling position. "I don't understand. Didn't you feel something just now? Didn't you feel anything?"

She was up quickly on one elbow, her hand reaching out to touch his face. "Matthew," she said softly, "of course I did." She lowered her head, and when she looked back up at him there was pain and confusion in her face. "I don't know what happened. I truly don't, Matthew. But whatever it was, I can't let it go any further. I want to be true to my husband." She suddenly bowed her head and was silent.

"I thought that what just happened between us was something special," Matthew said quietly.

Her hand reached out and found his. "It was, Matthew. It truly was. I've never done anything like this ever before." She looked searchingly into his face and leaned forward. "It *was* special, Matthew. *You* are special. I shall always remember you—and this moment—for the rest of my life. You must believe me."

He couldn't understand her position, and Coleen leaned forward and squeezed his hand when she saw his misery.

"You're a good man, Matthew," she said, her voice both urgent and pained. "Someday you'll make some woman most happy, I know. And once this war is over, the king will probably end up knighting you, declaring you the hero who saved the colonies from this revolution."

Matthew clamped his eyes shut and drew in a deep breath. She thought of him as a Tory. Of course . . . And what would have happened if she had declared her love for him only to find out that he was a patriot? What a fool he had been.

"I too shall remember this moment," he replied in a low voice. "For I truly do love you, Coleen. You'll probably never know how much." He bowed his head in frustration. "I'm sorry if I pressured you. I never want to cause you hurt or pain."

Coleen smiled softly, her hand touching his shoulder. "You didn't pressure me—nor are you capable of inflicting hurt or pain. You're not that kind, Matthew. But things will never be any different than they are. I'm only glad that I have you for a friend, a true and deep friend."

Matthew kept his eyes to the ground in front of him. He knew he couldn't meet her eyes. Not just yet. He had to have time to heal a bit. But he would never forget this moment. Not for one minute would he ever forget.

28

FOR TWO WEEKS Matthew kept away from the Waterford house and barn. His excuse to Colin and Martha was that he was needed at the Staten Island British encampment.

"Spy business, you know," he said as he packed the remainder of his things.

"But surely they don't need you all night," Colin objected.

Matthew grinned and winked at his young friend. "And surely you don't need me around at night, either." He had already stumbled upon Colin and Martha in bed, and wondered how they had gotten past the watchful eye of Coleen.

"Matthew," Colin answered seriously, placing a loving arm around Martha, "I hope it isn't because of us that you're leaving."

"No." Matthew looked around the small room to make sure he hadn't forgotten anything. "I'm glad you two are together. You make a fine couple."

"Of course my parents don't know of this arrangement," Colin said.

"But they suspect," Martha added wisely.

Colin shrugged. "I don't care. We shall be married as soon as this war is over. In the meantime, I see nothing wrong with what we're doing."

"I see no reason why you two shouldn't enjoy each other either." Matthew said, "and I don't judge you for it."

"I think Coleen sees it as a sin," Colin said with a wide grin. "At any rate, there's not much she can do about it."

Matthew glanced up at the loft, wondering if she was up there listening. The softness of her skin still burned on his lips.

She was his reason for leaving, although he had convinced himself that he was needed elsewhere. The British had made no attempt to get in touch with him, which suited his purpose just fine. He walked along Statan Island's shoreline, appearing absorbed in the water's edge, in stones, in his own thoughts, but eying the encampments and the unending activity of the boats in the harbor.

Most of the troops and provisions were now being ferried across the narrows to Long Island. The huge force of battleships slowly sailed past to head either up the Hudson or the East River, the dull thuds of their cannon tumbling back across the water as the ships bombarded the patriotic defenses on the Manhattan and New Jersey shores. Matthew knew he should relocate to Long Island, where the British command was stationed. Only his hunger for Coleen kept him on Staten Island, and he finally began to feel the futility of staying on any longer.

It was the day he had finally decided to act. With heavy heart Matthew had trudged to the Waterfords' house to say his goodbyes to the Pages. He had just walked through the front gate when he spied the brown-garbed figure on the porch rocker. Even from that distance, the red hair was unmistakable.

"Nathan!" Matthew exclaimed in a hushed voice, glancing around to see if anyone else was nearby.

"It's Samuel now." Nathan Hale grinned, shaking Matthew's hand firmly. "Samuel Johnson."

"Not very original of you," Matthew laughed.

The red-haired schoolteacher shrugged. "It was the first thing I could think of when I introduced myself to your friends."

Matthew grabbed him by the elbow and walked to the edge of the yard. "How did you get here? And how did you manage to find me?"

Nathan grimaced and leaned against the fence. "It was not easy, my friend, but General Washington gave me several names you had given to him. It was not that difficult to locate the Pages once I was here on Staten Island."

"Washington?" Matthew could feel the excitement boiling in his veins.

"He's desperate. We haven't heard a thing on what the British are doing. It's been almost a month since our defeat, and the British still haven't made any moves. There's just the occasional shelling from their blasted ships."

"But surely his other spies have found out something."

"Apparently not. Neither Washington nor Congress can figure out why Howe hasn't attacked New York yet. With water on both sides, there's no way to defend the city. That's as far as the British will get, of course. I guarantee you that!"

"And what does he need from me?" Matthew asked.

"Anything. We're desperate for information." Nathan suddenly grinned. "You must see how desperate they are if all they could find is someone like me to look for you."

Matthew studied him seriously and shook his head. "You volunteered, didn't you? No one else would be mad enough to come through such British strength."

"Let's just say that I've come to agree with you— military life *can* be quite boring. I wasn't doing anything. I was actually very glad to get into this spy business, even though I've yet to learn all the tricks of the trade."

Matthew clapped him on the shoulder. "Well, you must be pretty good, Nathan. You've made it this far at least."

"It's the getting back that worries me."

Matthew laughed softly. "You've come just in time. I was going to tell my friends I had to leave. I was going over to Long Island to gather information."

"Then my timing is perfect."

Their timing was not perfect from there on. For one thing, Matthew missed the one person he had really wanted to say goodbye to; Coleen had departed with the Waterfords for some shopping. Colin and Martha had disappeared somewhere along the shoreline, and only the elder Pages were at home to receive his goodbyes.

Their timing was little better on Long Island. They had found an almost deserted countryside. "But where is everyone?" Matthew asked a sergeant standing guard over boxes of provisions.

"New York," the man replied, missing the exchange of alarmed glances between Matthew and Hale. "Ol' Black Dick landed on Manhattan a couple of days ago."

"My god, we're too late," Nathan exclaimed as soon as they were out of earshot.

"Nothing's lost yet," Matthew said with determination. "We can still gather information. But we should act fast."

They walked a long distance without talk. Off to the right, Matthew could make out the distant Jamaica Pass where he had been so near death. Ahead of them were the passes used by the British to drive back the American forces.

"Do you know New York?" Matthew finally asked, trying to map out his course of action.

"I was just a lad when I visited. I have a distant cousin who owns a tavern there."

"Do you know where it is?" He glanced over at Nathan and saw the red head bob up and down. "Good. If anything should go wrong and we separate, we shall meet there."

"It's called the Cedar Tavern. My cousin's name is Samuel Hale."

"Can he be trusted?"

"He's my cousin," Nathan answered, giving Matthew a quizzical look. "He's family."

Matthew smiled and shook his head. "You *are* new to this business, aren't you? The safest thing is not to trust anyone, not even family."

"But this is different, my friend," Nathan responded good-naturedly. "The Hale family has very close ties."

"All right then," Matthew agreed, "we shall meet

there." He glanced again at his friend. "You really don't know much about spying, do you?" he asked cautiously.

"No one had much time to tell me anything. All I've known to do so far is not to wear my uniform, and not to give my name."

"You might as well give your true name. It's harder to remember a false one." He sighed as they continued their walk. "There's so much to warn you about and so little time . . ."

New York was virtually British-held. Rumor had it that General Clinton was as far north as Kips Bay. Murray's Hill was captured, as well as both sides of Manhattan on the Hudson and the East rivers. A contingent of Americans had been stranded at the toe of Manhattan, but had been lucky enough to escape through the swamps and low hills in the middle of the British forces.

"By God, we made it," Nathan whispered as they walked through the deserted streets of the city after Matthew had talked their way by a patrol of Highlanders he had recognized from Long Island.

"Don't even say it," Matthew warned. "Remember, you're a British subject now. You've got to think like them. It's their city now, and it's the 'damn rebels.'"

"Damned rebels, is it?" Hale muttered. "Tell me, how can you stay so calm and think that way, Matthew?"

He had to think seriously about his answer. "Maybe it's because I've lived with them. Maybe it's because I'm not always so damned sure whose side I'm on." He shrugged at Hale's look of astonishment. "Don't worry, Nathan. I'm a patriot. It's just that I can't quite bring myself to hate the Tories as completely as some of the rebels do."

They spent the next day drawing maps of the British breastworks along the river, estimating the number of cannon that were being towed from their positions at the bottom of the city to the new British lines in the north.

"I hear the fighting, Matthew," Nathan said, looking out from their position on the roof of the abandoned barn, "and I don't like it. My comrades are out there in the thick of battle, while I'm here, hiding, obscured from any danger."

"It won't be much longer, Nathan," Matthew answered, glancing at the large mass of troops off to their right. "It looks as though Howe has finally placed his troops and you can take these notes back to Washington."

Nathan was silent as he listened to the sharp crackle of musket fire and the dull reports of cannon in the distance. "People are dying out there, Matthew," he murmured. "Look at those red coats—so many, so many."

It was growing dark when they stepped out of the barn door and started back toward the town. "The stink of war," Nathan remarked, wrinkling his nose at the air. "Smoke, gunpowder and death."

"Mostly smoke," Matthew said. "Look!" He pointed to their right toward the river. A black mass of smoke billowed skyward from the waterfront.

"By God, they've set New York afire!"

By the time they had made their way into the heart of the city, most of the town was ablaze. The streets were filled with screaming and pushing crowds, running about helplessly. It was a panic and Matthew and Nathan had to struggle to keep their footing. They pulled apart flailing and clutching arms and hands, hurtling themselves through the mass of hysteria.

"We've got to get you to the river," Matthew shouted out to his friend. "We've got to find you a boat to ferry across."

Nathan nodded his understanding. "I'll follow you," he shouted out.

It was several blocks before Matthew turned to make sure Nathan was behind him, but his friend was nowhere to be seen in the crowd. "Nathan!" he shouted, but his voice was drowned out by the noise of the mob. "Nathan!"

Matthew looked for some signal as he was tossed about in the crush of panicked New Yorkers.

A hand reached out and grabbed at him, a grimy face raised up and angrily shouted at Matthew. "Goddamn rebels set fire to our city!"

Matthew pushed the man aside, his eyes still searching out his friend's face. "Nathan!" He started back, shoving through the tide of people who surged down the street. "Nathan!"

He stopped and looked around beside a building that was as yet untouched by the raging fire. Nathan Hale was nowhere in sight. He kept calling out his name but it was fruitless.

Matthew took a deep breath to clear his head. There was only one thing to do. Somewhere in this city was the Cedar Tavern owned by one Samuel Hale, cousin to Nathan. It was his only hope.

It took Matthew far longer than he had expected to find the tavern. He had to fight his way through desperate crowds and avoid the fire, and many of the landmarks he was looking for had been destroyed in the blaze. It was well into the early morning hours before Matthew stumbled into the Cedar Tavern.

"Hold there!" A red-coated corporal reached out and grabbed him. Matthew looked about in confusion. The room was filled with a handful of armed soldiers. In their grasp, Nathan Hale stood tall and proud.

"Nathan!" Matthew gasped and yanked his arm free. "What's going on?"

Nathan cast him a cold smile. "Poor boy," he said his voice amazingly clear and steady. "Please do not think ill of me 'cause I hoodwinked you."

Nathan addressed the soldiers nearest him. "I'm afraid I was using this poor lad. Being new to the city, I asked him to act as my guide. And while he showed me around, I jotted down a few things of interest, as you've already discovered."

"Spy!" the corporal snapped out, his hand lashing out against Nathan's head. "You not only make plans of our fortifications, but you set fire to our city."

Nathan raised his head and stared down at the military figure. "My good man, the city is not yours. It is ours, or it is no one's."

Matthew listened in shock. "Corporal—"

The soldier whipped around to glare at Matthew. "So help me, you be quiet. You've done quite enough." He stared at Matthew angrily. "That is, unless you want the same fate as this spy will be getting."

Matthew glanced up at Nathan and met his cold blue eyes. There was a stern look from the redhead, warning him to remain quiet. "I—"

"You're in enough trouble for aiding a spy," the corporal barked out. "Now, unless you want us to bring you in too, keep out of our business!"

Matthew knew what he had to do, but the urge to speak out was unbearable. His fists and jaw were tightly clenched as he shifted his gaze to Nathan.

"You'd best do as the man says," Nathan responded in a casual manner. He looked around at the quiet saloon. "I know what has to be done. And you, my innocent young friend, I am sure you too have the inner strength to do what you know must be done."

"That'll be enough of you!" The corporal stepped forward and shoved Nathan backward to be grabbed by the other men. "We'll be taking you to headquarters. I'm sure they know what to do with spies!"

Matthew could feel the swelling of anger and pain in the back of his throat and he tried to swallow it down. There was but the briefest exchange of glances as Nathan marched past him and out the door.

The corporal looked around to make sure his men had left. He then turned to a tall redheaded man standing behind the counter. "Thank you, my friend," he called out and tossed the man a small leather bag.

Matthew stared in shock at Nathan's cousin. So this was family, was it?

He swirled around and grabbed at the corporal's red coat just before he stepped out the door. "What's going to happen to him?" he asked hoarsely.

There was a mocking grin on the corporal's face as he shook free of Matthew's grip. "What do you think we do with spies?" he snarled. "Hang him."

Matthew was oblivious to the laughter of the soldier as he disappeared into the night. He was oblivious to almost everything around him except the pounding of his heart and the anger that seemed to rise from his stomach and spread over his body. There it was in all its ugliness. Hatred. He had found the enemy and he hated.

29

HE ARRIVED too late. The crowd had already dispersed and there were only a few small children running about, their parents sitting on the grass, picnic baskets spread before them. They paid little heed to the horse cart that was just pulling away from the gallows, a long wooden casket in its bed.

Matthew watched until the car rounded a far corner and was gone from sight. It didn't seem possible. It had happened so quickly and he would still be waiting outside the garrison walls if not for the idle chatter of some guards.

A spy was to be hanged, they had said. A heathen rebel spy caught setting fire to their city. A self-confessed spy with copies of British fortifications and positions. There had been both admiration and a morbid glee in their voices.

Matthew grabbed hold of a tree trunk to steady himself as the sickening heaviness of truth swept through his body. Slowly, he sank to his knees, his head sliding along the smooth bark, his eyes moistening. Oh, Nathan . . . Oh, my dear friend . . .

Matthew carried that memory with him as he made for Connecticut. He knew he had to get away, from New York, from the British, from Washington, from the war, from everything. He was tired! God, how he was tired! Somehow he didn't care who won the battle. He didn't care about anything—not even Coleen, he told himself.

It felt good to be home, to see the small house, the neatly trimmed lawn and the smiling faces of those he cared about. He knew Deborah sensed something was wrong with him. She stepped away after receiving his hug and eyed him with that "what's wrong" look she had, but there would be time for talk later.

His father was older and it saddened him to see the shoulders sunk forward, the back that once was straight as oak now humped and bent. Had he been gone that long?

Mark was much the same. He had fashioned a wooden leg for himself and could get about with amazing agility. He was still every inch the ardent young patriot. "You mean you just up and left the fighting?" he asked aghast. "You left 'em? But the damn British are driving Washington out of New York. Maybe you could have helped."

Matthew sighed and stretched his tired feet out in front of him, content to stare at the toes of his boots while answering. "Washington had already given up New York, Mark," he replied. "There was no way he could stop them."

"By God," Mark exclaimed fiercely, "give him a few good men and we'd stop them redcoats."

"Good men die too," Matthew answered moodily, feeling suddenly sad and alone.

"Is that what's wrong, Matthew?" Deborah asked, as she sank to her knees in front of him and took his hands in hers. Her grasp was tight. "Is that what's wrong?" She searched into his eyes. "It is, isn't it?"

Matthew returned her look and nodded, not daring to speak.

Deborah bent forward and folded her arms about him, holding him tightly, rocking him gently, saying nothing. Matthew clamped his eyes shut tightly and fought back the tears. . . .

It was the next day that he finally mustered up the strength to tell them about Nathan Hale. Once that tale was told, so came the rest of his story. Or parts of it. But he could not tell them he was a spy, and the web became more and more complicated as he tried to account for the time he'd spent away from home. He hated the lies, the half-truths, and finally, in the middle of a tale, he stopped and looked at them in sullen defeat and stormed out of the house. It was no good, not with his own family. He was through with the lies, the poses and evasions. No more . . .

There was no mention of the war from then on. Matthew dived into the business of coopering as though he had never been away, and for the next few months he pushed himself as hard as he had ever done.

"You should go out, Matthew," Deborah said one evening as they strolled down the path near their home. Already the air had the sharpness that foretold an early winter, and she buried her head into the collar of her coat and hooked her arm through his for warmth.

"And what about you?" he asked good-naturedly. "I never see you go out."

She laughed. "And who would I go out with? There isn't an eligible man anywhere for miles around. The war, remember?"

"What about your John Langley Hunter?" he asked. "Haven't you been seeing him?"

There was a pause before she answered in a soft serious voice. "He writes as often as he can, but travel is difficult with the war." They had taken several more steps before she continued. "I'll see him again— as soon as he has a chance to get away."

"I'm sure you will," Matthew answered confidently. "But there has been no one else?"

She shook her head and turned hesitantly to him. "And what about you? You have not found anyone?"

Matthew debated whether he should go into it. "I found someone," he finally answered, "someone very special. Unfortunately, she comes from a Tory family."

"Oh, Matthew," Deborah responded, "that should make little difference. We were all Tories not too long ago. Certainly politics aren't going to get in your way, are they?"

"She doesn't know I'm *not* a Tory," he said quietly, refusing to look down at his sister for her reaction.

"But how can that be? She doesn't know you're a patriot?"

"It's a complicated story," Matthew answered, "made even more complicated by the fact that she's already betrothed. It's a problem I'll just have to get over," he concluded, forcing a lighter tone.

Deborah chose to remain silent for a few moments.

"You know that Chaning Wilson is still unattached."

"I'm afraid I'm past the Chaning Wilsons," he said wryly. "I'm past quite a few things."

Coleen Page was not one of those things dismissed so easily. The first snows came, the last month of the year came and still his dreams and idle thoughts were of Coleen. Surely she must be married by now. Did she ever think of him, he wondered?

"Matthew Bell?" The officer stepped forward, his hand reaching for Matthew's. "My name is Colonel Thomas French. I'm on General Washington's staff." He said the last with a meaningful look, eyes steady on Matthew's.

"Colonel!" Matthew hesitated, conscious of Deborah and Mark silently watching them from their chairs in the living room.

"Perhaps I might have a word with you—in private?" The officer gave a slight bow to Matthew's brother and sister.

Deborah caught on immediately. She grabbed Mark's arm and pulled him out of the room. "Come, Mark," she said to the youth, "I want a word with you."

The colonel waited until the door was closed, then stepped closer to Matthew. "We've been looking for you for some time now," he said in a low voice. "It was the general himself who suggested you might have returned to your home." His disdain for Matthew was obvious, but Matthew only returned his stare defiantly.

"Well," the officer said wearily; "now that I've found you, I have been asked by the general to give you certain instructions."

Matthew eyed the man warily. "Since when does the general send others to do his work?"

There was impatience in French's voice as he responded. "Since the general found it impossible to run around the countryside looking for you. Since the general has been somewhat occupied trying to keep the British down. Since the general has taken to riding up and down the front lines in full view of the enemy, without so much as a farthing for his own safety, because that is what he believes a leader should do for the morale of his men. Since the general—"

Matthew raised a hand and shook his head with a grimace of embarrassment. "All right," he murmured, "I understand. I was only surprised because in the past he's always done this sort of thing himself."

"Of course," French answered, reaching inside his jacket to extract a folded piece of paper. "Which is why he wrote this letter of introduction."

Matthew unfolded the document and read it through twice before nodding and handing it back to French. "He speaks most highly of you, Colonel."

"We can get down to business then?"

"We can get down to why you were sent here, Colonel," Matthew answered with a slight smile. "But whether or not I accept this mission will be *my* decision."

Colonel Thomas French nodded and pulled Matthew over to the small sofa. "General Washington wanted me to tell you he wouldn't be asking you to take on this mission if he didn't feel it was of the utmost importance and that he had no one else to turn to." French drew in a deep breath and leaned forward. "General Charles Lee has been captured by the enemy," he said, his voice almost a whisper.

"Lee?" Matthew asked incredulously.

"He was captured by his old regiment, in fact. A stupid mistake, but that's past and done for. As you probably know, the general regards Lee as his most valuable leader, and his capture poses a great threat."

"I realize Lee was the best tactical man we had," Matthew said, "but surely the general has just as capable men left."

"We have many capable leaders, Mr. Bell. But few with the military training and know-how of Charles Lee. We need every intelligent mind we can get, more now than ever. Washington feels that losing Lee is like losing an entire army."

"And just what is it that I'm supposed to do?" Matthew asked slowly.

French drew in a deep breath and straightened himself. "The general asks that you return to New York City where Lee is imprisoned, and see if there's a way we can get him out."

"But he must be guarded by hundreds!"

"It will not be an easy task, we realize," French answered, "but we have to try. The general feels that your experience and the contacts that you've established might be especially helpful in finding a way to free Lee. That, my young sir, is quite a compliment."

Matthew felt a small thrill that drew him toward the mission, an excitement he thought he had discarded several months ago.

"The city is British held now?" he asked.

"They control most of the island now. In fact, most of the original Tory families have moved back from Staten Island."

Matthew started at the news but made no reply.

"There are others, of course," French said after a long silence, "but none equipped as you. Time is of the essence, Mr. Bell, and the general has made it clear you are the most fit." There was a hesitation as though he had saved the best for last. "We're not saying we shall lose because of Lee's capture, nor are we saying we shall win if we have Lee back. We're saying that our spine is broken and it will heal much faster if we have Lee back with us."

Matthew struggled within himself. He already knew he would go and he wondered why he had succumbed so quickly. Was it Coleen who drew him back to New York, or was it some other need, just as compelling?

30

I T DIDN'T seem possible that a little over a year had passed since he had first met Coleen, at the Page's Christmas party. Matthew stood across the street from the familiar structure where he had been accepted as family. The snow fell gently against his face as he blew into his cupped hands for warmth. His feet were wet from having trudged through the snow drifts of the first January blizzard.

There were dim lights cascading down upon the silver shadows from the front windows. Matthew wondered whether the Pages had found their home intact when they had returned. Was Coleen there? Was her major?

The city had changed. There were only traces of the American defense works along the river fronts. There were ruins of barns and warehouses, including Mahler's cooperage, which had been destroyed in the cannon fire of the British warships. And there was still the charred evidence of the horrible fire from that summer. British and Hessian troops had swarmed in to scavenge whatever they could for the winter in the name of King George. The soldiers' families had come next, along with the Tory families from Staten Island. New York was firmly a British stronghold.

Yet Matthew felt safe there. He was sure his identity as a Tory was secure, and he was confident he could rely on the Pages' endorsement if he were questioned. He had no reason to believe Major Whitehead suspected him as a double agent. He had not seen the major since the Battle of Long Island, but there was nothing to link him with the Americans. His only real problem was the intense anger that began to boil at the memory of Nathan Hale. The man's death was still etched too deeply in his mind to forgive or forget.

Matthew turned away from the Page house and slowly walked back to the Waterfront. He couldn't bring himself to go to the door. Not quite yet.

The old boarding house was very different from what he remembered. Raucous laughter filtered from the stairwell and there was a stench of stale ale. The door to Martha's apartment opened at Matthew's knock, and a beefy red-faced man peered out. "We're filled up," he said gruffly. He started to close the door but Matthew held it ajar.

"Where's Martha?" he asked.

"Martha?"

"Yes, the owner of this building, Martha Dundee." Matthew tried to peer over the man's massive bulk. The once neat and tidy room was now cluttered with clothes, boxes, and brightly colored material. Two women, one naked except for bloomers, were sprawled on the couch.

"She don't own this place. I do!" The man's eyes narrowed suspiciously.

"Did she sell it to you?"

The big man sneered. "I got this place fair and legal. What's it to you, anyhow?"

"Martha is a friend of mine. I'm trying to locate her."

The man laughed. "She's down at canvas town, most likely. Or shacked up with some gent. It's about the only way any gal's going to survive here." He winked at Matthew and jerked his head toward his room. "Ain't a bad setup to be in, eh? I can also earn me a few extra quid off them once in a while."

He saw Matthew's look of distaste and called out to him as he left the building. "Don't knock it, pure-heart. You'll be swimming in the filth like all of us soon enough. It's the only way of surviving in this town. You'll see!"

The night air smelled good and the silence was welcome as Matthew walked away from the boarding house. He wondered what had happened to Martha and Colin, whether they were still together. He had money in his pocket, a generous amount Colonel French had given him before leaving Wethersfield. But he had already discovered that funds would deplete quickly in this city. The prices of everything in New York had soared beyond belief. It was a good excuse for him to turn to the Pages for help. Besides, if he was going to find General Lee, where better to start than with John Page and Major Whitehead?

Coleen opened the door at his knock and the two stared at each other silently. She had changed. There was a maturity about her, and now she resembled her mother more than ever before. The sparkle in her

green eyes was missing, and instead there was knowledge and a certain sadness. She was no longer a young
girl and he ached to know what pain had caused that
transition.

The whole house had changed. Furniture was missing, as well as the vases, paintings and knickknacks
that had decorated the rooms. And the elder Pages had
changed. John Page had greyed considerably in that
short time. There was a haggard, desperate look about
him, a strained and almost apologetic smile as he
greeted Matthew.

Lydia Page's bearing was proud and straight as
always, but there was a self-consciousness about her.
It was almost like a tarnished heirloom trying valiantly to retain its glory but unable to hide the dents
and flaws that came with age and mistreatment.

"Matthew." Lydia Page offered her cheek. "You
have found us once again."

"I do seem much like a homing pigeon, don't I?" he
responded with a forced smile. "I'm afraid one of these
days I'll find my roost either locked up or barred."

"No, no, my dear," Lydia Page answered, leading
him to a couch. "You shall always be welcome in our
house or wherever we are . . . But please tell us where
you've been all this time, what you've been doing."

He kept his story short, telling them that he had
wandered about with his red-haired friend until his
friend had met with an accident and had died. Sad-
ened, Matthew had returned home to Wethersfield,
only to return to New York.

"Ah, you poor boy," Lydia consoled with a pat of
her hand on his. "They still won't forgive you for not
becoming a rebel?"

Matthew dropped his head. How he hated to lead
these people on with a lie. "I found it better to leave,"

he answered, hoping it would satisfy her curiosity. Then he quickly brightened. "But I'm glad that you're back in your home."

Lydia Page glanced at her husband and waited for his reply. There was something wrong that they weren't telling him. He could tell by the way they exchanged hurried glances. He could tell by the way John Page stood by the empty fireplace, with head down, unmoving, and by Coleen's uncharacteristic quiet and reserve.

Matthew waited until the silence was too much for him. "I feel that I have come at an inconvenient time. Perhaps I should be on my way." He got up to leave, but all three stood up and spoke out.

"No, please, Matthew. You're welcome to stay." He waited, eyeing each one quizzically until they dropped their eyes.

"Something is wrong," he said hesitantly. "If it's nothing I've done or said, then perhaps it's something I may be of help with." He waited again before saying, "I *want* to help."

There was a long pause. Lydia Page kept her head down, her fingers interlaced in her lap. Coleen's head was also bowed until she glanced over at her father.

John Page frowned. "I'm sorry if we don't seem our usual selves tonight, Matthew," he answered in a deliberate voice. "But as you can see for yourself, these are not the best of times." His voice shook and he looked about the half-vacant room with glistening eyes. "In fact, these are very bad times. We've had to—had to sell some of our belongings to make things work out."

"We were forced to!" Coleen broke out, correcting her father. She turned to Matthew, and for the first time there was a spark of life in her eyes. "It was the only way we could get our house back. We had to sell our things so the authorities could find the proper papers."

John Page coughed and raised a hand for her to be quiet. "The people in charge have gotten a bit out of hand," he said slowly. "They're blackmailing, threatening and robbing us all."

"Can't the military do something about this?" Matthew asked.

"Military!" John Page snorted in contempt. "They're even worse. Soldiers are running about the streets without restraint. I hear New Jersey has become worse than Staten Island ever was."

"Certainly Major Whitehead has some influence," Matthew said, aghast at what he was hearing.

He noted the strain in Coleen's eyes as she glanced quickly at him, then dropped her head in silence.

"Winslow has apparently been very busy," John Page finally volunteered, with a definite note of sarcasm in his voice. "That is, he's been too busy to see his betrothed."

"Father!" Coleen said sharply. "I told you I had given him his freedom back."

John Page turned to Matthew with a disdainful look. "Our daughter," he explained in a controlled voice, "has given the major an opportunity to back down from their engagement."

Matthew shot Coleen a startled look. "You've broken off your engagement?"

"I have given him the opportunity to change his mind," she answered proudly.

John Page gave a humorless laugh. "He's been seen accompanying other women to the theater and cotillions," he said.

"Father," Coleen whispered, red-faced, "that doesn't mean Winslow has done anything other than act as an escort."

"With those painted whores?" her father exclaimed. "For a man betrothed to so openly display his appetite is completely lacking in manners and sensibility."

"And that is why I've allowed him to break the engagement if he so desires," Coleen answered wearily, sounding as though this had been a recurring argument with her father.

"If he so desires?" John Page said angrily. "No man shall treat my daughter disrespectfully. You should have broken that engagement yourself—not given him a choice."

"But Father," she exclaimed, "he's done us many favors and I—" she hesitated, realizing her mistake. She glanced at Matthew and reddened.

"You shouldn't stay engaged to a man merely because he knows the right people," Matthew said quietly, not daring to let himself hope too much.

"That's my point of view also, Matthew," her father responded. "I am not one of those fathers who marries off his daughters for wealth or advancement. I, for one, hope a marriage is conceived in love. If it is, everything else will come along." He looked at his wife and smiled.

"I agree," Matthew said after a moment of silence. "Love should be the most important thing between a man and a woman. It's what you feel about each other that's important."

Coleen looked up at him, her face going white, and then glanced quickly at her mother and father. With a startled cry she ran from the room.

John Page looked after her in amazement. "Well,"

he said, "maybe the lass still has feeling for Winslow." He shook his head sadly. "I don't know, I just don't know."

Matthew was perplexed himself. He had seen some hope in the thought that Coleen had been sacrificing herself, that she had planned to marry a man she no longer loved in order to insure her family's safety in these difficult times. But perhaps she still felt more for Whitehead than she would admit. Not once had Coleen given any hint that she even welcomed Matthew back. Not once a hint that she remembered what they had shared that summer day on Staten Island. Not even once had she shown any interest in where or what he had been doing.

"I haven't seen Colin or Martha," he said after a prolonged silence.

John Page coughed uncomfortably. "Colin no longer lives with us," he commented gruffly.

"What happened?"

There was a loud sigh before Page answered. "I told Colin we could not have that woman living with us once we came back to New York." He paused before adding, "So the two of them walked out on us."

Matthew was alarmed. "You asked them to leave?"

Page glared angrily at Matthew. "What in the name of God was I supposed to do? Allow that woman to stay under our roof, living in sin with Colin?"

It was Matthew who now became angry. "That woman's name is Martha, Martha Dundee. She is a decent human being who loves your son dearly, and he loves her." Matthew grimaced in annoyance. "I do not understand you. In one breath you tell Coleen she should only marry a man if she loves him. And in the next breath you're telling me that Colin and Martha shouldn't be together because they love each other? Frankly, sir, I do not understand your reasoning!"

"My reasoning is perfectly obvious," John Page answered, his voice rising. "That woman is a prostitute."

"*Was* a prostitute," Matthew corrected, trying to calm his anger. "I once explained to your daughter that there are people today holding high positions whose pasts have been far worse than Martha's. And there are people whose ancestors settling this land were harlots and criminals. You know that as well as anyone. People change, sir. It isn't what any of us were, but what we are now!"

"I shall not have a member of my family associated with a sordid past," John Page answered loudly.

Matthew went cold at the words. In spite of the love Page felt for his son, he had all but disowned him—and all because of meaningless conventions. What if Page knew Matthew was a patriot? That too must seem sordid to the man. And perhaps no less sordid to his daughter, he reminded himself.

Matthew stared heatedly at John Page and then wordlessly swung about and left the room.

31

"MR. BELL," Major Whitehead did not bother to rise from his desk, but leaned back in the chair, one hand tapping the wooden desktop as he stared at Matthew. "We thought you were dead."

"Not far from it," Matthew said. He was conscious that it took even greater effort than in the past to affect loyalty and respect. His contempt for the Tories was complete now, and only added to the disdain he had long felt for the pompous Whitehead. His job was to obtain information for Washington and this time he felt almost elated about his mission. "Dudley and I were captured. We made our escape but he died of a wound. By the time I got back, you had gone on."

There was a long pause, the tapping stopping only

a second before continuing. Matthew found himself staring at the fingers.

"Go on."

Matthew shrugged. "I went back to Staten Island. I knew you would find me there if you needed me. Then I decided to go home for a visit."

"And did they accept you with open arms?" Whitehead asked, a slight sneer on his lips.

For a brief moment Matthew felt like slapping the smug face but he had an act to follow. "I'm back here —for good now."

"These rebels are a stubborn lot, Mr. Bell, just like your family. But once the war is over and we've instituted some firm laws and punishments, they'll come about to our ways. Mark my word, you'll return to your little hamlet, Mr. Bell, as a hero. If you play your cards right you might even be given a position in your town that will bring in ample rewards. His Majesty rewards his servants most kindly—remember that, Mr. Bell."

"I've always tried my best, without regard to reward," Matthew said, having learned by now what the major most liked to hear. It had become almost a game to Matthew to see how smarmy he could be without raising Whitehead's suspicion. Suppressing a smile, he added, "I feel it's the least I can do for England in these troubled times."

"Well put," the major answered. He began to shuffle papers, indicating that he was finished with Matthew.

"I was wondering if there was any further need of my services," Matthew asked.

Whitehead arched an eyebrow. "This is winter, my dear boy. It's a time to relax and prepare for the spring."

Matthew cocked his head and put on an air of disappointment. "I was hoping there might be some kind of a job. I've found it difficult to find lodging and work."

"My dear man, both lodging and work are scarce here in the city. There's over thirty thousand people and only ten thousand jobs, and that's just for the civilians. There are almost a hundred thousand soldiers spread over the countryside with nothing to do until the spring, and clamoring to keep them occupied. I don't have time for you, not today."

Matthew stared at the major as he bent his head over his work. Whitehead was the only avenue to General Lee. He had only one chance. "I've heard there are jobs guarding prisoners," he lied. "I was hoping you could give me a letter."

Major Whitehead looked up at Matthew and studied him in surprise. "You want to work at the prison?"

"It's a job," Matthew answered. "It would help."

Again Whitehead studied him in silence, then reached for a piece of paper. "Well, if that's what you want, I'll write a letter of introduction. That's all I can do."

"That will be more than enough," Matthew answered with a pleased smile. "Your name carries quite a bit of weight."

"The Commissioner of Prisoners is a Mr. Joshua Loring," Whitehead said as he finished with the letter. "A warning, lad," he said with a stern look, "or perhaps some advice. Getting a job at the prison will depend upon whether Loring thinks you'll be of value to him. He's an ambitious man, if you know what I mean. You should be able to take advantage of that." He smiled as he creased the paper and handed it over to Matthew. "Also—I shall consider you still to be my man, is that clear? Anything you ever hear that may be of some use to me, I'll expect your report. These rebel prisoners might be of some use to us."

The fool, Matthew thought, containing the smile on his lips. Whitehead thought he was turning the favor to his own advantage, but it was possible he had unwittingly given Matthew the one bit of knowledge he most needed. "Ah, one more thing, sir, if you don't mind," Matthew said. "I was wondering if you know the whereabouts of Colin Page."

"Colin?" There was the slightest tinge of annoyance in Whitehead's eyes. "The Pages have moved back to New York, of course."

"Yes, I know," Matthew answered. "But I failed to ask them where Colin might be."

"The last I heard of the boy was when he came to me asking for work, just like you." The last was said with open sarcasm.

'And do you remember where you might have sent him, sir?" Matthew inquired, beginning to struggle with the false humbleness.

"The last I heard, he was a houseboy for one of Lord Howe's aides," Whitehead said impatiently. "And now, if you don't mind, I have work to do."

Matthew bowed and stepped back out of the office. He had learned enough and his heart skipped. If Colin was indeed close to Black Dick's headquarters, then Matthew had found a way into the British stronghold! Things were working out far better than he had hoped.

Joshua Loring was of average height, with black wisps of hair carefully brushed over his balding head, and small, darting eyes set close in his round face. Matthew knew at first glance that he didn't like the man.

"Where are you from, Mr. Bell?" Loring asked as he scanned the letter of introduction.

Matthew answered, studying the man as he reread the letter with his head bent close to the paper.

"Your family, Mr. Bell, are they affluent?"

Matthew smiled. "No, sir. My father is a cooper."

Loring bit his lip and sat back in his chair, eying Matthew over square-rimmed spectacles that were set on the tip of his nose. "A cooper, eh?" He hesitated, then looked at the paper again. "You work for Major Whitehead? You're a spy?"

"You're very good, sir," he answered. He felt he had better stroke the man's ego. "I've done some spying for the major. But there's little work to be done just now, and I'm starving along with the rest of New York."

Loring laughed. "Aren't we all though? So why did you come here? We don't pay much."

"The major thought I might be of some use to him if I worked with some of the prisoners," he said, assuming Loring would catch the meaning behind his words. This approach might be dangerous if the two men ever got together, but it was a chance that Matthew had to take. "I understand you have General Charles Lee. Congratulations!"

"I have Charles Lee?" Loring laughed all the louder. "Do you think his lordship would let such a personage rot with the rest of 'em? Lee is a special guest of his lordship. Why, he's better cared for than I am. Can you believe that? Bloody rebel bastard is being treated like some foreign dignitary. T'ain't fair, I say, bloody bastard!"

Matthew was taken aback. He hadn't expected this new information. As he was contemplating what to do Loring began to laugh again.

"I bet you were expecting to sit soft and pretty watching Lee, weren't you? That would be a soft job now, wouldn't it? Especially with him getting all those special privileges. You see," Loring continued, wiping his eyes and trying to suppress his laughter, "that's exactly the way I had it figured, too."

Matthew joined in with the laughter, beginning to understand more about Joshua Loring. Suddenly, he stopped and leaned forward, grabbing the man's sleeve to quiet him. "But there's more than that," Matthew said confidentially. "My real reason for being close to Lee is that we've heard that he knows exactly what Washington's plans are going to be come spring. If we can latch onto those plans, Lord Howe will be able to capture the entire rebel army."

"And just how are you thinking on loosening Lee's lips?" Loring asked. "Howe hasn't been able to do it yet, and there's no way he'll allow someone of Lee's rank to be tortured."

"That's what I was sent to find out," Matthew answered. "If I could find out Lee's weaknesses, we just might be able to get the information out of him without him knowing what he's done."

Loring blinked in confusion but nodded, unwilling to let on that he didn't understand what Matthew was saying.

Matthew leaned closer and squeezed tightly on Loring's arm. "And," he continued slowly, "do you realize what would happen to the man who brought that information to Howe?"

Loring sat back, a slow smile coming to his lips.

"That's right," Matthew went on, "Howe and His

Majesty would see to it the man was rewarded richly. Can you imagine their gratitude for helping to put an early end to the war?"

"My good boy," Loring said eagerly, "no one can do it alone. You'll need help."

"You might be right in that," Matthew answered, "but I must be careful who I take in. It must be someone I can trust implicitly, someone who will not tell anyone else," he said warningly. "I don't want to split the reward too many ways."

"I'm with you, boy," Loring answered. "Let me help and I can guarantee there will be only the two of us."

Matthew knew Loring wouldn't hesitate to find a way to eliminate him in the end. But that really didn't matter, for when the end came he and General Lee would be safely away.

"Then you think you can get me close to Lee?" Matthew asked.

"Close to Lee?" Loring exclaimed. "You forget who I am, boy. I have means of getting pretty much what I want."

"Without arousing suspicion?"

"Without even the blink of an eye!"

Matthew pretended to weigh his decision. Finally, he nodded. "All right, then you're in. But no one— no one must know, or there'll be nothing for either of us."

"I understand," Loring answered. "Believe me, young man, I've been in this kind of business several times and I know when to hold my tongue."

"Fine!" Matthew could hardly believe his luck. Surely this was going too easily. "Now how do you get me close to Lee?"

"You let me work on that," Loring answered. "I have connections with his lordship."

"I don't want to arouse anyone's curiosity, Loring," he warned. "People start inquiring why I'm here, they might catch on and get to the reward before I do."

"Before *we* do," Loring corrected. "Don't worry my friend. I am most careful. Trust me."

"I'll be back in a couple of days to hear your progress." He got up, suddenly eager to be out of this man's presence.

It took almost the rest of the day to locate Colin. Matthew had found that by boldly walking into General Headquarters he was able to ask a great many questions of uncertain soldiers who never even learned his identity.

He finally found the house where a young man of Colin's description worked. Matthew waited patiently across the street in the cold, eying the heavy-coated officers who came and went, a great many with beautifully dressed women on their arms.

It was into the evening hours when Colin finally came out the front door, wrapping a long scarf around his throat and trudging wearily down the steps.

"Colin!"

The boy whirled in surprise, and for a moment stood wondering who was approaching him.

"Matthew!" With a joyful cry, Colin grasped him around the shoulders with both arms. "Matthew! How good to see you!"

As Colin eagerly pulled him down the street, he threw out more questions than Matthew was able to answer. "You've got to give me time to breathe," Matthew laughed.

"I'm sorry," Colin answered smilingly. "Don't tell me anything. Wait until we get home so that Martha can hear too."

Matthew allowed himself to be led through the streets to the warehouse district, which had been untouched by the fires. Here, against the sides of the buildings, a makeshift city of built-up boxes, canvas, heavy paper and broken boards housed the poor and desperate. There was a stench of rotten garbage, sewage and opium that hovered in the close alleys as the two made their way between these hastily built structures. At this time of night, no one was in sight. No doubt they were huddled together in their hovels for warmth. Matthew wondered if it was to one of these pathetic shanties he was being taken.

They finally stopped at a door in an alleyway. Colin grinned at Matthew as he knocked. A few seconds passed before they heard the rattle of a chain as the door was carefully inched open. A face peered out, studied Colin for a minute, then opened the door wider to allow them to enter.

"Our doorman," Colin whispered as they passed the silent bulk of a sour old man to make their way down a darkened hallway. "He keeps the riffraff out." Colin laughed. "Actually, he comes with the rent—which I tell you, my friend, takes almost all Martha and I earn. But at least we're out of the cold, so I guess it's worth it."

He stopped at the end door. "Home," he commented, and knocked on the door twice, then three times.

Martha laughed in delight as the pale light spewed across the hallway and caught Matthew. She kissed him on the cheek, then stepped back, holding his hands in hers.

"Oh, Matthew, I wish you wouldn't stay away from us for such long periods. We fear for you."

"It won't happen again," he answered joyfully and

looked her over. There was still the same spirit, the same smile, but there was a worn look about her, as with Colin. It was obvious that they worked long hours. One brief look around the small apartment was enough to realize they were struggling. But their spirits were not broken.

"I heard you two were asked to leave the house," Matthew said. "I'm sorry."

"I'm not," Colin answered defiantly. "I guess you must also have heard that we're married!"

Matthew was startled but pleased by the news. "No, I hadn't heard. But I can't think of anything nicer. I congratulate the both of you!"

"Congratulations accepted, young sir," Martha answered with a happy smile. "That's one of our nicest presents—especially coming from you."

"I mean it," Matthew answered. "You're two of my favorite people and I know you'll have a successful marriage."

"It hasn't been easy but we'll make it," Colin answered firmly. "I've found a job as a manservant to Colonel Deatre and Martha cleans house not too far from here. It's hard work, but at least we have jobs and are earning money—which is more than can be said by most of the sorry lot you see around here. We'll make it, Matthew."

Matthew smiled. "I have no doubt about it. But if I can be of any help, don't hesitate to ask." He told them of his encounter with Joshua Loring and his request for a special assignment.

Colin and Martha exchanged secretive smiles at the news. "What's the matter?" Matthew asked.

Again, they exchanged knowing smiles. "I guess you haven't heard then," Colin remarked. "But it's all over the city. If anyone can get a favor I'm sure

Joshua Loring can. You see, one of the reasons he's got such an important job and why he can get anything he wants is because his wife is Lord Howe's mistress."

"Mistress?" Matthew exclaimed, dumbfounded. "How can a man allow that to happen?"

"From what I hear," Colin explained, "there wasn't much he tried to do about it. But he surely took advantage of the affair. It's quite out in the open, you know. That's the kind of man your Joshua Loring is, I'm afraid."

Matthew took a deep breath. If a man would allow his wife to become mistress to the commanding general for his own benefit, then there was no telling what else the man would do. Matthew would have to be wary.

32

Loring kept his word. When Matthew returned to the Commissioner's office, Loring handed him a piece of paper. "You're now assigned to guard General Lee," the man said with a satisfied smile.

Matthew stared down at the paper in astonishment. It was too good to be true. "I shall make good use of this, believe me," Matthew answered.

"And you won't forget me," Loring said warningly.

Matthew doubted he could ever forget Joshua Loring. As he made his way through the streets of the city, he turned his thoughts to his mission. If he was lucky, he might be able not only to free Lee but also to obtain Lord Howe's spring campaign plans. He would have to use Colin, of course, and that bothered him greatly. One of these days, however, Colin would have to find out he was a patriot, and their friendship would come to an end. The thought saddened Matthew, but he wouldn't allow himself to dwell on it.

"Goddamn it, boy, where in hell have you been?" The barrage was his first introduction to Howe's famous prisoner. Charles Lee, tall and angular, but for his pot belly, sat on a sofa, wearing only a wrinkled white shirt.

Matthew bent to place the tray on the table beside the couch and then straightened. "I'm sorry sir, but this is my first time at this."

"Goddamn fools," the general muttered, grabbing a biscuit. "This any way to treat a general?" He continued speaking even as he ate. "Did they tell you I used to command this troop? Eh? Didn't know that? Regiment never was any good after I left. Don't even know when to bring my breakfast!"

He began to toss parts of the biscuits over his shoulder, and Matthew saw two small shaggy dogs leap up from the far corner of the room and race to the tidbits. "Where's the meat?" Lee asked, lifting the covers on the hot plates. "Where's the meat?" he bellowed, beginning to toss things off the tray and then turning accusingly to Matthew.

Matthew was taken aback. "I didn't know," he stammered. "I thought—"

"Thought?" the man bellowed, rising to his feet. His chinless face darkened to purple and his eyes sunk deeper under heavy brows. "Since when does a common servant have the right to think? You ass! Where the hell is that sergeant?"

Matthew panicked. He couldn't lose this position because of one mishap. "Please, sir." He stepped forward, blocking the general's way to the door. "I'll fetch it immediately."

"You haven't got the brain of a flea," he yelled. He

glared at Matthew, then turned and kneeled before the two dogs. "Come here, cootches," he murmured, his voice going soft and warm. "Come to papa." The two animals, tails wagging, leapt to their master and began licking his face. "The bastard forgot to bring your food," he muttered, suddenly glaring at Matthew. "Stupid is going to fetch your food now." He glowered at Matthew and waited.

"Yes, sir," Matthew murmured and hurried to the downstairs kitchen. So this was the famous Charles Lee. He had heard the man was eccentric but this encounter surpassed anything he might have imagined.

Later that evening, he told Martha and Colin of his day with the general. "I've never met such a coarse, vulgar person in my life," he said, shaking his head in disbelief.

"I heard they're all like that," Colin answered. "I hear Washington eats with his knife and drinks heavily."

Matthew was tempted to refute the rumor but decided to let the matter rest. "They can't all be as bad as Lee," he commented.

"I heard from the ladies," Martha said excitedly, "that Lee has a woman in his room every afternoon and every night—all night long!"

"He's enjoying himself, all right," Matthew answered. The general was pampered by the British and it was obvious Lee liked the attention. So much so that Matthew was worried. Would the man turn against Washington and join up with the British? It wasn't difficult to imagine. Lee had been a British officer. He was probably all too aware that his confederates were somewhere out in the frozen wilderness of New Jersey, while he was living a carefree life in New

York. Would the man even entertain the idea of escaping?

For the next weeks that led into March, Matthew kept his eyes open, waiting for the right opportunity. Lee had little use for him, or for anyone else in the household that served as his jail. He seemed to prefer the companionship of his two dogs, who followed him everywhere—even to the dinner table, where they had their own chairs, one on each side of him. Lee found his only other acceptable companions in the constant stream of harlots coming and going from his bedroom. Matthew soon became used to the man's vulgarity.

"You Tories are asses!" It was Lee's morning greeting as Matthew entered to pick up the clothes strewn about the room during the previous evening's partying. It was not going to be a good day, Matthew could see. He decided it best not to respond.

The general was bent over a desk, its top covered with maps spread open on top of each other. He was in his usual garb, wearing only a soiled shirt that barely covered his buttocks and genitals. He kept shaking his head, as he pored over the maps. "Goddamn Howe . . ."

Curious, Matthew moved closer to the desk, trying to peer over the man's shoulder.

"What are you doing?" Lee suddenly looked around at Matthew. "You think you're a tactician, do you?" he snarled. "For that matter, you're probably smarter than Howe, that ignoramous!"

Matthew moved to the front of the desk to look at the maps. "Those are beautiful, sir," he said. Lee already thought him a dolt, and he was perfectly willing to play the role to the hilt if it would get him any information.

"Beautiful maps?" Lee snorted and shook his head. "Leave it to a bumpkin to call these things beautiful. But they'll do, they'll do." He leaned back and stared at the maps with a sigh. "Can you believe it?" he said, more to himself than to Matthew. "Howe's going to let a golden opportunity slip right through his fingers. Hell, any private would know better."

"What do you mean, sir?"

"This!" Lee pointed out the northern limits of the city along the Hudson River. "The British have had three months to plan their campaign and the fools come up with this idea."

"You mean Howe's spring campaign?" he asked quietly.

"You mark my words," Lee answered. "Seventy-seven will be Black Dick's downfall."

"You don't agree with the British plan?" Matthew didn't dare breathe, wondering whether he was stepping too far.

"I told Howe himself it was an absurd plan," Lee remarked with a sneer, "right to his face. I even showed him what to do, but do you think that bumble-head would understand?"

Matthew was silent, thinking of how to trick him into revealing the British plan. "I know Howe doesn't have the knowledge of the countryside that you do, sir," he said, "but I'm sure his lordship knows what he's doing."

"He *doesn't* know what he's doing," Lee answered savagely. Exasperated, he spun a map around. "Here, look," he said excitedly, tracing a route with his finger. "Howe's plan is to cut New England in half there." His finger traced the Hudson River up through Lake Champlain. "He'd send someone down from Canada and then come up from New York himself—he'd cut us right in half. Then he'd bring in St. Lager from the west and quarter New York State." He looked up at Matthew.

"Sounds like a good plan to me, sir," Matthew answered, his heart pounding with the fact he had just been informed of Howe's spring tactics.

"But it doesn't get us by the balls," Lee snarled. "Got to get your enemy by the balls—that's where it counts. Remember that." He rummaged among the papers and pulled out a sheet which he spread before Matthew. "Now here's the plan of a master tactician." His finger again flew over the paper. "We can go along with the idea of someone coming down from Canada, and even St. Lager coming in from the west. We can even send a small force from New York to the north, but they're all distractions. If I was Howe I'd send my best troops here—to Philadelphia. That's where our balls are, right there! Cut down the Continental Congress—cut off their center of command, and George will have nothing else to do but pack up and head back for the farm!"

Matthew left the house as soon as he could. Rescuing Lee was all but impossible, and Matthew wasn't sure it would be a rescue so much as a capture, after what Lee had revealed to the British. The most important thing was to get the information to Washington as quickly as possible. But before he went this time, he had to say goodbye to Colin and Martha and leave them the pouch of money he had been hiding.

Colin was late in returning to the small apartment. Matthew sat on the rocking chair watching Martha prepare a stew in the small fireplace. It was a cozy room, but these people deserved far more. "I want you to know," Matthew said hesitantly, "that you and

Colin will always be welcome at my home in Wethersfield."

Martha looked at him with a curious expression on her face. "Why would you say that?"

He shrugged. "So that you know—just in case. You two will always have a roof over your heads."

She studied his face, frowning at what she read in his eyes. "I thought you weren't welcome in your home," she said.

Matthew debated how to reply. "I consider you and Colin my best friends," he finally answered carefully. "I consider *you* even closer, if you don't mind. Can I trust you, Martha? I mean, can I trust you not even to tell Colin?"

"Never?" she asked.

"Not until I can tell him—at the right moment. I feel I can tell you now, but it will be more difficult for Colin. Can I trust you?"

"Are you sure you want to tell me? It must be terribly important. And why do you have to tell me in the first place? Is something wrong?"

Matthew shook his head. "No, but I do have to leave. I might not be able to see either of you for a long time, and there's something I feel I should tell you before I leave."

She took only a few moments before nodding her head. "All right then, Matthew. I shan't tell Colin, if that's what you wish."

Matthew took a deep breath and relaxed. "It's just that none of us knows which way this war will turn out. If it's a British victory, then you and Colin should have no worries. But if the rebels win, it's going to be very difficult for the two of you. I'm just saying that if things get out of hand, if you do have need of a roof —go to Wethersfield and look my family up. They'll welcome Colin. He is a good cooper and they can use him."

"But we're Tories."

"They'll welcome you. Believe me."

"And for this, you want my trust?" she asked, eying him with an expression that said she knew he was holding something back.

"I need you to trust me when I say you and Colin will be welcomed in Wethersfield, and to trust me enough not to ask how I know all of this."

"I'm afraid to ask," Martha answered slowly. "But I'm more afraid of what I'm thinking, of what I'm guessing."

Matthew swallowed hard. "Trust me, Martha, and please remain my friend. For I shall always be your friend, no matter what I'm thinking, of what I'm guessing."

Matthew swallowed hard. "Trust me, Martha, and please remain my friend. For I shall always be your friend, no matter what."

"Matthew," she whispered, "you're acting as though something terrible is going to happen to us."

"Nothing is going to happen," Matthew answered, and he got up to take her into his arms. "There are people who think there are things that are more important than love, than friendship. I hope we don't fit into that category."

"Oh, Matthew," she whispered, "I don't know what to think. You scare me sometimes. There are times when you are someone quite different, almost a stranger."

Matthew sighed and pulled away, smiling down at her. "I shall always be your friend."

They both swirled about as the door burst open and Colin came in, out of breath. He closed the door quickly and leaned against it, catching his breath as he stared wide-eyed at Matthew.

"What's wrong?" Matthew asked, an odd sensation in the hollow of his stomach.

"I don't know," Colin answered, "but they're looking for you. They've been questioning me for the last hour, and now they've gone to my family's house."

"Who? Who's looking for me?"

"Soldiers! Major Whitehead!" Colin gasped. "They've got a warrant for your arrest!"

"Do they know where I am?"

Colin shook his head. "They tried to follow me, I'm sure, but I lost them," he answered. "Matthew, why are you under arrest? What have you done?"

"I don't know," Matthew answered, trying to think what to do. "It could be for a number of reasons. I quit my position guarding Lee and left without notice. Maybe that's why." But somehow he knew it had something to do with Loring.

"I think it's more serious than that," Colin answered. "Winslow was really angry, asked a lot of questions about you, wondered where you've been, what you've been doing, who you know."

"What did you say?"

Colin grinned slyly. "I told him I hadn't seen you since Staten Island."

Matthew smiled with his friend. "Thank you. You said Whitehead was going to your family's house?"

"He's searching everywhere," Colin answered. "He said something about Coleen probably knowing where you would be."

Coleen . . . He wondered whether Whitehead would tell her he was a rebel spy. The major had certainly guessed his identity; one didn't go about looking for a servant who deserted his post guarding a general.

But what bothered Matthew more was that Coleen would be told his secret by someone else. He had wanted to be the one to explain to her. But it was already too late.

"I've got to get out of here," he said, walking across the room to get his coat.

"No," Colin answered and blocked his way. "You've got to stay here. You're safer here. Right now Whitehead has guards at every exit out of New York watching for you. Wait here until they get tired, and then you can go. Or maybe by that time we can find out why you've been placed under arrest. Maybe it's just a mistake."

"I doubt it," Matthew answered, reaching again for his jacket.

"Please, Matthew," Colin begged, "stay here with us, where you'll be safe."

"I don't want you to get into trouble."

"Trouble? For protecting a friend?" Colin smiled and led Matthew back to the couch. "They can send me to prison, as far as I'm concerned. I'd still help you."

Matthew stared at Colin and was flooded with love for this young man. "All right then," he answered with a smile. "I shall stay here, but only for a couple of days. Then I must go."

33

AFTER TWO days, Matthew was ready to try his escape from the city. The longer he stayed, the more he was jeopardizing Martha and Colin. Besides, he was too restless to stay cooped up in the small room much longer.

He was packing his things when there was a soft knock on the door. It was too early in the afternoon for it to be Martha or Colin. And it was too gentle a knock for Whitehead or one of his soldiers. Curious, Matthew pressed his head to the door and waited.

There was a second, more insistent knock, and this time Matthew called out, "Who is it?"

"Matthew? It's Coleen! Please let me in."

Matthew quickly opened the door and beckoned her inside. "How did you find this place?" he asked anxiously, taking a look down the hall before closing the door.

She was breathless with excitement and hurriedly drew off the fur bonnet and shook her blonde hair loose.

"Matthew," she demanded, "what is going on? Why is Winslow hunting for you?"

He hesitated, yearning to tell her everything, yet afraid that whatever small relationship they did have would end forever when she knew the truth. "How did you find me?"

"I made Colin tell me," she answered, looking about the room. "Is this where you've been living?"

"Just for the last couple of days," Matthew responded. "This is where Colin and Martha live."

"It's awful," she exclaimed, and turned back to him. "I didn't know."

"You should try to change your father's mind about them. They are married, you know—and they're good for each other."

"Oh, Matthew, I've tried but . . ."

"But not hard enough, is that it?"

Coleen sighed. "We miss Colin terribly—and we worry about him. It's just—it's just that it's most difficult, knowing what Martha was and . . ." She let her thoughts trail off.

It was Matthew's turn to sigh. "People have to adjust to change, Coleen. Just look at the colonies. We're all witnessing a great change. No matter who wins, this thing is going to affect us all. I know changes are difficult but they're not impossible to endure. Martha's past is just that—the past." He wondered if he dared. "It's the same with the war. If the British win, the rebels will have to forget what has happened and

change back to the old ways. If the rebels win, the
Tories will have to change and adapt to the new ways.
The choice is up to each individual—and to how much
they love the country. In a way, it's the same with
Martha and Colin. Forget Martha's past if you love
Colin. In time, with patience and understanding, you'll
see her as I see her—as a gentle woman full of love
for Colin."

Coleen was looking up at him, close enough so that
he was suddenly conscious of her lavender fragrance.
Her hand slowly came up and touched his cheek. "So
gentle, Matthew," she murmured. "What are you doing
in this dreadful place at this dreadful time?"

For a moment he hardly dared move. Then he took
her hand and pressed it against the side of his face as
he stared into her eyes.

"Sometimes I see you as a stranger walking among
the ruins of this war, so out of place," she said. "What
is it you're searching for?"

He tried to shrug it off. "I'm not sure," he answered.
"Maybe myself."

She smiled wistfully. "Maybe that's what it is.
There's a side of you that I always feel is just beyond
reach."

He brought her hand down and edged closer to her.
"Coleen," he murmured, "I don't always know *what*
I'm doing in this war. But I do know that every time
I'm close to you, I feel good, and warm. I feel it's
right. Do you?"

Her expression didn't change. She kept searching
into his eyes. "I don't know," she answered softly. "I'm
confused. I don't know how I feel, or how *to* feel, or
who to feel for."

He took her hand, noticing how warm it was.

"Changes, Coleen—they're difficult to comprehend, difficult to go through—but they can bring all sorts of new and wonderful things."

They gazed at each other silently. His heart beating furiously, Matthew slowly bent his head, half expecting her to pull away or cry out. But she didn't move. She closed her eyes and her lips opened slightly.

He placed his lips on hers, finding them soft and full and warm. She strained toward him and brought her arms up and around his shoulders. His hands pressed into her back, and he could feel her stomach flattened against his, her breasts, round, yielding against him.

He brought his hand to the neck of her dress and touched the top button. She pulled back just enough to look at him waiting, her hands clutching his elbows. Slowly, deliberately, he unfastened the first button and pulled apart her collar. He put his hand against the moist warm skin of her neck and pulled her head forward, kissing her gently and then pulling back to wait for her to open her eyes and look up at him. His hand found the second button. He slowly unfastened it and pulled the material apart, now exposing a white lace undergarment and the curve of her cleavage.

He waited again, half expecting her to stop him. Then he moved on to the third button, which he unfastened more quickly this time. As he pulled the top apart, her hand came up and grabbed his. She had a confused, almost frightened look. "I'm cold," she whispered, suddenly shivering.

He nodded toward the small bedroom. "There a bed in there, warm blankets. I'll get some more in the cupboard."

She smiled gratefully at him and went through the door, leaving it partially ajar. He could hear the rustling of clothes.

He gave her plenty of time, pacing the floor as he waited. He didn't understand this girl at all. She was not like the others, not like Channing or Louisa. He was quite sure he would be her first. And yet there she was, undressing with hardly a word—for him.

When he pushed the door open, he found her lying almost in the middle of the small bed, her blonde hair spread across the pillow like a shawl. She watched him with wide eyes as he closed the door and approached the side of the bed.

He wanted to hurry but knew he had to be gentle and allow her time to get used to him, to get used to a man. He unbuttoned his shirt and slowly drew it off, conscious of her gaze as he continued to undress. When he was naked he sat on the edge of the bed and looked down at her.

"Matthew," she said in a hushed voice, "I hope you don't mind but . . . It's just that I—I've never done this before and I guess I'm a little afraid."

Matthew tenderly kissed her nose. "Don't be afraid. I promise I won't hurt you."

"Oh, Matthew," she answered, "I know that. Maybe that's why I'm doing this. I wanted someone gentle— to be my lover."

"Shhh," he whispered. He drew the cover back and buried his mouth over the rigid nipple that was turned to him. Her skin was cool, refreshing and sweet. He pushed down the blankets of the bed, his hands roving over skin that was soft as satin.

Her body became rigid for a moment, but then she moaned and pressed her hands on top of his head as his lips and tongue traveled across to the other nipple. Their bodies began to writhe and he lay down beside her, pressing his hardness against her thigh, his hand reaching down to the dark triangle of hair.

He could feel her quiver and hold her breath as his fingers gently parted the hairs to find the moist folds of skin. She was already wet and he slowly massaged the folds, marveling at the warmth, the sensual tingle that her excitement seemed to spread from his fingertips up his arms and through his body to the tip of his penis.

He put his hand over hers and brought it down to cover his erection. She touched him tentatively at first, letting his hand guide her until she was rubbing the tip along her inner thigh. She turned her body so that her face sank into Matthew's neck, her lips caressing him softly below his ear. He pressed his head close to her. The tip of his penis found the coarse hair between her legs and rubbed into the moist folds of skin.

"Oh, Matthew," Coleen whispered, "I want you. I want you to make love to me."

He moaned and lifted himself on top of her, careful to keep his weight on his elbows and knees. He reached down between their legs and pressed the tip of his penis into her, entering her slowly, pressing as far as he could without resistance. Never had he felt such pleasure.

Coleen moaned. She arched her back to help him break the maidenhead. Her fingers dug deeply into his back. "Oh God, Matthew," she gasped.

"Gently, my love, gently," he murmured into her ear.

She moaned again between gritted teeth, straining against him. Then, with a suddenness that took both their breaths away, his penis slid into her. She gave a sharp cry and her arms tightened about him.

"My love," Matthew murmured, not daring to move, wanting to enjoy every last sensation, every last minute. They clutched at each other, and for that moment all else was forgotten.

34

MATTHEW BLINKED his eyes as he awoke and looked down at Coleen. Her head lay over his arm and close to his shoulder, the mass of soft hair tickling his nostrils. He pressed his hand softly upon her bare shoulder.

He lay back against the pillow and eyed the ceiling, unconscious of the dirt and cobwebs in the corner, absorbed only in his own contentment. The girl amazed him! Never had he even dared dream that they would share an afternoon like this. He wondered whether Coleen would still go through with her marriage to Whitehead. Lord knew that Matthew would now do his best to discourage that idea. Coleen would never have consented to bed with him if she were truly in love with the major. It seemed safe now to believe that any thought of marrying Whitehead had been more out of concern for her family than for her own happiness. The Pages would prosper with that marriage. But would they be happy?

Matthew suddenly remembered that Colin and Martha would be coming home fairly soon. It would not do to have them find Coleen in bed with him. He bent down and kissed her lightly on the top of the head.

She stirred, her hand coming up and caressing his shoulder. Suddenly he could feel her tense up, and she pulled away from him.

"Aye," he said, smiling down at her wide eyes, "we went to sleep for a while."

"Will they be home soon?" she asked, pulling the covers closer under her chin.

"We have time." He wanted to take her in his arms again but there was a stiffness about her that held him off. "What's the matter?"

"I don't know," she whispered, barely loud enough for him to hear.

"Second thoughts?"

Her eyes came up swiftly to meet his. "Oh, Matthew," she murmured, and her face was full of despair. "I don't know. I just don't know. I feel so—so—"

"Shhhh." He put his finger to her lips and then cupped her chin. "What we did—there was nothing wrong. It was a beautiful experience, one I shall cherish all my life. When two people are in love, it's—"

Coleen was shaking her head. "But that's just it. I don't know whether I love you. I don't know whether I'm in love with anyone. I'm confused. I don't know why I did that. I don't know why."

"One shouldn't go around planning to make love,

Coleen," Matthew answered. "I've dreamed of making love to you, for I love you dearly. But I haven't been going around planning to seduce you. I was just as surprised at what happened as you were. But I *am* pleased—and I hope you are too."

"Oh, Matthew—"

The clamor at the front door was so loud and startling that Coleen clutched at Matthew. They held each other, waiting, barely breathing. When the knock on the door resounded again, they both jumped. Matthew slid his feet over the side of the bed. "You stay in here and get dressed. I'll see who it is."

Matthew pulled up his pants and reached for his shirt. "Don't worry," he said, trying to ease the fear that was on her face as she stared out of the room toward the front door.

Matthew closed the bedroom door after him and leaned against it to take a deep breath. The pounding at the front door began again, this time with such strength that he knew it was being forced. He watched helplessly, knowing there was nothing he could do, as the wood splintered at the latch with each repeated blow. Finally the door flew open.

"Well, Mr. Bell." Major Whitehead strode inside, brushing past the soldiers who had forced the door and looking around the empty room. "We've found you!"

Before Matthew could react, two soldiers entered, followed by Captain Magnus DeWitt. "What's this about?" Matthew demanded, his anger getting the better of any fear he had felt.

"Oh, come now," Whitehead answered, taking off his gloves and placing them carefully alongside his cap on the table. "Don't tell me you haven't been expecting us."

"I don't know what you're talking about." Matthew had to will himself not to look at the bedroom door and give Coleen's presence away. Instead, his eyes followed DeWitt, who began picking up things and inspecting them.

"Mr. Bell," Whitehead said as he dropped into a chair that faced Matthew, "you have a habit of disappearing at very odd moments." He paused, then pursed his lips. "You also have a habit of asking a great many questions that do not concern you."

"I'm a spy," Matthew said. "I thought you would want me to ask questions and seek out information."

"When your questions concern British matters rather than American matters, then it begins to worry me."

"You seem to have something specific on your mind, Major," he said, a sudden chill coming over him as he wondered if it was all up.

"Yes. Yes, I do," Whitehead answered. "I find it very strange that you've made inquiries to young Colin Page about his association with Colonel Deatre's work."

"Why wouldn't I ask him? He's my best friend," Matthew answered. "He's even allowed me to share this apartment with him."

The major gave him a thin smile. "How convenient. And how convenient for you to have become good friends with the Pages. They've opened a great many doors for you, haven't they? They even allowed you to come with them to Staten Island where our headquarters were. Why, I do believe it was the Pages who introduced you to me. How convenient that I, too, took you under my wing." His tongue made a clicking sound and then he went on in a low, almost conversational tone of voice. "Mr. Bell, do you know how we treat spies? Are you aware that we hang spies?"

"But I'm your spy," Matthew answered calmly.

"Mr. Bell, you might have hoodwinked me in the beginning, but I'm not entirely the fool. I've had a long talk with Mr. Joshua Loring." He waited with a smile of satisfaction as he saw Matthew's face whiten. "Ah," he chuckled, "I see we're hitting a soft spot. You see, Mr. Loring doesn't trust you. He was very upset when you disappeared from your job. Said something about your having cheated him out of a great deal of money."

"What kind of lies has that man been spreading?"

"No, Mr. Bell, no lies. We've checked out his story —even so far as visiting with General Lee, who corroborates what we've found." He paused, eying Matthew with triumph. "You're an American spy, Mr. Bell —and we have enough facts to place you under arrest."

Matthew's glance shot to the door but the two soldiers anticipated him and placed themselves to block any exit. Captain DeWitt stepped out of the shadows and stood in front of Matthew. "Mr. Matthew Bell, by order of General William Howe, you are placed under arrest for spying on His Majesty's forces."

"It's all pure conjecture," Matthew exclaimed. "You have no proof—just hearsay and suspicions."

"Ah," Major Whitehead answered, "we British are not as inept as you seem to think, rebel! We've suspected you for quite some time and Captain DeWitt and his men have done investigations on you." He nodded to the other officer.

"We realized there was room for error in such suspicions, Mr. Bell." DeWitt smiled coldly, politely.

"You see, we don't make accusations without foundation. One of the easiest ways of finding out whether you truly are a rebel was to go directly to your home town. A very capable agent of ours had a most interesting talk with your family—who, I might add, never suspected they were talking to a British agent. They somehow gave the man the impression your sympathy lay with the Americans." He paused, letting the impact of his words sink in. "And then I looked up who the commanding officer was in Wethersfield." He turned and snapped his fingers at one of the guards.

The soldier opened the door and beckoned to a figure who quickly came in from the dark hallway.

"Scott!" Matthew blanched as he stared at the sullen face of his old nemesis.

"That's him," Scott said, "and he's no loyalist, or you can have my rank. He's a rebel!"

Matthew glared at the lieutenant. It was over.

"I guess that about does it," Whitehead said, and rose to his feet. "You'll need your shoes, Mr. Bell." He started for the bedroom but Matthew stepped in his way.

"You have a confederate in there?" Whitehead asked, trying to push past him.

Matthew stood his ground, but the two soldiers rushed up, pinned his arms and pulled him aside. "There's a lady in there," Matthew said, giving the major a dark look. "There's no reason to get her mixed up in this."

"One of your trollops?" Whitehead sneered and stepped through the bedroom door.

Coleen staggered back until she fell against the side of the bed. She pressed the top of her dress to her shoulders and stared up at Whitehead in terror.

He looked down at her, at first in shock, then in

contempt. He straightened to his full height, spun on his heel and slammed the bedroom door shut behind him.

"We'll hang him now—right here!" he barked. He looked to the rafters.

"Major!" DeWitt exclaimed and came around to grab at Whitehead's sleeve. "We can't! We've got to find out what he's told the Americans!"

"We hang him here!" Whitehead began a frantic search of the room, hunting for rope. "We hang the bastard here!"

"No!" DeWitt dragged Whitehead to a corner, where the two began a hushed conversation. Every once in a while, Whitehead would utter a vehement "no" and each time DeWitt would place a restraining hand on his arm.

Matthew watched in horror. Whitehead would truly have his revenge if he were hanged in front of Coleen. He turned to Scott, but the lieutenant only smirked.

"Don't look at me for support. I'll be the first to pull on the rope." Scott stepped in closer and eyed the bedroom. "You have someone else's wife in there?" he said, giving Matthew a knowing look.

There was no warning of what happened next. The officer's leg came up between Matthew's thighs and Matthew couldn't swerve fast enough. An excruciating pain knocked the wind out of him as the knee slammed into his groin. The two guards loosened their hold and he doubled up and fell onto the cold floor to writhe in pain, his hands digging down to cut the throbbing that flowed through his muscles.

He was barely conscious of DeWitt and Whitehead rushing to his side. "The bastard deserved it," he heard Whitehead exclaim. "I say we hang him!"

"No," another voice answered. A hand reached out

and touched his face. "Not now, at least. We have to find out what he told the Americans."

Matthew tried to relax. His eyes were screwed shut in pain, but he knew they were hovering over him, waiting patiently. He could smell their polished boots, hear their whispers. What kind of death awaited him? And Coleen—had she heard it all? Would he ever have the chance to explain it to her?

35

T HEY MARCHED HIM through the streets down to the old brick building at the Battery where Matthew had received his first assignment from Major Whitehead. It was a forbidding-looking structure, separated from its nearest neighbor by a small tree-lined park. The East River ran about a hundred yards to its rear.

The early April wind was still chilly, especially blowing in from off the great harbor. Squads of soldiers worked in the distance, moving crates of supplies and barrels of food and drink from the constant flow of shipping traffic that busied the port now that the ice had melted. Howe and his aides were no doubt in one of the nearby brick buildings, busy over maps as they prepared for the spring campaign of 1777. Matthew wondered whether Charles Lee had convinced

Howe to attack Philadelphia rather than advance northward up the Hudson.

He was searched thoroughly by a disinterested sergeant, whose fingers dug in ruthlessly to all parts of his body. Both Whitehead and DeWitt had disappeared upon entering the building, and only Scott stayed close.

"You have nothing better to do, Scott?" Matthew muttered as he was finally allowed to don his clothing.

"Believe me, Bell," the officer replied, "I'm enjoying this immensely."

They took Matthew to the basement, a dark and musky smelling hole that was cold and wet. In the rear, iron bars separated two cubicles from the rest of the room.

"Your home." Scott waved a hand to one of the open doors. He waited until Matthew walked through, then slammed the door and watched as the sergeant turned the big brass key. "You'll be here until we're through with you. Then I imagine you'll be taken to one of our prison ships. I'm sure you've heard a great deal about them," he added, laughing as he turned and followed the sergeant up the steps.

A door clanged shut, leaving the room in darkness, and the sound of their footsteps faded. Matthew waited for his eyes to adjust, but there wasn't even a glimmer of light. He remembered seeing a small cot to his left, and with outstretched hands he shuffled forward until he bumped into the bed.

Yes, he had heard of the famous prison ships. Several large vessels were anchored somewhere out beyond the harbor, far enough away so the stench of their human cargo could not drift ashore; far enough way, it was said, so that no one could hear the screams and the moans, and no one could witness how many bodies were thrown overboard to the sharks. Most of the tales were hearsay, of course; no man had ever returned from such imprisonment. Was that any better than the fate that had awaited Nathan Hale? Maybe hanging was the more humane treatment.

Matthew sighed and lay down. All the lies and deceptions were in the past. It seemed ironic that the best way to trick the British now was with the truth. If he could convince them that he hadn't had a chance to relay Howe's spring campaign to Washington, then they might stick with the battle strategy that Lee believed to be so foolish. And Washington might have a chance.

Whitehead had believed his lies for so long. Would he believe the truth? Time enough to tell. First they had to make him admit he was a spy.

"Mr. Bell!" Major Whitehead had come into the room. Two soldiers had come hours earlier and dragged Matthew from the cell to the center of the large basement room, where they had placed a high stool. Lamps were lit in a circle around him, making it impossible to see beyond the cast of their yellow shade. He had sat there, silent, unable to guess whether the soldiers were still out there beyond the lamps. He had heard the upstairs door open, followed by the sound of footsteps. Then the major had stepped into view, staring at him silently, then grabbing at a chair that was handed to him from the shadows and sitting directly in front of Matthew.

"Mr. Bell," he said again, his voice low and stern. "To save us all time, will you admit to being a spy?"

"I have spied for you, yes," Matthew answered, determined that he would not make it easy for them.

"Come, Mr. Bell," the major said in a weary tone. "Are you ready to admit that you're a rebel spy?"

"I don't think you have anything that can prove that I might be."

"We don't have to prove anything to you, Mr. Bell. We have enough facts to convict you in any court of military law. We are merely giving you an opportunity to make it easier on yourself—by allowing us to be a bit more lenient with you."

"Lenient?" Matthew smirked. "A short time ago I was employed by your people—and now you have dragged me from my lodging and thrown me in this hole, accusing me of all sorts of things. You call that being lenient?"

The major kept looking at Matthew with the same expressionless face, his eyes hardly blinking. Even after Matthew had finished, Whitehead kept on with his stare, long enough so that Matthew wondered whether the man had even heard his words. Finally, the officer drew in a deep breath and lifted a hand. One of the soldiers came to his side, carrying a long-handled object that resembled a handmade hearth broom.

"Have you ever seen one of these, Mr. Bell?" Whitehead asked, patting the broom he held. "It comes from India, of all places—made of bamboo. A most interesting instrument, I might add." He picked at one of the bamboo slivers and lifted it away from the others. "A very simple thing, actually—a couple of bamboo sticks tied together and then slivered." He touched the edge of one of the slivers. "Very sharp. Full of tiny slivers too. They say this thing can slice a man's skin and infect it so badly that it never heals. Far worse than any mere whip."

He lifted his head and nodded to the soldier, who came over to stand behind Matthew.

"And now, Mr. Bell," Whitehead continued, "I will ask again. Are you a rebel spy?"

"No."

He had expected the blow, and after the initial shock of pain across his back it wasn't as bad as he had anticipated. Slowly, Matthew opened his eyes and looked at Whitehead.

"Same question, Mr. Bell," the major said evenly.

"Same answer," Matthew replied firmly.

This time, the blow was harder and the pain deeper, sending Matthew into a moment of dizziness. He could feel that his back was wet, and knew by the looseness of his shirt that it was in shreds. "Do your best, Whitehead," he muttered.

"My best?" the major answered, sitting back and crossing his booted legs. "I won't have to go that far, Mr. Bell. We've just begun—and we have plenty of time. You're the one whose time is running out." He nodded, and again there was a solid whack to Matthew's back. The pain shot clear through to his chest, this time drawing a scream that could not be held back. He tried to stretch the tightness from his back, but every time he moved a new pain shot through him.

The Britisher was on his feet and pulling on his white gloves. "We're going to leave you now, Mr. Bell. There's a fine play being presented tonight that I don't want to miss. Enjoy yourself in the meantime, for we shall return in the morning."

The circle of light was empty, and for a moment Matthew thought he was alone. Suddenly, the two guards came into the light and took hold of his arms.

A scream of pain came from his lips as he was dragged back to his cell. It felt as though someone was pulling the skin from his back. He screamed again, louder this time. He struggled to get away, but he was thrown on his back and a knee was pressed down on his stomach. He was being tied to the bed, on his back, arms and legs underneath the cot. The slices on his back dug into every nerve. It felt like a million slivers were being pushed into his skin and every movement only made it worse.

How long he was unconscious he had no way of knowing. He was suddenly aware that it was dark and quiet and that he was alone in the cell.

The discomfort was bearable now. Or was he merely so worn out that he didn't care anymore? His arms and legs ached even more than his back. He knew he had to move them and concentrated on flexing each limb. Sometime later, he fell into an exhausted sleep.

He didn't realize it was morning until they assisted him up the stairs and out a back door into the early morning light. At first he was almost blinded by the glare and shielded his eyes with his hands. A bucket of water was suddenly thrown over his body and one of the guards laughed. Angrily, Matthew turned on him.

"You stink, rebel," the man laughed, pointing at Matthew.

The smell suddenly reached his nostrils and Matthew looked down at himself. He was covered with sweat and blood and excrement. Humiliated, he hobbled to the nearby water trough, where he washed his clothes and then himself, each movement slow and painful.

For the next five days, the routine never changed.

Whitehead appeared to ask his questions, watched as Matthew received his two thrashings, and then left, returning at the end of the day to repeat himself. Each morning Matthew was taken out behind the building where he was allowed to wash. As each beating passed, it became more difficult to move; every pull of a muscle seemed to encourage the bamboo splinters to dig deeper into his back.

"Mr. Bell!" Whitehead leaned forward in his chair on the fifth day and inspected Matthew. "This is getting ridiculous, don't you think? We cannot continue this charade much longer. You've proven that your endurance for pain far exceeds most men's, and I, for one, congratulate you. Please don't encourage us to continue. We might have to resort to more drastic measures." He waited, eying Matthew for some sign of acknowledgement.

"I shall be perfectly frank with you, Mr. Bell," he continued. "Pressure is being placed upon me to get information out of you. In other words, I've been given permission to do anything necessary to get this information. Do you understand?"

Matthew glared at him out of eyes dulled with pain.

"You force me to drastic measures, Mr. Bell. I'm going to get your confession, you'll have to realize that. Even if I have to drag in your confederates, I will get your confession."

"Confederates?" Matthew asked, confused.

"Come now, rebel," Whitehead sneered. "Do you think you've fooled us into believing you acted single-handedly? Any idiot can easily see you must have received help. How else could you have survived here in the city? How else could you have gotten to Staten Island? How else could you have found sanctuary before your arrest? The questions go on and on and on. And I think the answer is quite obvious."

Matthew shook his head. "I had no one," he murmured.

Whitehead made little clucking sounds with his tongue. "Oh, come now. All I have to do is bring in Colin Page or his strumpet wife and I'm sure they'll admit everything. Once that is done, the Pages will have no choice but to confess their participation— even, I'm sure, my ex-fiancee."

Matthew picked up his head and stared at Whitehead. "You'd do that?" he asked hoarsely. "You'd drag them into this?"

Whitehead shrugged and examined the tips of his fingers with exaggerated casualness. "I'm not a vindictive man," he said. "I'm sure you look upon my actions as those of a jealous ex-suitor. Believe me, Mr. Bell, I'm not like that. However . . . I do have a job to perform, nasty though it might be. I suppose one could interpret the Pages' actions in several ways, of course. The choice is entirely yours."

"You wouldn't dare," Matthew exclaimed, unable to believe that Whitehead could be so monstrous. "The Pages are too well respected in the community."

Whitehead laughed derisively. "Do you think the Pages' position in this community will influence a military tribunal? And once we're finished, do you believe the Pages will have any allies?"

"But you know they're innocent!"

The major arched his eyebrows. "Do I?" he asked. "I just have your word on that now, don't I?" He paused, his expression becoming smug. "Imagine how disgusting this all must be to our lovely Coleen. What a shame to bring her down to all this. Imagine her shock on seeing you in this pitiful state. And all because you won't admit to something we all know as truth anyway." He paused again. "Come now, Mr. Bell, come to your senses. Is all this beating absolutely necessary? Is my bringing the Pages here and humiliating them necessary when we know the truth?"

Matthew found himself almost hypnotized by the monstrousness behind the major's smooth tone. "If there's one thing I'm glad I did, Whitehead," he said at last, "it's ending Coleen's relationship with you, you bastard."

"And you, Mr. Bell—a rebel and a spy!"

"And proud of it," Matthew responded angrily.

A slight smile turned the officer's mouth. "Well, at least we've accomplished one thing, Mr. Bell. We have the truth from you." He rose from his chair. "And now that the preliminaries are out of the way, we shall get down to more serious business. I rather doubt you'll enjoy the rest of your stay here."

Matthew watched him disappear into the dark perimeter. He heard the sound of boots going up the stairs, of a door being slammed. Then, unbearable silence. Matthew surveyed the circle of light, waiting for the guards to approach. Whitehead's last words rang through his head. The major was through playing games. Whatever treatment he had had before was mere child's play compared to what was in store for him.

No one approached his cell for days, except for the shuffling guard who slid a pewter dish filled with slop under the barred door. Finally, he was taken upstairs to the back, where he was allowed to clean his clothes and body. As he washed in the trough, Matthew looked about him, breathing deeply of the fresh air. He had lost track of time, but by the greening of the trees in the far park he guessed it was still early April. As he looked about the building, he caught his reflection in a window glass. His face was bearded, his eyes sunken. It was an image that haunted him as he returned to his cell, knowing there was yet more he must endure.

It was that afternoon that the beatings began. As before, Matthew was put into the middle of the circle of light, where he would sometimes wait for hours before Whitehead appeared. Then the questions began. Had he or had he not relayed to General Washington the information he had tricked out of Charles Lee? By what means had he passed on the information? Who else did he work with in New York?

Matthew answered truthfully to all of these questions, but Whitehead seemed almost determined not to believe him.

"Convince us, Mr. Bell. You still haven't convinced us!"

Whitehead and his soldiers would leave as quickly as they had appeared. That was when Leo came, looming out of the darkness, a huge, ominous-looking man whose face was set in stony impassivity. Leo administered beatings that Matthew was too weak to fight off now. They never lasted long, but they seemed designed to brutalize the few areas of his body that weren't already wracked with pain.

After the first few such sessions, Matthew came to believe that it hardly mattered how he answered Whitehead's questions. This was not simply a matter of interrogating a prisoner of war. It was a personal vendetta. There was no way Matthew could bring a halt to the beatings, much as he might wish it. He could only wait Whitehead out. . . .

He awoke knowing that someone was staring at him. He painfully turned his head and stared across the small cell to the tall figure on the other side of the bars. It was Lieutenant Fitchley Scott.

"Good morning," the lieutenant said, his voice ringing with false heartiness. "I wanted to be the first to let you know that you've seen the last of those nasty beatings."

Matthew struggled to sit up, his ears ringing, his arms and legs aching beyond belief with the effort.

"You'll be seeing a lot more of me, though," Scott went on. "In fact, I've volunteered for a little experiment. I'm sure it will work. It's something I once witnessed. You might enjoy it." He backed away as two guards came forward and unlocked the door.

Matthew was dragged to his stool in the middle of the room. But this time, a small table was placed alongside his chair. Leo came out of the darkness, grabbed Matthew's right arm and pulled it down upon the table, where he braced it with both hands.

"This is a punishment saved for common laborers, rebel," Scott said from his post across the table. "It occurred to me that being a cooper, you probably value your hands—as do most common laborers. They're your trade, your pride, your future." He unsheathed his saber and placed it across the table, sharp edge upright.

"We're going to eliminate your fingers—one at a time."

Matthew instinctively curled his fingers into a ball and began to struggle against Leo's tight grasp.

"It's no use fighting," Scott said, signalling the other two guards to come forward and help Leo grasp Matthew's arm against the table top. The big man dug into Matthew's palm, prying the little finger free from his fist and pulling it out straight.

"We'll start with the little finger and then, each day, we'll eliminate the others. If by some stroke of luck you've survived the loss of all five fingers, we'll start on your other hand. He smiled at Matthew's terrified gaze. "We'll start whittling you down inch by inch until you tell us what we need to know."

Matthew watched in desperation as Leo straightened the little finger so that the second knuckle was placed directly over the sharp blade.

"Now, rebel," Scott asked hoarsely. "Who did you give the secrets to? Who was your confederate?"

"No one," Matthew whispered, his eyes transfixed on the gleaming blade. "I didn't give anyone the information!"

He knew Scott was watching him closely, but he could not take his eyes off his hand. He saw Leo's fingers close tightly over his and then jerk downward.

The pain screamed through his entire body. His arm was quickly released and he grabbed for the hand. The blood spurted through his fingers and he looked around, his eyes wide with confusion and disbelief, his mouth drawn in a cry of agony. Then, mercifully, he fainted to the floor.

36

WHAT DAY is it?" Matthew watched the guard enter the cell and place a bowl on a small stool beside the cot. He had lain awake several hours, it seemed, not moving, merely staring into the blackness.

The guard turned to him in surprise and with a sly grin shook his head. "Ya mean what month, don't ye?"

Matthew furrowed his brows and tried to remember. "You mean I've been down here for more than a month?"

"Been *out*, is more like it," the man answered. Before closing the cell door, he looked back at Matthew with a frown. "You been delirious, I'd say. Out of your head."

Matthew waited, trying to bring back the memories. It was the same cell, that he knew. The guard was the same, although it was the first time he could remember the man actually entering the cell. Then he remembered.

He bent forward, stretching out his hand. It was bandaged, soiled enough to indicate it had not been attended to for quite some time. There were only four fingers, his small finger missing. He looked up at the guard inquiringly.

"Ya dropped off. Took you to the hospital where they fixed up your hand. Ya been barmy ever since."

"What day is this? How long have I been like this?"

'It's 'bout middle of June now—ya been out for nearly three weeks." He picked up the lantern and turned to leave.

"Wait!" Matthew called out, struggling to swing his legs onto the floor. "Don't leave." None of his limbs would respond to his command, and he fell back against the bed. "Where is everyone?"

"Ya mean the major and the rest? They waited for you to come about. Ya needn't worry no more about them bothering you. I heard 'em say they got what they wanted out of ya."

"How do you know? What did I say?" Matthew demanded.

The man shrugged. "I don't know the whys and wherefores. All I know is, the army's moved out—went toward Philadelphia, I heard."

No! What had gone wrong? He had told the truth and the British should be marching north to meet the Canadian forces, not to capture the American capital. What had gone wrong?

"'That's impossible! I told them the truth!"

The guard hesitated and leaned into the iron bars, looking sympathetically at Matthew. "The major said anyone who suffered what you did would hold back any secret. They knew you had told the Americans, so they changed their plans. I'm sorry, son, but that's the way it works sometimes. No matter how hard ya try, the answer always slips out one way or t'other."

Matthew sank back on the pallet. He felt his throat begin to choke up and he closed his eyes tightly. . . .

He was allowed to bathe in the horse trough each morning. The area was relatively quiet, the harbor empty of its usual contingency of war ships, the park and broad field adjoining the stone building void of activity except for the small command that was left behind to maintain the city. In the ensuing weeks, the guards became more relaxed, obviously enjoying themselves without so many officers hovering over them. They even allowed Matthew to lie against the building and enjoy the fresh air while they played cards.

Matthew enjoyed his new freedom. He went out of his way to be friendly and helpful to the guard detail, even going so far as to assist in some minor carpentry work. The exercise felt good but made him realize he was well out-of-condition. He was finally given some extra pants and a shirt, and for the first time in months he felt like a human being again.

One morning, he waited anxiously on the cot for his guards to take him for his bath. He had been studying the area surrounding the compound, and by now every detail was firmly etched into his mind. His only chance for escape was by running for the East River, where—with luck—he could swim to safety. It was a long run, and it would take careful planning to judge the exact moment when he wouldn't be intercepted by any of the soldiers.

He had been exercising in his cell, conditioning his legs and lungs for the exertion of his escape. The

cuts on his back had started to heal. He was inured
to the sting that jabbed into his spine every time he
moved his shoulder.

He had finally unwrapped the bandages several
mornings ago to wash the ugly seared flesh across his
knuckle. One of the guards had given him salve to
put on the wound, and it was already beginning to
look better. He knew it wasn't a terrible loss—he
could easily work without the finger. He had been
lucky that Scott had not taken more.

His mind flashed back to Mark, wondering what his
brother was doing. Mark had suffered a far greater
loss in the war than he had. At the time, Matthew
hadn't been able to understand his brother's attitude.
But that was before Matthew had known what it was
to have a cause to fight for.

Matthew had become so absorbed in his thoughts
that he was unaware of the uniformed figure standing along the bars, staring in at him. Suddenly, he
snapped his head up.

"Your endurance amazes me," Major Whitehead announced. "When we left you, I was sure it was only
a matter of time before you'd expire."

"I'm glad to disappoint you, Major," Matthew
growled.

"Ah, still the fighter, are you?" The officer chuckled.
"I've only come down here out of curiosity. And, of
course, to tell you how successful your assistance has
been to our army."

The major smiled when he saw Matthew blanch.
"You didn't think we'd be fooled for one minute by
your brave little act? There was only one reason anyone would go through what you did, Mr. Bell—and
that's to protect the truth. You *wanted* us to believe
you hadn't told Washington of our plans so that we

would march northward. Well, that's why General Howe changed his mind. That's why we've attacked your capital instead!"

"You've already attacked Philadelphia?" Matthew gasped.

The major shrugged slightly. "Of course. It's only a matter of time now before we actually take it. Your General Washington is running around, afraid to meet our forces head on. We've merely come back to replenish our supplies and prepare for our final attack."

"You'll never make it, Whitehead."

"You, dear boy, will never know. I've made arrangements to have you transported to a prison ship a week or so after we sail for Philadelphia."

"Sail out?" Matthew said.

"Yes," the major responded. "We're sailing south— and then directly up to your capital. Much better than overland, don't you think?"

A prison ship . . . Matthew knew he had to get away soon. Once they tossed him on a ship, there would be no escape.

He was kept below in his cell for several days after Whitehead's visit. The guards had returned to their sullen silence, fearful of the officers upstairs. Matthew waited impatiently, his ears and eyes straining for some sign to indicate the departure of the British army.

"They're gone!" The guard, probably almost as relieved as Matthew, shook his head in relief and opened the barred door. "Ya can get a bit of fresh air."

"What day is it?" Matthew asked, stumbling forward for the daylight.

"Early August now," came the reply.

Five months he had been in this hell hole. Five months. He took his time with the bath, meticulously scrubbing at his clothes, stretching out full length in the cool water and staring about at the deserted courtyard. To his left, the small park was green with grass and heavy foliage. Two figures enjoyed the early morning, seated on a bench under a large elm.

If he was going to escape, Matthew knew it would have to be during this morning bathing ritual. He studied the terrain that sloped to the distant river. It was all in the open with no concealment whatsoever. The guards' muskets were leaning against the side of the building next to where they sprawled playing cards. He could probably cover about a hundred feet before the soldiers would be able to aim their rifles, and at that distance their marksmanship would begin to suffer.

Matthew looked around for other soldiers. He had noted that a courier often appeared at this time of day; he would have to see if there was a firm pattern to the man's arrival. There was also a squad of soldiers that Matthew saw from time to time, possibly raw recruits being trained at a far barracks. He would have to make note of their habits too.

It was decided. One week—seven days—and he would make his escape or die trying. One week would give him ample time to study the habits of the guards and the courier and the movements of anyone else at this time of the morning. One week would give him time to exercise in his small cell for the long run to his freedom.

Every morning thereafter, Matthew would casually study his surroundings. The courier, he found out, came every other day; Matthew's run would have to come on the day the courier was absent. The squad of recruits had their close-order drill ten or fifteen minutes after Matthew began his bath. If he started before the recruits gathered outside, there would be no problem from them. Even if he found they had started their drill earlier than usual, he would still have a chance of beating them to the river.

There was one question that began to plague him the second day of his vigilance. The same two men appeared in the park again, as they did every day thereafter. Even more unnerving was that after he began to watch them he became quite sure that they, in turn, were either watching him or the building behind him.

On the fifth day, a wind swept across the field, hinting of a summer thunderstorm. When Matthew stepped out of the building, he found his first glance was toward the park. In a way, it was a disappointment that the bench was empty of its usual two visitors.

"It's going to be a good blow," one of the guards yelled out. He leaned against the side of the building and waited as Matthew nodded and bent to stick his head into the water and scrub his hair. "We need the rain," he finally answered in return. As he turned to grin at the guard, his eyes caught a figure standing at the corner of the building. The man was cloaked in a long brown cape, and Matthew knew instantly it was the taller of the two mysterious figures he had seen in the park. Once again, Matthew wondered if the presence of the two men had anything to do with him. And if so, had they been sent by Major Whitehead to keep an eye on him—or was it possible they had been sent by Washington to rescue him? He turned unobtrusively to look for the smaller companion from the park, but no one was in sight. The entire field was empty except for the slight wisps of dust the gathering wind was spewing about.

"I better be taking you in," the guard announced. "Storm's coming."

Matthew turned in time to see the guard reach for his musket and then stop short sighting the stranger. The cloak had parted revealing a pistol in the man's hand.

Matthew did not even hesitate. He ran forward and grabbed the musket from the wall, then looked past the guard to the figure. "Hunter!" he gasped as the man pushed back the tricorn that had been pulled low on his forehead. "John Langley Hunter!"

"Quick," came the strong voice, the pistol waving toward the door. "Inside before anyone sees us!"

Matthew quickly followed the guard and the tall Virginian inside and pulled the door shut. As he turned, he started, for Hunter's companion held a pistol on the two guards, who stood motionless against the far wall.

"Good," Hunter said. "We got them all together!" He inclined his head slightly toward the other figure. "I believe you two have met before?"

"Deborah!" Matthew stood still, completely dumbfounded, as his sister drew off her tricorn and shook her dark hair loose.

"Oh, Matthew!" She rushed to throw her arms about him. "Oh, Matthew, you're safe!"

They held each other in silence, swaying slightly, absorbing each other's love. They didn't even hear John Hunter's sharp command to the guards to head for the downstairs cells. It was not until the man came back alone that they pulled apart from their embrace.

"But how?" Matthew murmured, shaking his head in disbelief.

Deborah smiled and reached out to pull John Langley closer to her. "We've been hunting for you for months," she explained. "Your friends Martha and Colin Page appeared in Wethersfield and told us about your capture. We didn't know what to do. Finally, I wrote to John. He was the only one I knew who might help us."

John Langley Hunter came closer and put an arm around Deborah. "And a lucky thing. I was headed north to join Washington when I got the letter, and he gave me some valuable hints as to where you might be. I then went to Deborah, and she came down here with me—much against my will, I might add."

"It was only last week we found out where they had you," Deborah continued. "We had to wait until the British left and then we waited in the park. That's when we first saw you and where we made our plans."

"I never would have guessed those figures on the bench were you two," Matthew answered. "Not in a million years."

"While our luck is still with us, I would suggest we leave. We don't want anyone to find us," John Langley said. He grabbed a coat that was hanging on a hook and threw it to Matthew. "Here, put this on. We'll get you clothes later. Right now we have to get out of this city."

"Will you take me to Washington?" Matthew asked as he struggled with the coat.

"As soon as we return your sister. Right now, he's hunting for Howe and the British army."

"I think I know where they are," Matthew answered as they made their way for the door.

"Good God," Hunter exclaimed. "Then we'd better make haste."

Matthew reached out and stopped him. "There's one thing I have to do before I leave." They turned inquiring faces to him. "It won't take long. And it's something I have to do."

37

MR. PAGE, please," Matthew begged, placing a foot in the doorway. "Please, I've got to talk to Coleen!"

"How dare you show your face here!" John Page drew himself up indignantly and tried to force the door shut. His gaunt face was rigid as he frowned upon Matthew. "You betrayed us. And I, for one, will never forgive you!"

"Mr. Page, we have different political beliefs, it's true. But I've never betrayed our friendship."

John Page hesitated. "I doubt whether we shall ever resume what once was. And, we're separated by more than political preferences. There's a war going on, and we're on opposite sides. That makes us enemies, and neither you nor I can change that."

Matthew was conscious of the two mounted figures

waiting for him in the street. "May I at least say good-bye to Coleen?" he asked.

The elder Page sighed but did not move. "I'm afraid it's too late for that, my boy. She's suffered quite enough, thanks to you."

"I'm begging, Mr. Page," Matthew said, trying to keep his voice controlled. "It may be the last time I ever see her, and I must try to make her understand my feelings."

"It's a little late for that, isn't it?" Mr. Page asked dryly.

Matthew was growing desperate. Time was running out and he had to leave, but he knew he would never be able to rest easily if he didn't speak to Coleen one final time. "I love her," he said simply. "I love her with all my heart. I cannot ask your forgiveness any more than I can ask hers, for I acted as my beliefs dictated. I can't say I'm sorry for it either, because if it weren't for my beliefs I would never have met any of you. I don't know what to say to Coleen really, except that I love her."

"Father!" Coleen's hand slid upon her father's shoulder from behind and she came into view. Mr. Page stepped back, leaving them alone in the doorway, silently looking into each other's faces.

"I have to leave," Matthew finally said, yearning to take hold of her and bring her in close to him.

"You look so pale and thin," she said softly.

Matthew tried to grin. "I had to keep up my image, didn't I? I mean, we always seem to meet when I'm somewhat battered."

She searched into his eyes. "Are you all right?"

Matthew nodded. "I'll recover. It's just—it's been a long time, and I've thought about you so often."

Her hand came up quickly in warning. "Please—

no," she said firmly. "I don't want to hear those things."

"I can't help myself," he finally answered. "I know I've got to leave—and I can't bear the thought that we may never see each other again. I had to come to tell you I love you. I always will."

Again, her hand came up to stop him, but he reached out and grabbed it and held on tight. "I love you, Coleen. I had to tell you one more time before I left. And I had to know whether you have any feeling for me."

Coleen looked at him miserably and then bowed her head.

"I know there was something, Coleen," he whispered. "I know there was that day. Do you know what kept me alive in that prison? My ideals. I did what I did for the Americans because I believed in what they did. I don't think I fully realized it until I was in prison. I was determined to endure so that I could carry out those ideals. I had also found love—and I think that's what kept me alive too. I think that's what will keep me alive for however long it is until I come back here."

He stepped forward and clasped her hand in his. "Coleen, please, give me some hope. Give me something to live for—some hope for the future. Give me something to help me endure."

She slowly shook her head back and forth. "I can't," she finally whispered. "I don't know anymore." She stared up at him with tear-streaked eyes. "I don't know, Matthew. I thought there was something, but then—then it broke. When I heard all those awful things about you—when Winslow told me how you spied on us—it broke." She began to shudder and heave with sobs.

"Love doesn't have any politics, Coleen," Matthew answered softly. "If you love someone, it shouldn't matter what uniform they wear, what flag they salute. Look at Martha and Colin. It didn't matter what her past was—they were in love. And it doesn't matter to me that you're a Tory. I love you for who you are, inside. That's all that matters."

Coleen pulled away to lean against the door, her tears flowing freely now. John Page appeared and placed a protective arm about her shoulders, staring sadly at Matthew.

"You'd better go, son," he said softly, stroking the top of Coleen's head. "You've said your piece. Your friends are getting anxious." He gazed down at his daughter, then back at Matthew. "You better look to your own safety." It was the closest he could come to a kind word.

Matthew wanted to say more, but words seemed so inadequate. He reached out to touch Coleen's shoulder, then stopped.

"Goodbye, sir," he said firmly. He whirled and ran down the steps to his horse. Someday, he would return. No matter who won the war, by God.

As soon as the three rebels had escaped through the British lines and were back in American territory, they placed Deborah on a coach for Wethersfield.

"That was a foolhardy thing you did, coming to rescue me." Matthew kissed her on the cheek and smiled. "But I'm thankful you did."

"You be careful now," she answered. She turned to John Langley and kissed him softly on the lips. "Both of you be careful."

The two men rode westward in silence. They found Washington at the crook of the Delaware River just below Trenton. As they rode through the mass of tents and wagons, they saw that the soldiers were preparing to leave the area. Matthew and Hunter were directed to a large tent set apart from the rest. It was the first time Matthew and the command in chief had met without secrecy.

"We thought we had lost a valuable aide, Master Bell!" The general smiled and waved them to some chairs under the shade of a chestnut tree. Soon they were settled comfortably, each with a mug of tea. "You've caught us just in time," Washington observed. "We're breaking camp and moving north soon." He turned to Matthew. "I heard you were imprisoned."

Matthew responded briefly about his capture and imprisonment, leaving out the grimmer aspects.

"You bear the strain of torture," the general responded. "I've seen such eyes before, Matthew." He glanced at the scar on Matthew's hand, then slowly lifted his head to meet Matthew's penetrating gaze. "War brings out the worst in mankind, I'm afraid. I'm deeply sorry you had to suffer as you did. They must have been desperate for whatever secrets you had."

"I had learned the British plans and was preparing to bring them to you just before my capture," Matthew explained. "They wanted to know whether or not I'd passed on the information. I thought if I told the truth, the British would go ahead with their plans. From what Lee said, that would have given you a chance for victory, but . . . They didn't believe me. They thought I had given you the information and so they changed their plans and came south to attack the capital instead."

"So, that was it," Washington murmured. Suddenly he smiled and reached out to pat Matthew's leg. "My boy, you probably couldn't have planned it better. If

Howe had gone ahead with his original plan, I daresay New England would be lost to us now. Burgoyne is giving us enough trouble as it is, and Howe would only have added fuel to the fire.

"I don't understand," Matthew said. "Lee seemed to feel that—"

"The blunders of a genius can be as awesome as his success," Washington interrupted. "And it's possible he was simply putting on an act for you. In either event, Howe has done exactly as I would have wanted him to. He's split his army in parts. We still might have a chance to stop Burgoyne. And I'd much rather meet Howe here—in New Jersey." His face lengthened into a frown. "That is, if we could only find the rascal."

"You mean you don't know where he is?" Hunter asked in surprise. "The British set sail from New York long ago."

"We know that," the general answered. "And his ships have been at the head of the Delaware off and on for quite some time." Washington shook his head. "I really don't know what the man is doing. It could be a clever diversion to keep us here while his main force is actually headed northward. It's a game of cat and mouse. We're both waiting to see what the other is doing. Right now, he's disappeared completely."

"But he intends to attack Philadelphia," Matthew exclaimed, trying to recall Whitehead's last conversation with him in prison.

"They did," Washington answered. "Several times. Then they went back to New York and boarded their ships. That's where they are now—somewhere out in the Atlantic, trying to confuse us and doing a good job of it."

Hunter broke into the silence that followed. "You said you were moving north. You must have received word then?"

"Yes," Washington replied wearily. "Burgoyne has captured Ticonderoga and now there's no stopping him. I think Howe's gone north to deal the final blow. We're going up there to stop them."

"That's impossible!" Matthew stood and took a few agitated steps before facing Washington. "I'm certain the British intend to take Philadelphia. They told me they were sailing right up to the capital and would take it."

Washington shook his head. "We have scouts all along the Delaware and there are no signs of British ships. They must have changed their minds."

"Or are trying somewhere else," Matthew suggested.

"They might," Washington answered. "But I'm sure our scouts would have sighted them before now."

"Unless they went further south," John Langley Hunter said slowly, turning the idea over in his head. "They could have sailed further south." He turned to the general expectantly.

Washington thought about it but slowly shook his head. "No general likes long marches, Mr. Hunter," he finally decided. "It makes little sense."

"It does make sense," Hunter explained excitedly, "if Howe sails his ships up the Chesapeake."

"The Chesapeake?" Washington said. "But that's too far south." He frowned as he thought it over.

"That's probably what he's hoping we'd think. It's a long sea journey—but it's also a back road leading right up to the capital."

Washington reached over to a small table and unrolled a map. The three men bent over the paper and studied the waterway. "It's a daring move," Washington murmured. "And it would take a daring commander to undertake it."

"He knows you're waiting over here in New Jersey," Hunter said, his long finger tracing a circle in the area northeast of Philadelphia. "His army could be marching right up through the back door now and we'd never know."

Washington raised a solemn gaze to Matthew and Hunter. "If you two are correct," he finally said, "I've almost made an irrevocable mistake. As it is, we may be too late."

The big man stretched to his full height and drew in a deep breath as he surveyed the army that spread before him on the open fields. "Do you realize how pitifully small and unprepared we are? And if you two are correct, we'll be meeting head-on with the world's mightiest army. The only thing we have in greater supply than they do is spirit," he said. "Which is no doubt why we've been able to hold them off so long," he added in a suddenly brisk tone. "If you two will excuse me, I'm going to send scouts southward in search of the enemy."

38

H E'S DONE it to us again!" Washington muttered as he concentrated on a map that had been fastened to the side of his tent.

Matthew glanced over to Hunter and shrugged quizzically. They had been summoned to Washington's tent. After weeks of inactivity, they had both enjoyed the march through Philadelphia. Now that news of the approaching enemy force was filtering in, they were eager to be of use once again.

"I don't follow you sir," Matthew prompted the general.

"Howe! He's disappeared again. There's only about a third of the force across the river. Where are all the others?"

A vanguard of patriots had already met the front line of Howe's army, some 30,000 strong who had

suffered aboard the ships that had finally landed at
the source of the Chesapeake. The British had spent
almost a week recuperating from the confinement,
stale air and rotten food aboard the ships. Reports
from Washington's spies came in that the few horses
that had survived the trip had run amok in the
Maryland cornfields, literally eating themselves to
death. Probably the same number of men had died.
Finally, the redcoats had rallied and started their
journey toward Philadelphia. It was at the Brandywine River that Washington had set up his defenses,
daring the British to wade across the wide expanse.
Both sides dug in and prepared for the siege. The
British cannon occasionally sounded out in the summer heat, but they were merely testing the stamina of
the patient patriotic force that lay waiting.

"I need you two to infiltrate their lines and find out
where Howe is," Washington asked. He shook his
head, discouraged. "I've received reports putting him
at just about every possible location, and God only
knows which one is true. If the man risked his army
by sailing all the way down to the Chesapeake, then
he's willing to risk almost anything. He's damn clever.
And I must admit, his tactics are wearing me thin."

Matthew had already heard the talk that was spreading around the camps. Washington's indecision at
the Delaware had been bad enough, but now this
waiting at the Brandywine was causing all kinds of
speculation. "He's running scared," someone had said
over a campfire. "I told you his luck was running thin.
I say we need someone like Greene to lead us. Hell,
even Wayne!"

Matthew had seen Washington's officers lagging in
their duties, a great many of them having already
taken to the bottle, their indiscretions hidden from

Washington's disapproving eyes by their aides. It was as though many of the officers didn't care anymore—and this feeling was spreading to the troops. Of course, it didn't help Washington's cause any when orders were issued that barred the horde of camp followers from the encampments.

"By God," one of the soldiers remarked bitterly, "he's got his wife coming down to him whenever he wants—but we common folks can't have our funning! If you ask me, one of these mornings the general is going to wake up and find empty beds outside. I'm beginning to think of going home!"

Matthew studied the tall Virginian carefully. The shoulders tended to stoop a little more, the mouth was set in a rigid line, and there were dark shadows under the eyes. The man was tired, it was plain to see; he looked as though he carried the weight of the country.

"I think Howe's back here," Washington went on. "I think he would want me to attack thinking he'd gone elsewhere—just so he could swoop down on us."

"You have lookouts, don't you?" Matthew asked.

"Yes. I only wish I could trust their accuracy. There are a great many conflicting reports, and I don't know who to believe. That's why I want you two to head upstream to the north. We were going to attack the cannon but I've called it off until I know for sure where Howe is. I don't like this waiting any more than you do, but I see no other alternative. If you two can't find signs of the British, then it will mean Howe is somewhere to the south of us, waiting to bait us into a trap."

Matthew and John Langley Hunter followed the Brandywine toward its northern source. They carefully inspected the ground for signs of heavy movement at each fording path across the river, but they found nothing of any significance.

It was an early morning when they crested a ridge and immediately threw themselves flat on their stomachs at the sight before them. Lines of red-coated infantry, fanned out over the entire valley, were slowly trudging toward them.

"By God," Matthew breathed softly. "Howe!" He pointed to an area slightly to the rear of the main mass of troops where a large group of horsemen, surrounded by various bright red flags, watched the proceedings.

"The whole stinkin' force," Hunter exclaimed. "And they're coming right for our asses!"

"We better get back to warn Washington." Matthew started to edge off the top of the hill.

"You go," Hunter proposed. "I'll keep an eye on them just to make sure they don't disappear again . . ."

At the American encampment, Matthew backed away as he watched Washington's orders go into effect. His information had met with stern countenance and only one question.

"You have no doubt your information is correct?"

When Matthew nodded, the general reacted quickly. Couriers were assembled, the few officers nearby were summoned and the camp rapidly assembled.

They followed Stirling's and Stephen's troops northward, stopping opposite the British with a vast open field stretching between them in the valley. High on the opposing hillside, the British troops were resting. As the excited rebel army scattered for their defenses, the British appeared to remain calm in their pastoral setting, content to watch the brown-and-blue uniformed army prepare itself. Looking off in the distance, Matthew could easily make out the spot on the Brandywine where the British and Americans were still restlessly awaiting further orders.

And so they waited. Matthew had found a lone apple tree for shade within eyesight of the dismounted Washington and another imposing figure whom someone had pointed out as Nathanael Greene, the great Rhode Island hero. These two generals were surrounded by other officers, who seemed to be bickering over battle positions. Washington would take each man aside, his head bowed in soft conversation as he tried to soothe wounded pride and win complete cooperation.

As the heat of the day topped and shadows began to lengthen under the trees on the hillsides, there was definite activity along the British lines. Music began to filter down and across the field as the British band struck up. Slowly, in unhurried and assured pace, the British force made its way down the hill, approaching as though there was no such thing as opposition. The effect was profound, Matthew saw as he looked about him at the nervous rebel army standing ready.

Suddenly they could hear the muffled sound of the British artillery beginning its bombardment of the rebel troops at the Brandywine. Washington nodded to Greene and the two men mounted, giving final instructions to their generals. Matthew followed when the two men rode off to the Brandywine, where the rebel troops were concealed in the woods, lying low as the fire from the other side exploded over their heads. The small group of horsemen stopped to survey the scene. Washington motioned General Greene off to take command of the troops near the southern end of the river, where it bent at a place called Chadds Ford. Then he anxiously looked around at Matthew.

"I want you to stay here," he yelled over the roar of gunfire. "Get word to me if there are any changes. I'll be with my troops in case you need me." Without waiting for a reply, he and his aides rode off.

Matthew settled beneath the trees on a hillside that offered a sweeping view of the river. Puffs of smoke rose over each side in a bombardment that lasted well over an hour. Behind him, he could hear the reports from the fight against Howe's forces. It was going to be quite a battle. . . .

The sun was making its final arch toward the horizon when the course of the battle changed. Matthew saw them coming out of the smoke like rats from a burning building. Green-coated cavalry and infantry scurried down the far embankments and hit the water with a splash. There were cries of warning all along the wooded area as the rebel forces took up their positions and started firing at the approaching British. By the time the first British soldiers began to wade out of the river lines of infantry were still pouring out of the smoke and into the water on the opposite shore.

Matthew was instantly on his feet, grabbing for the reins of his mount. This was an all-out assault. Already the Brandywine flowed red with blood, bodies floating face downward along the embankments or slowly washing downstream. Directly in front of him, rebels were running out of concealment, bayonets flashing, war cries breaking the air with shrill audacity. They met the Britishers struggling out of the water, almost helpless in their heavy wet uniforms and fatigued with the effort of crossing the wide river. The Americans held their own, once in a while actually halting and driving back the human chain coming across the river.

Suddenly, from the right, new gunfire and screeching war yells shook the American line. British troops came into view, a contingent of Howe's army having broken through the American lines.

There were cries of panic as the Americans were caught between the two forces of Britishers. Some fought valiantly, clubbing their way backwards to the safety of the trees, or falling in a suicidal attempt to hold the line.

Matthew looked around him. From his vantage point, he could see the American lines begin to sag, pulling back from the mass of British soldiers. It was time for him to get help.

It was another hour before he was able to find Washington. The horizon was beginning to match the redness of the battlefield that spread before them. Washington and his officers closed their horses upon the lines, oblivious to the close rifle fire as they struggled to prevent a retreat.

"The British have crossed the river," Matthew yelled out, pulling in close beside the general. "I don't think they can hold!"

The Virginian frowned at the ribbon of red coats advancing across the fields. "We cannot hold," he said angrily, "but by God, they shall not forget this battle!" He turned to Matthew.

"Search out Greene or Sullivan or one of the others," he answered heavily. "Instruct them from me to make an orderly retreat." He looked around sadly at the ragged line of patriots. "Tell them I'll hold open the road to Philadelphia for them, but they must hurry. The darkness will help."

"We'll make it, sir," Matthew promised. His tone made Washington snap his head up and stare at him. "We'll make it, sir!" Matthew repeated.

There was a sadness in Washington's eyes. "I have

failed in this battle," he said, his voice hollow. "I underestimated the enemy badly. They've paid dearly for this victory, but I've lost some dear friends and too many gallant souls have suffered. We may lose again, Matthew, but I shall never make another such mistake."

Matthew was stunned by the words, panicked that a man of Washington's strength would ever admit failure. Washington was the one man who could inspire such a rabble force to overpower the mightiest army of the world. It was Washington who inspired these farmers to place their lives before such an awesome spectre and to believe they could win. If Washington's strength waned, so waned the strength of his army, of the hopes and ideals for which they fought.

"We'll make it, sir," he said again, almost choking on the words.

He had to repeat those words over and over as the sun disappeared and the faint Indian summer moon shone over the road that led to Philadelphia. The retreating army was quiet, tired and drawn of its fiber. The only thing that made their spirits rise was word that the enemy too had had enough of the carnage and were not in pursuit. The British had paid dearly for their first step towards Philadelphia.

39

THE NEXT WEEKS found the two armies virtually playing hide and seek. Washington's forces tried valiantly to regroup while keeping the British at bay. The city of Philadelphia was being evacuated as rapidly as possible, the Congressional Records being carted off to New York, along with most of the Congressmen.

John Langley Hunter had just relayed the bad news that General Anthony Wayne's rear guard action had been stopped by an overwhelming bayonet charge.

"It isn't going well for us," Hunter exclaimed, taking a long swallow from his mug. The tavern at the edge of Philadelphia was deserted except for the bartender and a few local citizens.

"It will," Matthew answered emphatically. "Washington has gone up to Reading Furnace to fetch supplies there. Once he's back, we'll give the redcoats their due."

"You maintain your optimism well," Hunter said with a sad smile. "If only more shared the same feeling."

"We've got to believe," Matthew said determinedly. "We're so close to victory I can smell it!"

"It's the smell of death in your nostrils. That's the only smell around here . . ."

Matthew shook his head and stared at the mug in his hands. He wished he was back home now, that Coleen was there waiting for him. The memories seemed almost unreal, from so long ago.

"Don't look up!" Hunter's hand fell on his in a strong grip, full of warning. "Don't look up," he hissed.

Matthew froze. All he could see from his bowed position was the bartender, who stood stock-still, his gaze fixed on the front door behind Matthew. Hunter was also staring past Matthew's shoulder, his muscles taut, his eyes unblinking.

There was the sound of footsteps coming in, booted steps that were cautious, followed by two, maybe three other men. Out of the corner of his eyes, Matthew saw the polished black thigh boots of a grenadier.

"We don't want no trouble with civilians," a voice barked out.

Matthew felt Hunter's hand nudge him and he slowly lifted his head and turned to look up at the red-coated soldier who was staring down at them.

The soldier inspected both Matthew and Hunter carefully, then went about the room looking at each person. Finally, he stopped at the door and faced the silent room. "Your city is now in the hands of His

Majesty, King George the Third!" Swiftly, he turned around and marched out of the room.

"My God!" Hunter breathed.

It was impossible! Matthew started to rise but Hunter pushed him back into his seat.

"You can't go out there!" he exclaimed, keeping his voice to a whisper. "You might be recognized. Stay here until it's dark—then we'll slip out."

"But the British are here!"

"So they are. And there's naught we can do about it. I'm sure Washington and the others already know about it."

Matthew was numb with disbelief. "I didn't think it would ever happen. I thought for sure we could stop them."

"And we will," Hunter said in a hushed voice. "We will! You wait and see—the general will get it back!"

They found Washington north of Germantown. "As long as we control the Delaware, the British are isolated from the rest of the world," their commander answered calmly. "I've asked for reinforcements from the north and they're arriving each day. Perhaps we should attack before the British get too settled in our city."

Several days later, Washington called in both Hunter and Matthew. On his desk were numerous maps and papers. "We shall attack," he started ominously. "It's a plan that calls for good timing, and good communications. I've instructed my officers and I feel they know their parts. However, on these foggy mornings, and in the heat of battle, confusion often reigns." His face set grimly as he eyed Matthew and Hunter. "I need you two as my eyes, my ears. I am not going to have Howe surprise me again as he did on

Long Island or at the Brandywine. This time it is I who will be presenting the surprise."

The British were indeed surprised, although not quite as Washington had expected. Anthony Wayne's Pennsylvanians, who had survived the slaughter only weeks before, sought out revenge once they were set back in action. Their first encounter with the British was a massacre, Wayne's men bayoneting anyone they could find, including those who were wounded or trying to surrender. So vicious was their vengeance, it was the first time the British had had to sound a retreat.

As news of Wayne's victory spread across the army units, a new upsurge in morale pushed the Americans forward. So vigorous were the charges that the redcoats were often caught in their camps still preparing for battle, their only choice to run in retreat. The Americans fought savagely, almost as if they had lost their senses in the soul-wearying demands of battle upon battle. As brutal as their attacks were, nothing ever shocked Matthew quite as much as a scene he witnessed while watching the American advance from atop a hill. It was the moment that the tide seemed to turn irrevocably against the rebels.

To his left, approaching hurriedly to aid the front lines, a troop of Americans suddenly came upon fellow rebels lying in wait for a British attack. So sudden was the appearance that the rebels started firing on each other.

Matthew could not believe his eyes. He raced his mount down the hill, yelling out a warning. The gunfire was so fierce that both units panicked, each thinking they had come upon a much superior British force. As Matthew reached the battlefield, he was met by scrambling men, pawing over each other in an attempt to escape.

"Hold back!" he cried out, wheeling his horse back and forth. "Hold your positions—they're friends!" But it seemed only a matter of seconds before Matthew found himself alone, an eerie stillness having settled over the field, broken by an occasional moan from some dying soul.

He sat on his mount, dumbfounded as he took in the deserted field of dead rebels. This was not possible. How could an army so close to victory succumb to such a mistake? Matthew spurred his horse. He had to find Washington and relay the news.

He found the general in the middle of Skippack Road amidst occasional gunfire. He was mounted on his white horse, trying to block the string of men who slowly shuffled past but their eyes were downcast and they remained deaf and unheeding, no matter what Washington shouted out. By the time Matthew reached him, the general was silent, moodily watching his soldiers trudge past.

"Look at them," he said softly. "Look at those poor devils. They've given until there's no more to be squeezed out of them."

"General, what's happened?" Matthew asked, his voice hushed with distress.

The man shook his head, his eyes following each face as it passed. "Everything," he sighed. "Wrong roads, wrong timing, fog too thick to know whose shoulder is rubbing against you—you name it. Providence was against us."

"We're retreating?" Matthew asked incredulously.

"They're retreating," Washington answered, nodding toward the pitiful human beings dragging past them. "I cannot ask any more of them—not now."

"You're giving up?"

Washington's head snapped around angrily, his blue eyes cold with anger. "Giving up? These men are retreating because they're exhausted. They've done the work of three compared to the British; those odds are difficult in any man's book. They're retreating, Mr. Bell, but they are not beaten. Nor am I—not by the long of it."

"I'm sorry—sorry, sir," Matthew stammered. "I didn't think you'd give up."

Washington reached over and touched Matthew's shoulder kindly. "We're all tired, Matthew. But we're not beaten. Just keep thinking that. We still have our forts on the Delaware. We still have an army—which, once rested, will be back on its feet."

His army rested a good distance from Germantown, safe from Howe's threatening presence.

"The man amazes me at times," Washington declared one night. He sat with Matthew and John Langley Hunter, watching the glow of an October moon over the army spread out before them in the open field. "He's had plenty of opportunity to attack us while we were down."

"He's concentrating on the Delaware," Hunter commented. He had already reported his findings to Washington on his return.

"We will hold," Washington said emphatically. "We will hold!"

"We need a miracle," Matthew answered with a sigh. "That's what we need, a miracle!"

Washington smiled to himself. "What? Are you losing your faith, Matthew?"

"I can understand your having to think we'll win, General," Matthew responded, his eyes tracing various designs in the faint stars breaking the dark veil of the night. "But as your ears and eyes, I have to tell you what I see. And that is that your army is discouraged. It's tired, it's hungry, and it doesn't want to fight anymore."

"It is all those things. You're right, Matthew," Washington replied with a sigh. "All, that is, except the last. They *will* fight! They still believe, and as long as they believe, they'll still fight—until the last drop of blood falls, if necessary."

Matthew knew he couldn't say more. It was not his place to argue, nor was it his desire to do so. Matthew knew he would continue the fight for as long as Washington asked it of him. And so, probably, would all those men resting in the fields.

"Well," Matthew said quietly, "we could do with a bit of luck."

The bit of luck arrived the next day by courier. Washington's tent suddenly erupted with men scurrying around to pass the news. Soon there were cheers and occasional gunfire. Matthew beckoned to Hunter and the two walked over to the tent to satisfy their curiosity.

"Your prayers were answered," Washington announced as they entered. It was the first time in months that Matthew had seen a smile on the general's lips. "Here—a communique from the north," he said, pointing to a piece of paper on his desk. "Burgoyne has surrendered!"

"Burgoyne surrendered?" Matthew repeated, grinning at the news.

Washington nodded enthusiastically. "One of Britain's ablest generals and finest armies—and we have beaten them!" He slammed his fist onto the table and stood up. "Do you realize what that means? It means, by God, that none of this has been in vain." He strode from behind the desk. "It means that now maybe France and the other nations will join our side and give us aid. By God, lad, Providence has finally favored us!"

40

MATTHEW SHUFFLED his numb feet and dug his hands deeply into his greatcoat as he stood before his commander in chief.

"You look as though you haven't eaten," Washington commented, his breath coming in small puffs in the frigid air. When Matthew failed to reply the general cast him a questioning look. "How long as it been?"

Matthew shrugged and kept his eyes averted. "No more, no less than the others, sir," he answered. Actually, he had forgotten the last time he had eaten anything even resembling a nourishing meal. He scavenged the fields like most of the others, but with the winter cold, it was becoming increasingly difficult to find any kind of food. Except for the officers' mounts, horses had long ago been sacrificed to feed the motley army. Weakened by starvation, the soldiers were more often at rest on the cold ground than standing on their feet.

The only activity of late had taken place at the remaining American garrisons guarding the Delaware River. British warships had bombarded both forts, one on the New Jersey side, the other on an island near the Pennsylvania shore. The battle had been furious, with one of the British ships blown up by a lucky shot that illuminated the sky for miles around. There was not much Washington could do for the defenders but keep sending in what small supplies he had left and replacing the soldiers who were killed. At night, rebel boats would slip up to Fort Mercer, the island fort, under the noses of the British, while Matthew and others took supplies to Fort Mifflin on the New Jersey shore. But in the end, the supplies had finally run out, and now they watched the final attack of the British. Washington had sent John Langley Hunter and one of his aides, Alexander Hamilton, northward to the victorious American army for reinforcements, but so far no one had responded to his call.

"We're fading, my friend," Washington confided, turning from Matthew to the scene before them. It was evening and they stood watching the continuing British bombardment of the Delaware forts. "Fading—but not beaten. If we can only hang on until winter, then maybe we can get our rest and regroup. Just a few more weeks and then . . ." He sighed heavily and his voice trailed off.

Matthew stared at the broad back. He was reluctant to remind Washington of the seriousness of the condition of his troops, but certainly the man knew how exhausted they were. Howe kept up his persistent attacks, and the most the rebels could do was to fend off the wave of redcoats, not even pretending to think of an offensive. They were all praying for the snows. If their two forts could hold off the British guns, Philadelphia and Howe would then be cut off from supplies and would have to retreat to New York to spend their winter.

"Have you ever prayed for snow?" Washington had glanced up into the bright starlit sky.

"I'm not sure which is the more gallant way to die, sir," Matthew replied, trying to lighten the mood. "The British or freezing to death!"

The man smiled. "Right now," he answered, "I'd rather take my chances with the weather."

Matthew stared at him, bewildered. Where the Virginian got such great faith, he did not know. Washington often walked through the ranks of men scattered about the countryside. He had seen their rags, their feet poking out of shoes tied with rope and cloth. He'd seen the sunken eyes and ravaged faces of starvation. They were exhausted. Who wouldn't be? These brave souls had been fighting an army three to four times their size, well supplied for the rigors of war. And yet here was their commander in chief, still standing tall under the pressures of his own exhaustion and worries, confident of the nobility of his purpose, and knowing that he was in disfavor with half the country.

It made Matthew's own worries and problems seem insignificant as they waited for the morning sun to brighten the distant hills. But with the first greying of the sky, the shelling of the small blockhouses on Fort Mercer began again.

"My God," Washington gasped. "Can you believe that noise!"

It was a continuous roar. Every British cannon

aboard the warships had opened fire, with a continuous barrage that seemed to last not for minutes but for an eternity. As the noise went on, Washington drew closer to the edge of the roof.

The island was a mushroom of smoke now and the British ships drew in nearer. Washington placed a long spyglass to his eye and carefully studied the scene. "The British are throwing grenades from their masts!" He snapped the glass closed. "It cannot continue. We'll have to evacuate. We're out of ammunition. All our soldiers can do now is sit there and take the bombardment. And then what?"

And then what indeed. Matthew had no answer. He glanced toward the distant battle and his shoulders sank in dejection. "They've stood their ground so gallantly," he murmured.

"We're no match for their guns, but we'll have another chance to make a stand," Washington announced. He turned to study Matthew. "It's not that bad to take a step backward. Not as long as you know you can proceed by two or three huge steps at another time."

"How do you know we'll be able to?"

Washington pursed his lips and turned to the smoke-filled horizon. "Faith," he finally answered. "Faith that what we're doing is right."

"Faith hasn't given us food or clothing or ammunition!" Matthew burst out, unable to contain his bitterness and frustration.

"Faith doesn't *bring* you these things," came the slow response. "You do that yourself because your faith makes you believe you'll find the things you need. You, of all people I know, Matthew, should know that. It's part of your way, isn't it?"

Was it? Matthew wondered. He shook his head. "I

don't even know what faith is," he responded bitterly.

"I think you do," Washington answered. "Look around you. The soldiers at Mercer and Mifflin, everyone in our army has faith—faith in our country, faith in each other, faith that what we're doing is right. Don't you have dreams you hope will come true?"

"I have dreams—and hopes," Matthew acknowledged, Coleen's image coming painfully to mind.

"Then put faith in them. Know they will come true," Washington answered.

"It sounds too easy . . ."

"You have faith in God. Have faith in yourself, Matthew," Washington answered as he turned to leave. "Have faith in what you think and in what you do."

Matthew watched the figure ducking through the door and disappearing down the stairs. Was it as easy as he made it sound? How could one have faith without at least some assurance things would work out? There had been prison. Was it faith that he would get out that had made it possible for Deborah and John Langley Hunter to rescue him? Or was it coincidence, mere happenstance? Would he have made good his own release without their help?

Was it because of his faith that he had been able to spy for the Americans for so long without being caught? Because of his faith that he had not been hanged or killed? Matthew rubbed at his hand and stared down at the spot where his little finger had been. His brother Mark and all those souls buried across the countryside had paid dearly for their faith. Faith that they could win? Matthew glanced at the British warships still pounding away at the small fortification with their resounding guns. With all the setbacks of the last two months, and now Washington's decision to evacuate and leave the Delaware to the British,

was there room for faith that victory would still be
theirs? Matthew shook his head and turned to follow
his commander. He would try—try as hard as he
could. But the way he felt at that moment, he doubted
he had the strength for such a task.

The last of the three hundred soldiers from Fort
Mifflin and Fort Mercer had been quickly pulled
ashore a half hour before the sun broke over the
horizon the next day. Matthew had waded into the
icy waters to carry out the wounded, struggling with
those who grasped onto him in desperation. His
clothes were caked with their blood, his mind filled
with memories of ghastly wounds, mangled limbs
and shock-worn faces that stared at him in childlike
horror and bewilderment.

Matthew was among the many who spent the next
weeks scavenging the countryside, often walking miles
pulling a small cart which he kept filling with twigs
for kindling, roots for eating. He begged with the
farming people for whatever they could spare. Whenever he found a deserted barn, he would grab anything that could offer warmth or food. And yet with
all his endeavors, there never seemed to be enough.
No sooner would he arrive back at the camp than
desperate hands would empty the wagon.

It became a nightmare for him. He was driven to
go out in search of more, but it seemed that he found
less and less and less. . . .

"I haven't seen you for some time," Washington said
from his chair, studying Matthew carefully. "You
don't look well."

"It's just the cold, sir," he answered. He dug his
hands deeper into his threadbare coat to try and stop
his shivering.

Washington sat silently for a moment, knowing that Matthew, like so many others, was so overcome with exhaustion and despair that he hardly knew what day it was.

"You have been my ears and my eyes, Matthew Bell," he said at last, "and you have never failed me." He was silent again as though struggling over the words. "I've had many faithful and helpful aides, but none I felt I could confide in. You share secrets that I share with no one." He sighed. "You've been my release, Matthew. You've never given me cause to doubt my faith in you. You've been of invaluable service to me—to your country. I'm afraid there has been little reward for you. I can only remind you that you have been watching the birth of our new nation. Very few have had that opportunity, and I hope you carry the memory of that honor with you forever."

Matthew blinked in weary confusion, "I'm not sure what you mean, sir."

A patient smile touched Washington's mouth. "I guess I'm rattling on. One of these days you'll understand. Part of it is that faith we were talking about a couple of weeks ago."

Matthew shook his head. "I'm afraid I don't have the strength you do, sir."

"It will take one proof and that will be all that's needed. Just one proof that faith works, and you'll be a believer."

"I'll take about anything right now," Matthew answered. "I need some kind of hope."

Washington tapped a finger on the desk in front of him and tried to smile. "We prayed for snow and we got it, didn't we?"

Matthew shrugged. "The British have the Delaware and our capital. They're snug for the winter."

"And we have our snow," Washington reminded him. "I asked the Congress for permission to set up winter quarters near Wilmington. However, it seems the Pennsylvania legislature wants us to stay near the British troops to protect the country from any possible attack."

"There's no food around here," Matthew protested.

"I know," the general answered. "But we've been ordered to stay for the winter. I want you to go ahead and survey the site for me. We'll follow shortly."

The place that Washington had pointed out to on the map was Valley Forge, a windswept plateau that sloped to the distant bluffs of the Schuylkill River, an area that had been occupied and destroyed by both British and American forces.

Nearby, a village of stone houses surrounded an old ironworks. At one end the charred remains of a sawmill and what had once been storage sheds for American supplies were mute reminders of a British raid only weeks before the first snow had turned the British forces back to Philadelphia for the winter.

Matthew stared at the rolling field on a dark day that shoved a cold wind against his back, a sure sign that another snowfall could be expected. My God, Matthew thought, shaking his head. Was this all that lay at the end of a year's struggle? Was this the fate of those half-dead troops who would soon be shuffling their way toward him in hope of rest and warmth to tide them through the winter months?

Matthew stared up into the heavens ignoring the wind that buffeted against him. "Faith?" he called out. "How can I have faith with all of this?" He sank to his knees on the cold ground and began to cry.

Matthew spent the night under a grouping of small trees at the far end of the plateau. He had torn branches from the trees to cover himself, but in the morning he awoke shivering and numb. There was a faint grey fog misting the area, and a light drizzle which soon turned to sleet and snow.

As he watched the ground before him begin to turn into a blanket of white, Matthew sat huddled in a tight ball, his mind blank, his face sullen and forlorn. God, how he wished he was back in Wethersfield! He could feel the warmth of the fire in the great stone fireplace, smell the aromas of dinner from Deborah's kitchen, enjoy the laziness of rocking slowly in the old rocking chair, his mind at rest as he stared into the flames.

Coleen . . . Beautiful warm Coleen. It warmed his body to think of the girl, the memory of their love-making stirring deep within him. Would he ever return to New York? If he found her, would she even look at him?

She had to! There had been too much between them. He had felt too much. He had to believe she would be waiting, he had to have faith. . . .

They came in two rows, an endless ribbon of rags, some not even bothering to look up as they passed Matthew. Some half-carried, half-dragged their friends, sick with fatigue, sick from starvation.

And on they came, silent, barely alive, mechanical in their movements, too tired, too sick to react to the desolation of their new home. The able lay aside whatever they had been carrying and ran for the wooded section, bringing back limbs and branches for shelter and for fires. And still they came, shuffling by, dropping to the ground and stretching out, huddling against one another for whatever comfort they could find against the snow and the cold. As the campfires were lit, the sick were dragged closer to the warmth. There were no quarrels, no fighting or struggling to get to the fires. They were all too tired.

Was this the American army that had stopped the might of Britain? Was this the foundation of the new nation? Was this the army that would bring the redcoats to their knees? The only answer Matthew found was his bitterness over their suffering.

Washington and his staff came into view hours later, slowly walking their horses beside the last of the army. He stopped and looked at Matthew, his face wet from the snow, white hair plastered to his head. There was no need of words between them. The general turned to his aides, his orders crisp and firm. They rode off to do his bidding.

"It isn't heaven," Washington remarked softly, "but then neither is it hell. We shall endure Matthew. It's going to take more than the British to stop us. It's going to take more than the elements to stop us."

"We cannot survive this!" Matthew had to yell to be heard above the wind-driven sleet that now came slicing across the plateau.

"We will! We will survive!" Washington pulled his cloak about him and surveyed the mass who lay before him. "We've got to!"

"Your faith is going to keep them warm? Feed them?" Matthew yelled out angrily.

Washington's eyes suddenly pierced into Matthew's with such an intensity that Matthew drew back, startled. "My faith—their faith—your faith, yes! At the moment, that's all we have—faith! But by God, it's enough!"

Matthew backed away as Washington mounted his horse and urged it into a gallop. Suddenly, Washington wheeled the animal around and trotted back.

"I forgot," he said reaching inside his jacket. "Your

friend Mr. Hunter returned and gave me this. It's a letter that was sent to your home at Wethersfield." The general handed an envelope down to Matthew. "I hope it is good news," he said, nodding encouragingly before he rode off toward the distant stone houses.

Matthew watched him in silence, then glanced down at the paper. His name was written on the envelope in an evenly inked scrawl that was unfamiliar to him. He stuck the letter under his clothes and ran to the nearest grove of trees for shelter.

His hands shook with the cold as he tore at the envelope hunched over to protect it from the rain. He turned the paper over, searching for the signature.

Coleen! His heart jumped and he closed his eyes in disbelief. She had written! She had written to him! He clutched the letter tighter, as though seeking her warmth, and breathed in deeply to calm himself.

With shivering fingers, he slowly held out the letter and tried to accustom his eyes to the dim light and delicate scrawl.

"Dearest Matthew . . ."

A warmth began to spread over him. He straightened and felt a new power surge through him.

Faith! Faith, indeed!

His eyes searched out those words once more.

"Dearest Matthew:

"I can no longer contain myself. I have to let you know that I love you. . . ."

*FIRST IN THE DRAMATIC NEW
FREEDOM FIGHTERS
SERIES:*

Tomahawks
and
Long Rifles

by Jonathan Scofield

*BEGINNING THE SAGA
OF THREE AMERICAN FAMILIES—
AS PASSIONATE AND DIVERSE AS
THE LAND FOR WHICH THEY FIGHT
AND OFTEN DIE . . .*

In this blockbuster lead-off novel in the FREEDOM FIGHTERS series John Langley Hunter, the tall, red-headed Virginian, fights his first battles with young Colonel George Washington, loses his child-bride to a brutal enemy, meets his friend—and rival—Magnus DeWitt in the climactic battle of the French and Indian War on the Plains of Abraham—and has a fateful romantic encounter with the lovely, strong-willed Deborah Bell of a hardy Connecticut clan.

BE SURE TO READ
TOMAHAWKS AND LONG RIFLES
—ON SALE NOW FROM
DELL/BRYANS

THIRD IN THE DRAMATIC NEW
FREEDOM FIGHTERS
SERIES:

The King's Cannon

by Jonathan Scofield

Young Schuyler DeWitt joins the Rebel cause when his Tory brother, Magnus, betrays his best friend to the gallows and steals the passionate bond-servant who is his obsession.

Meantime, the lovely Clarissa Hunter—sister of the heroic Virginian, John Langley—faces a hard choice: her virtue—or the precious cause of American freedom.

As General Washington's beleaguered army faces a bloody final showdown with the awesome British forces of Lord Cornwallis, Schuyler and Clarissa race against time—and the determined Magnus DeWitt—with the message that may turn the tide.

BE SURE TO READ
THE KING'S CANNON—
COMING IN MAY
FROM DELL/BRYANS

FOURTH IN THE DRAMATIC NEW
FREEDOM FIGHTERS
SERIES:

Guns at Twilight

by Jonathan Scofield

A few short years after the American Rebels had vanquished the Redcoats and won their hard-earned freedom from the British monarch, the tables were turned, and soldiers of the Crown sacked Washington, and sent President James Madison and his wife Dolly scurrying across the Potomac.

Youthful Carson DeWitt, despite the royalist machinations of his conniving uncle, Magnus, went to war in his nation's cause, and despite a romantic scandal that temporarily lost him his commission, managed to join his countrymen in a gallant attack against its powerful enemy—and to find true love in a most unlikely quarter.

DON'T MISS *GUNS AT TWILIGHT* —COMING IN JUNE FROM DELL/BRYANS